JABOTINSKY

Jabotinsky

A Life

—◆•◆—

HILLEL HALKIN

Yale

UNIVERSITY

PRESS

New Haven and London

Yale University Press books may be purchased in quantity for educational, business, or promotional use. For information, please e-mail sales.press@yale.edu (U.S. office) or sales@yaleup.co.uk (U.K. office).

Set in Janson Oldstyle type byTseng Information Systems, Inc.
Printed in the United States of America.

Library of Congress Cataloging-in-Publication Data
Halkin, Hillel, 1939-
Jabotinsky : a life / Hillel Halkin
pages   cm — (Jewish Lives)
Includes bibliographical references and index.
ISBN 978-0-300-13662-3 (alk. paper)
1. Jabotinsky, Vladimir, 1880–1940. 2. Revisionist Zionists—Biography. 3. Zionism—Biography. I. Title.
DS151.Z5.H36 2014
320.54095694092—dc23
[B]   2013041102

A catalogue record for this book is available from the British Library.

This paper meets the requirements of ANSI/NISO Z39.48-1992 (Permanence of Paper).

10   9   8   7   6   5   4   3

CONTENTS

1

The Young Jabotinsky

ALTHOUGH THE LONDONSKAYA in Odessa was the most palatial hotel my wife and I had ever stayed in, our room was a simple one on the top floor, where the servants' quarters once were. The grand suites started on the floor below, past which the elevator didn't go. To reach it we had to circumnavigate a long, dark hallway and climb down a narrow flight of stairs. Only then did we emerge in the broad corridors with their high, carved wooden doors, chandeliered ceilings, elaborate parquet floors, stained-glass windows, and great carpeted stairway sweeping down to the lobby as though for a Tsarina to descend on to a ball.

It wasn't all genuinely Tsarist. Built in 1827, the Londonskaya was extensively renovated at the start of this century after falling into disrepair during the long years of Communist rule. So was the entire old center of Odessa, which was founded in 1794 by Catherine the Great, on territory wrested from the Turks, to be Russia's Black Sea gateway to the world. Set on a flat promontory overlooking a gulf into which empty three of Europe's greatest rivers, the Danube, the Dniester, and the Dnieper, its once-again stately streets with their lan-guorous names—Pushkinskaya, Longeronovskaya, Richeliev-skaya, Yekaterinskaya, Deribasovskaya—abut a strip of leafy greenery sloping down to a busy port. A few hundred yards to the Londonskaya's left, at the foot of a commanding statue of Odessa's second governor, Duke Armand de Richelieu, dressed in the toga of a Roman senator, the slope is cut by Odessa's famed "boulevard of stairs." Their nearly two hundred broad steps were made an icon of the city by Sergei Eisenstein's Soviet-era film *The Battleship Potemkin* with its melodramatic scene of troops firing, during the 1905 anti-Tsarist uprising, on a crowd of demonstrators that flees, falls, and tumbles down them, followed by a sleeping baby in a runaway carriage.

Farther away from the water, past Cathedral Square and its neoclassical Church of the Incarnation, renovated Odessa comes to an end and leaves the rest of the city still molder-ing. "It's all a big show," we were warned in advance by an ex-Odessan in Israel. Still, it's a fine show, especially if you've come to it on the trail of Vladimir Jabotinsky, the great Zionist politician and writer who was born in Odessa in 1880. Although Jabotinsky left Odessa when he was seventeen, lived in it only intermittently thereafter, and said a last goodbye to it before World War I, a part of him always remained there—and what remained in him of it, the city he grew up in, studied in as a boy, worked in as a young journalist, and wrote his wonderful novel *The Five* about, was either in or just beyond the elegant downtown above the sea now restored to its former architec-tural glory.

A gift of the sea is what the most gorgeous of its creations, Odessa's opera house and municipal theater, looks like. One of the first buildings you come to if you turn away from Richelieu

upon leaving the Londonskaya and head in the opposite direction, its curving, sand-colored walls and conch-white pillars
and porticos suggest a great, intricately whorled seashell. The
story is told, tempting to believe, that its Italian construction
workers sang arias as they laid and plastered its bricks. Unable
to get a glimpse of its interior, I had to content myself with a
description by *The Five*'s narrator, a young journalist attending
a performance of the opera *Mona Vanna*, of its "blazing crys-
tal, gilt, caryatids, and red velvet chairs" that reflected "all the
splendor of our carefree, contented Odessa."

Carefree, contented Odessa! Never mind that by *The Five*'s
end the city has become a bubbling stew of popular discontent,
rising ethnic tensions, and that fumy mixture of decadence and
revolutionary ferment that heralds the explosive ends of epochs.
While this was the Odessa that Jabotinsky said farewell to and
that helped make him an active Zionist, the Odessa he looked
back on nostalgically was a lighter-hearted place. A *gneyvishe
shtot*, "a thievish city," he once called it, using a Yiddish expression that meant not only that it was a freewheeling town
in which one had to survive by one's wits, but that its roguish-
ness stole one's affections. "Nowhere," he wrote in his memoirs, "but in Odessa—that is, in the Odessa of those years—was
the air ever so full of soft gaiety and light intoxication, without the slightest hint of psychological complications."[1] One of
the striking things about these memoirs when compared with
the reminiscences of other Jewish authors of the age who were
raised in the *shtetlakh*, the villages and provincial towns of the
Tsarist empire, is their untroubled sense of at-homeness in the

---

1. Jabotinsky published two volumes of autobiographical writing, *Memories
of a Contemporary* and *The Story of My Life*, which appeared in 1932 and 1936,
respectively, though parts date to earlier years. In this book I have generally
referred to them both as his "memoirs" without bothering to distinguish between them.

world. "I have friends and acquaintances from many places [in Russia]," Jabotinsky remarked,

> and I have often heard them speak of their formative years and felt (I'm referring to the Jews among them) that they grew up in an atmosphere thick with the grimness and bitter salt of Jewish tragedy. . . . Perhaps Jewish society in such places was more deeply and consciously "Jewish" and far better educated in Jewish terms. Yet I've always thought that in their psyches, from childhood on, these Jews lived in a harsh climate, under gray skies—always in a state of war in which they had to fight their way forward while defending themselves against countless enemies. This may have been, I admit, a better training ground for a Jewish existence; it created more profound, perhaps more finely attuned types. Odessa was never profound about anything—but for that reason it never pecked at the soul. Having no traditions, it didn't fear new ways of life or doing things. This made us Jews more temperamental and less hungry for success; more cynical, but not so bitter.

Odessa was indeed a unique place for nineteenth-century Russian Jews, the only large Russian city they weren't barred from. For Jewish inhabitants of the Pale of Settlement, the extensive area of rural western Russia to which they were legally confined after its acquisition by the Tsarist empire in the 1772, 1793, and 1795 partitions of Poland, cities like Moscow, St. Petersburg, and Kiev were out-of-bounds; special permits, obtainable only by a limited number of wealthy or professionally trained Jews, were needed to live in them. Newly established Odessa, to which the Russian government sought to attract settlers, was the exception. Drawn by its boom-town economy, Jews flocked to it. By 1850 there were more than fifteen thousand of them, comprising twenty percent of the city's residents and over fifty percent of its merchant class; thirty years later, they were a quarter of a population that had swelled to three hundred thousand. A main street was named Yevreskaya or "Jews' Street," and "living like God in Odessa" was a proverbial Jewish way of saying "living high." The impressions of a provincial Jew arriving in the city for the first time are conveyed in a letter sent home to his wife by Sholem Aleichem's comic fictional character Menachem-Mendl, who has gone to Odessa to seek his fortune. "Words fail me," he writes,

> in describing the grandeur and beauty of the city of Odessa, the fine character of its inhabitants, and the wonderful opportunities that exist here. Just imagine: I take my walking stick and venture out on Greek Street, as the place where Jews do business is called, and there are twenty thousand different things to deal in. If I want wheat, there's wheat. If I feel like wool, there's wool. If I'm in the mood for bran, there's bran. Flour, salt, feathers, raisins, jute, herring—you name it and you have it in Odessa.

Menachem-Mendl, who ultimately loses his shirt in Odessa's stock market, was writing about 1900, when no other major European city apart from Warsaw had such a high proportion of Jews. Yet Odessa's Jews differed from Warsaw's. Although they, too, were mainly Yiddish-speaking emigrants from the shtetl, they were at a greater remove from it geographically and psychologically. The first wave of them had come, often from considerable distances, to a new city with no Jewish institutions, and while these were built in the course of time, Odessan Jewry remained less traditional and less subject to rabbinical influence than other Eastern European Jewish communities. Warsaw's wealth of neighborhood synagogues, yeshivas, and Hasidic courts was not duplicated by Odessa; though the latter had its share of observant Jews, it had more than its share of laxer ones, and observance, too, took on more liberal forms in it. The Yiddish maxim that *zibn mayl arum Odes brent der ge-henm*, "the fires of hell burn seven miles around Odessa," alluded as much to the alleged impiety of the city's Jews as to its brothels, gambling houses, speculators, racketeers, and port full of sailors and adventurers.

Ethnically, too, Odessa was unlike Warsaw. Warsaw had Jews and Poles, a large minority and a larger majority, each speaking its own language, living in its own social and economic world, and regarding the other with distrust. Odessa had only minorities. An international city from the start, its first planners and rulers were French and Italian aristocrats brought from abroad by Catherine and her successors; for a while, in fact, before yielding to Russian, Italian was Odessa's lingua franca. Jews, Russians, Ukrainians, Poles, Moldavians, Greeks, Turks, Tatars, Azerbaijanis, Georgians, and Armenians mingled in its streets as equals. Of these groups, Jews were the largest, and while exposed to prejudice and even occasional anti-Semitic violence, they were not generally scapegoated or discriminated against. In a place where each "us" had many "thems," no single "them" was deemed the exclusive menace that Jews were elsewhere.

As a result, Odessa's Jews, who viewed the Russian language and its culture less as assimilatory lures or dangers than as a practical means of intercourse with their often equally non-Russian neighbors, underwent Russification more quickly than did the Jews of the Pale of Settlement, where the Tsarist regime sought to impose it from above. The son of small-town, Yiddish-speaking parents, Jabotinsky is a case in point. His father Yona—"Yoyne" to his Jewish friends and Yevgeni Grigorievitch to his Russian acquaintances—came from Nikopol, a river port on the Dnieper; his mother, Chava or Eva Zak, from Berdichev, a Ukrainian shtetl so heavily Jewish that even its Christians were said to know Yiddish. Yet though Chava spoke Russian so poorly that, as Jabotinsky put it, she "wreaked havoc" on it with every sentence, it was in Russian and not in Yiddish—as it would have been in Warsaw—that he was raised.

Scolded by his Russian nanny if he uttered a Yiddish word, he nevertheless heard enough of what he called his mother's "juicy Berdichev Yiddish" to acquire a passive knowledge of it that, with the help of the remarkable linguistic facility he was gifted with, he fully activated as an adult.

The Jabotinskys lived on Bazarnaya Street, a fifteen-minute walk from the municipal theater. The two-story, grey stone building whose top floor they rented is still standing. Although like most of the houses of old Odessa it now faces a mournfully rundown courtyard entered by a gateway whose keeper and gate have long vanished, it was a dignified middle-class residence in the late nineteenth century. Yona Jabotinsky was a grain agent, a profitable occupation at a time when Russia exported, via the Black Sea, vast amounts of Ukrainian wheat to Western Europe. An employee of the Russian Navigation and Commerce Company, the largest of the wheat-exporting firms, he plied the towns along the Dnieper, arranging for the purchase, transport, and storage of the annual crop and its loading onto the boats that brought it to Odessa. Long after his death at an early age in 1886, he was affectionately remembered by his associates as a hearty, good-natured man with a gift for getting along. He died of cancer after an extended stay for medical treatment in Germany that ate up the family's savings, leaving Chava Jabotinsky a hard-pressed widow with her six-year-old son Vladimir or Volodya (his Hebrew name of Ze'ev was rarely used), and her ten-year-old daughter Tamara or Tania. Jabotinsky's lifelong dislike of Germany and the German language—in which, too, he developed an adult fluency based on a childhood foundation—went back to his association of them with his father's illness and death.

Chava opened a small stationery store on the corner of Richelievskaya and Yevreskaya Streets, opposite the Great or Choral Synagogue, Odessa's largest place of Jewish worship, renowned for its children's choirs and operatic cantors. (Its congregants were described by Menachem-Mendl, accustomed to the more intimate and less decorous services of the shtetl, as sitting as silently as theater goers while "chewing their cud in their little prayer shawls and ritzy top hats. . . . Try praying loud enough for God to hear you and a beadle comes over and tells you to hush!") The family moved to cramped quarters in the courtyard behind the store, and soon afterwards, to an even smaller attic apartment nearby, where it barely managed to make ends meet with the assistance of Chava's elder brother, a well-off businessman.

A second brother, a lawyer, tried convincing Chava to send her son to a vocational school to learn a trade, but the advice was indignantly rejected as unbefitting a boy from a good Jewish family and Volodya was enrolled in a private Russian elementary school. Jabotinsky's short story "Squirrel," whose nine-year-old protagonist lives in an unnamed Black Sea city with his widowed mother, depicts this as a progressive institution. Run by two women whose young charges called them by their first names alone, it had the reputation of being "a crazy establishment" because of its unheard-of practice of co-education. To encourage a spirit of sharing, the boys and girls were divided into couples that pooled their lunchboxes. If he happened to have a sardine, the narrator writes, his partner got the tail, "or even the body if she was nice that day," in return for which he was given half of her corn cob, although he sometimes had to pull her hair to remind her that she had already eaten its first half.

Though fatherless, Jabotinsky had by his own testimony a happy childhood. A high-spirited, independent, self-confident boy, he was remembered by a friend as once answering, when asked whose son he was so that he might be punished for a misdeed, "I'm just me." Another time, slapped by a Russian army officer for playing too loudly in a courtyard, he hurled himself at his far larger assailant and tried striking back. Perhaps his buoyancy came from the personality of the father he had not known for long; perhaps from the love and devotion of a mother who scrimped for his education by such things as eating the stale remains of the bread she bought every day for her children; perhaps from the streets of Odessa, in which he roamed freely without supervision, often playing hooky from school. Classrooms bored him. Writing decades later as a parent himself, he would say:

> I've seen children who loved their schools. I envy them—but to tell the truth, I understand them no more than a blind man understands what sunlight looks like. To this day my instinct, which no other father would probably admit to, is to hate good students, those that always do their homework. The only kind I've ever loved were the mischief makers.

Like all Russian high schools at the time, Odessa's had a Jewish quota, and Jabotinsky's first applications to them were turned down. Only after attending a special preparatory school, from which he was nearly expelled for helping a classmate cheat on a Latin exam, was he admitted to the Richelieu Lycée; there he put his talents to better use, earning pocket money by writing compositions for his classmates. (At the start of one school year, he recalled in a later newspaper column, he produced an essay on "My Summer Vacation" for a large number of clients, taking care to invent a different summer for each.) Often, he cut classes to wander in the port and fish from its stone piers, and he preferred spending the hours after school with friends to preparing lessons. These were not always passed frivolously. He and his friends read serious books, and a group of them even produced a newspaper called *Pravda*, "Truth," using a hectograph or primitive printing device on which copies were made by being pressed on an inked screen. The paper's irreverent contributors had to be censored by its editor to keep it from being banned by the school authorities, and Jabotinsky's column, he later boasted, was blue-penciled the most. It was the start of his journalistic career.

Most of his friends were Jewish. As he was to recall:

> There were about ten of us [Jewish students] in our class. We sat together, and if we met in someone's home to play, read, or just "shoot the breeze," it was always by ourselves. Not that some of us didn't have Russian friends—I myself, for example, was on very good terms with Vsevolod Lebedentsev, a capital fellow . . . but though I often visited him in his home and was visited by him in mine, it never occurred to me to introduce him to my "gang," just as he never introduced me to his—nor did I even know if he had one. And even stranger was the fact that my Jewish gang had nothing Jewish about it. The literature we read wasn't Jewish, and we argued about Nietzsche, morality, and sex, not about the fate of Russian Jewry, though this was ultimately our fate, too.

Vsevolod Lebedentsev went on to study astronomy and join the Russian Social Revolutionary Party or SR, the main rival on the Left of the Russian Social Democratic Workers Party or SD, which spawned both Lenin's Bolsheviks and the anti-Bolshevik Mensheviks. Arrested in 1908 for his role in an unsuccessful plot to assassinate Grand Duke Nicholas, he was hanged with the other plotters. He and Jabotinsky remained friends long after their school years and Jabotinsky once visited him in his observatory, where he described him gazing at the stars "like one of the stokers of the furnaces of eternity," recording their motions with the same methodical precision with which he planned his abortive bomb attack.

Of formal Jewish education, Jabotinsky had little. When he was six, his mother taught him the Hebrew alphabet, and a while later, a young neighbor, struck by his intelligence, offered to give him free Hebrew lessons; the volunteer was Yehoshua Ravnitzky, who was later to collaborate with the poet Chaim

Nachman Bialik on their "Book of Legends," a monumental
anthology of rabbinic midrash. When it was time for his bar-
mitzvah, Volodya was passed on to more professional hands,
which he left upon turning thirteen. Yet Ravnitzky had done
his job well: Jabotinsky's earliest surviving letter in Hebrew,
penned at the age of twenty-three, was written to him, and long
before that, as a teenager, he made a Russian translation of a
nineteenth-century Hebrew poem that he and Ravnitzky had
studied together, Yehuda Leib Gordon's "In the Depths of the
Sea." A long, rhymed narrative about the expulsion of the Jews
from Spain in 1492, it had orotund lines like,

> The Daughter of Israel was driven from Spain.
> Upon Gaullish gates she knocked also in vain.
> Europe let her sons choose between dungeons and graves,
> Or else face the exile's fate on the waves.

On the whole, there is little basis for the common assertion
that Jabotinsky's Zionism was a purely adult development and
that he came from an assimilated or partially assimilated Jewish
home. In his memoirs, it is true, he wrote that, apart from his
lessons with Ravnitzky, he had "no inner contact with Judaism"
and its customs when young, and that the synagogue and its
rituals did not appeal to him. Yet in the same reminiscence, he
stated that his observant mother kept a strictly kosher kitchen,
lit candles every Sabbath eve, and scrupulously recited the daily
prayers, and that

> had a Christian boy asked me what I thought of the Jews, I
> would have answered that I "liked" them well enough, but a
> Jew would have gotten a different—and more naive—reply.
> [This would have been that] I knew that some day we would
> have our own kingdom and that I would go there to live.
> After all, my mother, my aunts, and even Ravnitzky thought
> so. I just didn't have a clear notion of it. It was something

taken for granted, like washing my hands in the morning or having soup for lunch.

The word for "kingdom" in this passage, which was written in Russian like nearly all of Jabotinsky's belletristic work, is the Yiddish *mlukhe*. Although Theodor Herzl only burst upon the Jewish scene in 1896–97, Zionism had made its earliest appearance in Eastern Europe when Jabotinsky was a child, with Odessa as one of its main centers. The Hibat Tsiyon or "Lovers of Zion" movement, the first organized attempt to sponsor modern Jewish settlement in Palestine, evolved in the early 1880s, in part under the influence of the Odessan physician Leo Pinsker's "Auto-Emancipation," a treatise written in the wake of an unprecedented wave of pogroms that swept southern Russia in 1881. (More than anything, it was these pogroms, which also triggered the start of a massive emigration to America, that aroused the interest of Russian Jews in a possible return to Palestine.) It was in Odessa, too, with Pinsker as its head, that a Society for Aid to Jewish Farmers and Artisans in Palestine, better known as "the Odessa Committee," was established. The committee, which had offices on a lane off Yevreskaya Street, helped to fund early Zionist projects and assist Palestine-bound emigrants, many of whom sailed from Odessa's port. The future Jewish "kingdom" had an embassy, so to speak, around the corner from where the Jabotinskys lived.

Apart from native Odessans like Pinsker and Ravnitsky, many prominent Zionist activists and intellectuals came to live in the city in these years. Among them were the Hebrew novelist and publicist Moshe Leib Lilienblum; Lilienblum's ideological rival, the Hebrew essayist Asher Ginsberg or Ahad Ha'am, one of the most influential Zionist thinkers of his age and the editor of the prestigious Hebrew journal *Hashiloach*; such friends and colleagues of Ahad Ha'am as Mordecai Ben-Ami and Elhanan Levinsky; the Hebrew literary critic and historian Yosef Klausner; Bialik; the Hebrew poet Sha'ul Tchernichovsky; the future mayor of Tel Aviv Meir Dizengoff, and others.

A number of these men were associated with *Hashiloach* and with Bialik and Ravnitzky's Moriah, an important Hebrew publishing house of the day; some were active in the city's Jewish Historical and Ethnographic Society, in its Hebrew and Jewish studies classes given at the Jewish library on Troitskaya Street, a block from the Jabotinskys' home, and in its Beseda (Russian for "Conversation") Club, a regularly convened Jewish discussion circle. All mingled with each other and with such non-Zionist Odessans as the great Yiddish and Hebrew fiction writer Shalom Abramovitch, known by his pen-name of Mendele Mocher Seforim, and the eminent Jewish historian Simon Dubnov. For a while, in the early 1890s, Odessa was also the home of Sholem Aleichem. In Jabotinsky's teenage years, it had the most vibrant Jewish cultural life of any city in Europe, and while he seems to have taken no particular interest in this, it was too much part of his surroundings for him to have been unaware of it.

All this does not add up to an "assimilated" Jewish background. Why, then, did the myth of one develop? In part because, to other Eastern European Zionist leaders of his generation like Chaim Weizmann and David Ben-Gurion, Jabotinsky really did seem a kind of half-breed. The Weizmanns and Ben-Gurions were products of the shtetl. They were raised in Yiddish; were given their first education in the heder, the religiously Orthodox Jewish schoolhouse in which secular subjects were rarely taught; socialized as boys exclusively with other Jewish youngsters; and learned the languages of the generally anti-Semitic Poles, Lithuanians, Ukrainians, and Belarussians among whom they lived only later. Their world was divided into Jews and non-Jews, the latter viewed as alien and hostile. Ben-Gurion, who in the 1930s headed the more diplomatically and territorially compromising Zionist Left against the more militant Right led by Jabotinsky, once remarked that the latter was the only Zionist politician he knew who had not the slightest instinctive fear of Gentiles and could never be intimidated by them. Although this was meant as a compliment, the inference was, as Weizmann was to put it more baldly in his autobiography *Trial and Error,* that Jabotinsky had something "not at all Jewish" about him.

This might have been a reasonable way of describing Jabotinsky had he grown up elsewhere than Odessa. Only in Odessa could an Eastern European Jew feel both deeply Jewish *and* totally at ease among non-Jews, because only there did Jews and non-Jews mix in truly neutral spaces. Early on in *The Five,* the narrator, recalling his years as a young Odessan journalist who frequented the town's Writers' Club, remarks:

> Looking back on all this some thirty years later, I think that the most curious thing about it was the good-natured fraternization of nationalities. All eight or ten tribes of old Odessa met in that club, and in fact it never occurred to anyone, even in silence, to note who was who. . . . In our homes, it seems, we lived apart . . . but we had yet to wonder why this was so, unconsciously considering it simply an indication of temporary oversight, and the Babylonian diversity of our common forum a symbol of a splendid tomorrow.

It was Yehuda Leib Gordon who had famously counseled Russian Jews, "Be a Jew at home and a human being when you leave it." Yet while societies in which one could live Jewishly in one's private life and as a citizen of the world outside it existed in many places in Europe in the second half of the nineteenth century—in Berlin, Paris, and Vienna, for example, all capitals of countries where Jews were fully emancipated, or in Herzl's Budapest—this was possible in Tsarist Russia in Odessa alone. It was not as an assimilated Jew that Jabotinsky grew up there, but as the anomaly of a Western or Central European–type

Jew in Eastern Europe. The feeling of many Eastern European Zionists that he was not one of them—"the inner life of Jewry had left no trace on him," wrote Weizmann—was of a piece with their attitude toward Western and Central European Zionism as a whole.

Such feelings were also had about Herzl. He, too, was raised more Jewishly than was commonly acknowledged by his Eastern European critics, who misattributed much of what they disliked about him to a total absence of Jewish roots. Nor was it only they who thought his Zionism derived from a born-again sense of Jewish identity that he did not grow up with. Many of his followers also regarded him as a Moses-figure, a Jew raised in Pharaoh's court, as it were, with no sense of connection to his fellow Israelites. Part of the fascination of Moses' story lies in his having adopted the persecuted people of his ancestors when he could have led the privileged life of an Egyptian prince, and a similar legend accrued to Herzl. Unlike the Zionism of the Weizmanns and Ben-Gurions, which aspired to solve not only the Jewish predicament but their own predicament as Jews, Herzl's Zionism seemed disinterested and therefore grander, a selfless act of devotion to his rediscovered brethren with whom he, the acclaimed European journalist and playwright, was under no compulsion to be associated. For his self-sacrifice, Jews felt awe and gratitude; by it their self-esteem was heightened, since his giving up so much to be their savior could only mean they were worth giving it up for.

Jabotinsky, a rising star like Herzl in the worlds of journalism and theater when he abandoned both for full-time Zionist activity, was to inspire similar emotions. But the parallel is not just between him and Herzl, or even between him and young Western European Jews of his era. It is also between him and many young Jews of our own age, whose upbringing, while not at all like Weizmann's or Ben-Gurion's, is a great deal like Jabotinsky's in Odessa. Whether acquired at home, in school, in the synagogue, or elsewhere, their Jewishness must compete with other possibilities of self-definition. Weizmann, though he could have decided after settling in England to devote himself solely to his work as a chemist without getting involved in Zionist politics, could not have decided not to live as a Jew. He already was one through and through, and it would have been psychologically impossible for him to have lived simply as an Englishman or private individual without Jewish ties and obligations.

This was not true of Jabotinsky. Odessa had instilled in him, alongside his Jewish identity, a potentially non-Jewish one as well. In one of his early Zionist essays, he recalled walking there with two Jewish companions and seeing a Jew with the long ear locks and caftan of the shtetl approach them. Although the man clearly felt nervous to be so conspicuously Jewish in a Russian crowd, he was also, Jabotinsky reflected, more sure of himself than were they, who had "from childhood on grown up with the knowledge that we were Jewish but didn't have to be."

He had a choice. Indeed, when he dropped out of high school at the age of seventeen and set out for Western Europe and for Italy, where he led a boisterous life for the next three years in an entirely non-Jewish environment, it seemed he had already chosen.

"Going West" was not an unusual thing for a young Russian Jew to do. At the turn of the century, whole colonies of such youngsters could be found in various European cities, especially in Germany and Switzerland. Most were students at universities that, unlike Russian ones, permitted them to matriculate without a high-school diploma; a smaller number were members of revolutionary movements in flight from the Tsarist police. Jabotinsky must have known more than one Odessan who had taken such a route before him.

What was unusual about his decision were two things. The

first was that he was already close to the diploma that was beyond the reach of most young Russian Jews. In another year,
he could have taken his final exams. Passing them would have
opened the doors to a Russian higher education and professional career, walking away from which for an adventure abroad
seemed reckless even to himself. When asked "Why, for God's
sake?" by his family and friends, he couldn't "for the life of me,"
he wrote, have answered them, since the only word to convey
the willful nature of his decision was "Because."

The second thing, which partially mitigated the folly of
the first, was that he left Russia with the promise of foreign
employment. The year before, he had published an article in
a local Odessan newspaper criticizing the Russian high-school
grading system; now, he talked the paper's editor into offering him the job of correspondent in either Bern or Rome, two
European capitals it was not represented in. Although his pref-
erence was for Rome, his mother insisted on Bern, where there
were other young Russian Jews like himself. In the spring of
1898 he departed for Switzerland via Vienna, traveling by train
through southern Ukraine and Galicia.

The journey was his first contact with the shtetl. He found
it depressing. The sight of so many Jews with their queer dress
and manners, living in poverty and seeming abjectness, filled
him with an "instinctive revulsion" that afterwards, he wrote,
took "an unceasing effort to overcome." This effort would already be apparent in an essay he was to write five years later,
in which he called on Jewish intellectuals to reject the "slav-
ish" adoption of anti-Semitic stereotypes of shtetl Jewry. At the
time, however, he recalled: "I looked away in silence and asked:
Can this people be mine?"

Journalism, which was his ambition, was not an academic
subject in those days, and he enrolled in Bern's law school as the
best alternative. A hotbed of political radicalism, Bern's Russian student community was in any case less concerned with

formal studies than with its fierce quarrels between SD's and
SR's, Mensheviks and Bolsheviks, believers in a spontaneous
revolution staged by the masses and proponents of the guid-
ing role of a conspiratorial elite. Russian revolutionary lumi-
naries like Lenin, Plekhanov, and Trotsky, all in political exile
in Switzerland, spent much of their time in Bern, whose Jewish students, as described by Chaim Weizmann, then working
on his doctorate in nearby Freiburg, were in awe of them and
excitedly debated the differences between them.

Jabotinsky, who had no clear political views of his own,
was a spectator at these debates. The only time he actively participated occurred at a lecture given by Nachum Syrkin, one
of the founders of socialist Zionism—an ideology ridiculed in
radical circles, which, in Weizmann's words, "stamped as unworthy [and] intellectually backward . . . the desire of any Jew
to occupy himself with the specific suffering and destiny of
Jewry." As Jabotinsky remembered it:

> It was then that I gave the first speech of my life—and a
> "Zionist" one at that. I spoke in Russian and what I said
> was: I don't know if I'm a socialist, because I'm not yet well
> enough versed in the theory of it, but I'm certainly a Zion-
> ist, because the Jewish people is a dreadful one. Its neighbors
> hate it for good reasons. Its only hope of avoiding a "Bar-
> tholomew's night" is to move to Palestine.
>
> The chairman of the meeting . . . translated the gist of
> my remarks into German as follows: "The speaker is not a
> socialist because he doesn't know what socialism is, but he
> is a confirmed anti-Semite and wants all of us [Jews] to run
> away to Palestine before we're slaughtered."

The massacre of "Bartholomew's Night" (the actual events
took place over a period of several weeks) involved the murder
of tens of thousands of French Huguenots by Catholic mobs in
1572, and Jabotinsky's dry, self-deprecating humor in relating the

evening in Bern is typical of his autobiographical writing. Conveyed by it, though, are some of the main features of what was to become his mature Zionism: its ambivalence toward the common Jew he both identified with and shrank from, its conviction that anti-Semitism had objective causes that were not merely the delusion of anti-Semites, and its premonition of the doom lying in wait for the Jews of Europe unless they left it in time.

In all of this, Jabotinsky was the Zionist politician most like Herzl. It is curious, therefore, that his memories of Bern make no mention of the first Zionist Congress that met in nearby Basel a year previously; there Herzl had steered Zionism in a new direction by converting it from an uncoordinated series of Jewish colonization projects in a Palestine ruled by an unsympathetic Turkish government to an international political movement, institutionalized as a world Zionist Organization, whose goal was obtaining an official charter from the Turks for massive Jewish settlement. Yet if Herzl and Zionism were not on the minds of the young Russians Jabotinsky befriended in Bern, Zion remained, for whatever reason, on his mind. In addition to writing several newspaper pieces during his stay there (the first, presumably for lack of a better subject, dealing with a local inhabitant accused of stabbing a fellow townsman for drowning a mouse), he composed a sentimental ballad about Jerusalem. In it, the city appears as a snow-white woman to the poet camped beneath its walls with an Arab guide, who tells him: "God has sworn that in this country / Hebrews once again shall dwell." The female apparition shares this hope. Concluding on a Zionistic but anti-religious note, the poem describes how

> She summons to the homeland's ranges
> From the Exile's darkest ends
> A people weary and exhausted
> By its God's endless demands.

After several months in Switzerland, Jabotinsky departed for Rome. He had probably intended to do so all along, and having wanted to get away from Russia, he was now eager to get away from Russians and their ideological quarrels, too. In a humorous poem, he described a nighttime walk in the Alps with a young lady who, when he sought to engage her in a romantic conversation, responded by asking if he was a Marxist. Before he could coax a kiss from her, he had to explain that "Only cowards and tame spirits / Need a god to whom to bow. / The highest type is he who has / No labels pasted to his brow."

Rome was relatively Russian-free. Jabotinsky's three years there were for him, as his friend, political colleague, and eventual biographer Joseph Schechtman was to put it, a "tremendous experience." Arriving in the autumn of 1898, he registered for classes in the law faculty of the Sapienza, the city's ancient university, and set about learning Italian, eventually mastering it so well that he could pass for a native, even if Romans thought he came from Milan and Milanese that he was Sicilian. (Years later, Schechtman wrote, he witnessed Jabotinsky chat with five Italian waiters in a London restaurant, speaking flawlessly in the local dialect of each.) He quickly made friends and embarked on a bohemian student life that was less political, more fun-loving, and more to his liking than Bern's.

Despite having developed rapidly since becoming the capital of a reunited Italy in 1871, Rome was still a compact city, not much larger than Odessa; its greater part consisted of an old historic center divided into fourteen *rioni* or neighborhoods, most on the left or east bank of the Tiber and two, Borgo and Trastavere, on the right bank. During his stay, Jabotinsky lived in Trevi, Borgo, and Campo Marzio, where he rented a room on the Via della Croce, a small street leading from the fashionable shopping avenue of the Via del Corso to the Piazza di Spagna. He changed addresses often—sometimes to move in with new roommates, sometimes because he could not pay the rent, and sometimes because his landlords threw him out. "The constant visitors, the singing, the clinking of glasses, and the loud arguments always ended," he wrote, "with my being asked to pitch my tent elsewhere."

One place he pitched it in was later described by him in a short story called "48 Via Montebello." A second-story apartment near the Piazza delle Finanze, it had five rooms and as many occupants: the narrator, a thinly disguised Jabotinsky; his friend Goffredo, a fellow law student, aspiring playwright, and ghostwriter of parliamentary speeches; Goffredo's teenage girl-friend; his younger brother, a high school student; and a young decadent poet. One room, set aside for a study, had a work table with four places: the high school student's, piled high with text-books; Goffredo's, set with a stack of writing paper and Nietz-sche's *Thus Spake Zarathustra* in Italian; the poet's, with the same writing paper and the same book in French; and the narrator's, with "nothing at all." Mornings started with the girl-friend serving the four young men tea in bed; evenings ended with a communal meal, several liters of cheap wine, and Italian and Russian songs accompanied by the poet on his mandolin. "Those were good times," the narrator recalls. "We didn't go to a single lecture at the university, we let nothing worry us, and we did no one the least bit of harm."

Jabotinsky probably did attend some lectures, although perhaps never on a regular basis. An official academic record issued to "Vladimiro Giabotinsky" shows him registering for six courses in his first year in Rome, four in his second year, and none in his third. At the bottom of the document is typed *No ha superato esami*, "Received no passing grades."

It wasn't for lack of illustrious teachers. Besides auditing classes of the philosopher Benedetto Croce, he took Roman Law with Vittorio Scialoja, a future minister of justice in the Italian government; Institutions of Roman Law and History of Roman Law with Gaetano Semeraro, a respected scholar who had served in Parliament; Political Economy with Angelo Messedaglia, a former Italian senator; and statistics with Eteocle Lorini, a world expert on monetary policy. Even more renowned were Enrico Ferri, with whom he registered for Law and Penal Procedure, and Antonio Labriola, who lectured on Moral Philosophy and the History of Philosophy—the former a founder of modern criminology, the latter a noted Marxist theoretician. Both were men of the Left, and if Jabotinsky had not already found out by now, he would have learned from them what socialism was. He was, he now decided, definitely for it. In Rome, too, left-wing ideologies were *bon ton* in student circles. Fascism was still far away, and the bourgeois democracy that Italy practiced was considered a philosophy for the middle class and middle-aged.

A good deal of his time was spent in the Piazza di Monte Citorio near the Tiber, where the Italian parliament had its seat. He had by now switched newspapers and was writing several times a week for the Odessa daily *Odesskaya Novosti*. As a correspondent expected to cover Italian politics, he put in long hours in the legislature, livening his accounts of what he called its "usual pandemonium" with as much human interest as he could muster. There were non-parliamentary topics to write about, too, such as Italian literature, theater, and opera, the street life of Rome, the Mafia, the Papacy, an Italian expedition to the North Pole, Jabotinsky's own travels in Italy, and most dramatically, the assassination of King Umberto I by an anarchist in the summer of 1900. Local crime was also a useful topic. The murder in Borgo of a local champion at the board game of *mulino*, and the arrest and trial of two men from the rival *rion* of Trastavere, accused of killing him to avenge his beating their own best player, was good for a number of stories.

When such material ran thin, Jabotinsky, who had taken to signing his pieces with the pen name "Altalena," an Italian word meaning "seesaw," fell back on his own life and its escapades, such as the time he and his companions ransomed a young lady of ill repute from a brothel, leading her out in a torch-light parade; the time he challenged a friend to a duel that was averted at the last moment; and the time he went on Goffredo's behalf, dressed in a black suit jacket, yellow gloves, checked yellow pants, black cape, and battered straw hat, to ask "Signorina Emilia," a seamstress married to a coachman, for the hand of her daughter Diana.

Goffredo's girlfriend Diana is also a character in a short story bearing her name in which she, Goffredo, and the narrator become entangled in an emotional triangle. Their relationship takes an unexpected turn one day when, sitting with the narrator in the Caffè Aragno, a favorite haunt of politicians, artists, and intellectuals, Goffredo challenges him to a competition for Diana's affections. Her being his girlfriend, he declares, gives him no rights over her, inasmuch as, the narrator is told by him,

> we people of the upper flight could afford to do away with such obsolete phraseology: there was no such thing as "right," there was only force and struggle for power—for power over a thing, or power over a woman.

Loath to make Diana, whom he is fond of, a test case of Goffredo's newly acquired Nietzscheanism, the narrator replies, "My dear chap, I don't want a row with you; please go on enjoying your luck and leave me alone," and is answered:

> "But there need be no row! Just the contrary, we must remain friends as we are; our friendship will only be purified by the fact of our honestly and openly isolating the struggle. It's quite simple."
>
> "You're a child," I said. "We'd hate each other on the second day."

The argument continues at a music hall and tavern until the worn-down narrator agrees. After all, he confides to the reader, "I really did want to make love to Diana just like he did, and even better than he could. [And so] I turned to him and said savagely: 'All right. I accept the challenge.'"

Yet things get ironically complicated. The narrator, uncertain whether he is motivated more by sexual desire or the determination to best Goffredo, flirts with Diana but makes no real advances; Diana, though having no scruples about going to bed with him, is too afraid of Goffredo to take the initiative; Goffredo, consumed by jealousy, is sure the two are having an affair when they aren't. Coming home one night to find a cruel letter from Diana, the narrator writes a sonnet in Italian. (Its first stanza apparently alludes to an incident that befell Jabotinsky as a teenager in Odessa.)

> There is a sea that men call Black, though it
> Shone sapphire long ago when, on the land,
> A gypsy with a vampire's eyes said, "Sit,
> And let me read your fortune in your hand.
> I see," she said to me, "your name is Pierre.
> Your mother's dead. The years ahead will start
> And end serenely. But I see here
> A wanton woman who will break your heart."
>
> The years went by. My mother's still with us.
> In her flows the proud blood of her race.
> My name, if truth be told, is Vladimir
> And my whole life has been tempestuous.
> And yet it was no lie: fool that I was,
> I let that woman drive me to despair.

The *donna indegna*, the "wanton woman," was all of eighteen and Jabotinsky's own "tempestuous" life had not yet completed its twentieth year, but the poem has a precociousness that belies this. The story ends with the narrator's return to

Odessa. The train for Vienna is already pulling out when Goffredo appears on the platform. Running to keep up with the narrator's moving car, he exclaims:

> "One word! If there has been anything, just say yes; if nothing, say no. I'll stop here if it embarrasses you, you'll shout from a distance, only please loudly. Only *please* do shout. I implore you. You have poisoned me, crushed me to earth, do release me."
>
> . . .
>
> Quite unwillingly, I laughed and drew away from the window, and the train rushed on.
>
> Never mind: in Odessa I soon received a letter from him containing his usual foul language; there was also a sealed envelope from Diana, which I sent back unopened.

Whatever the element of invention in stories like these, which were written many years afterwards, they tell us much about Jabotinsky's life in Rome. Goffredo, whose actual name was Roberto Lombardo, and Diana, which was how his girlfriend Antoinetta preferred to call herself, were real people. We know this from a letter Jabotinsky wrote in December 1902 from Odessa, to which he had returned a year and a half previously, to his Roman friend Arrigo Razzini, a fellow law student who went on to become a well-known legal commentator and historian. One of the earliest of the many thousands of Jabotinsky's correspondences in our possession, it asks: "Has Roberto really married Diana? You know that I don't understand him. Where did he get such nobility of character?" He was not displeased by the news, Jabotinsky wrote Razzini, because "it was I who first proposed to Antoinetta on Roberto's behalf." And he added: "Do you remember it? What happy years those were, what wonderful times!"

That they were. Looking back on them, Jabotinsky was to call Italy his true "spiritual homeland," and while he spent only a small part of his life there, it was a formative one. He had left Odessa an adolescent and he came back a grown man, having matured intellectually, emotionally, sexually, and artistically. Another poem he wrote while in Rome, this one in Russian, is called "Piazza di Spagna." It begins with a sketch of the square near which he lived on the Via della Croce:

> I'm ravished by you, Rome. Your mountain
> Of deep blue sky broods with sad majesty.
> The flowers planted by Bernini's fountain,
> Bloom autumnally.
>
> All pleases me: the little streets, the piazza,
> The old, twin-towered church, up to which curls
> The dragon's stairway with its touring knots of
> Country girls.

The twin-towered church was Trinita de' Monti at the top of the Spanish Steps, which seem to ripple up to it from the fountain below. (Bernini's sculpture of a half-sunken boat, its eye-like porthole jetting water and its bowsprit sticking up like a narwhale's horn, may have suggested a dragon rising from the depths.) The piazza had its flocks of tourists then, too, mostly rural Italians come to see their capital. But the simple charm of country girls is not for the poet. A city child himself, his heart belongs to the elegant daughters of Rome:

> I see them on the Corso, the patricians,
> The proudest and the boldest of their sex,
> Their furry boas hiding from my vision
> Stately necks.

Draped in the long, stylish "boa constrictor" muffs of the period, the temptresses of the Corso are alluring, even though the poet knows they are out to subjugate, not to be conquered. He knows, too, that, like the city that raised them, they evoke desire that will be dashed to the ground, and that their life of urban refinement is made possible only by the exploitation of the laboring masses. Still, he is enamored of them, as he is of Rome and the cosmopolitan glamour of the age. "Piazza di Spagna" ends with a fin-de-siècle flourish of jaded bravado:

> Their smile is false, their friendship knavery,
> Their wealth plundered from a thousand others' share;
> Their jewels glitter with the tears of slavery—
>   And I don't care.
>
> My times! I was born a son to you.
> I see your splendor and your squalidness.
> I love each blemish, large and small, in you,
>   Each poisoned kiss.

Rome opened Jabotinsky's eyes not only to a sophistication far greater than Odessa's, and to the cultural treasures of a country that embodied every stage of Western civilization in art, architecture, music, literature, and science, but to a way of life that was both cultivated and passionate, contentious but tolerant, light-hearted yet earnest, hedonistic while respectful of the pursuits of the mind. Though the most southern and Mediterranean-like of Russian cities, Odessa was ultimately a provincial town, without a history, without traditions, without a folk shaped and molded by long centuries, without the liberal political structure that alone could protect its diversity from eventual effacement. Rome was the real thing. It was the beating heart of a country that had been freed in a long struggle for independence led by the intrepid figure of Garibaldi, whose Italian nationalism was tempered by a democratic humanism, and it left Jabotinsky with a lifelong vision of what a decent, free, and pleasurable society could be like—the society he was to want for another former and future people of the Mediterranean: his own.

This people did not occupy his thoughts while in Rome. If to Odessa he owed the possibility of a non-Jewish self, in Rome he lived this self to the full. So little did Jewish concerns impinge on him there, he later wrote, that he was unaware until afterwards that some of the Italian students and professors he had known were Jews like himself. Nowhere do his memoirs mention the one significant Jewish encounter from this period for which there is evidence, which can be found in a little-known recollection by the Tel Aviv physician, author, and Revisionist politician Ya'akov Veinshal. In this account, Veinshal writes of being told by Jabotinsky about several meetings had by him in Rome and Naples with the Sephardi Zionist adventurer Yosef Marcou-Baruch.

Marcou-Baruch, who killed himself in Florence in 1899 after an unhappy love affair, is an extraordinary if now forgotten figure in Zionist history. Born in Constantinople in 1872, he led the life, inspired by Garibaldi, of an anarchist and would-be liberator of his people. Constantly on the move from one European city to another and frequently arrested and imprisoned for his views, he sought to spread the gospel of a Zionist army that would conquer Palestine from the Turks and even preached it as an Italian delegate to the second Zionist Congress in 1898, at which he was a considerable embarrassment to Herzl. Whether it was he who sought out Jabotinsky or vice versa is unclear; his possible influence on the development of Jabotinsky's thought must remain a matter of speculation.

To Arrigo Razzini, Jabotinsky wrote from Odessa: "Remember I told you this and mark it well: never turn back from an adventure and never ask yourself where it leads."

When Jabotinsky traveled to Odessa in June 1901, it was to spend his summer vacation there and return to Rome. His plans changed when *Odesskaya Novosti*'s Jewish editor Ossip Kheyfets, impressed by his Rome correspondent's popularity with the paper's readers, offered him a job at a good salary as a regular columnist stationed in Odessa. For a twenty-one-year-old journalist with three years of experience the proposal was irresistible, and Jabotinsky accepted and moved back to Odessa and his mother's apartment.

Odesskaya Novosti was a liberal paper, founded in 1895. A sketch drawn by its cartoonist Mikhail Linsky in the early 1900s shows a seated Kheyfetz, one finger lifted in admonishment or emphasis, lecturing a staff that is not paying him the slightest attention. In one corner, Linsky is talking animatedly to the cigar-smoking Russian impressionist painter Piotr Nilus while the well-known Jewish journalist Semyon Gerts-Vinogradsky listens. In mid-room, the Jewish writer Ossip Abramovich, one of the founders of Odessa's Writers' Club, stands with several men at a lectern, and the popular columnist "Flitt" converses with an unidentified dwarf. In the opposite corner, behind Kheyfets's back, the writer Alexander Fyodorov sits on a low cabinet beside a young man, his swinging legs encased in tight pants and leather boots, who has been identified as Jabotinsky. A closer look, however, reveals him to be Jabotinsky's friend Korney Chukovsky, later to become a well-known Soviet-period author of children's books. A bulldog sniffs at the boots.

Kheyfetz gave Jabotinsky a free hand, and his columns (or feuilletons, to use the French word for a European form that was longer and more literary than the Anglo-American column) touched on a wide variety of subjects. Russian politics, dealt with by others, was not one of them. Jabotinsky discussed books, theater, intellectual trends and developments, local issues and events, chance episodes and encounters, and whatever else he cared to reflect on. Among the first pieces written by him were a review of a performance of the opera *Faust;* an account of an exhibition of southern Russian painters; a discussion of corporal punishment in Russian schools; a reflection on household servants; an essay on the Italian poet Gabriele d'Annunzio; and a description of an Odessa fire. In the months that followed, the suicide of a streetwalker led to reflections on the profession of prostitution, the expulsion of a fraternity student for making anti-Semitic remarks to a defense of the right to free speech even for bigots, and the death from encephalitis of a boy in Moscow to a critique of Russian education. This began:

> A young boy sits trying to solve a complicated problem in arithmetic, keels over, and dies. It turns out that he's come down with brain fever.
>
> It happened not long ago in Moscow. The boy, whose name was Volodya Fodin, was twelve years old.
>
> I haven't the slightest doubt that the problem that killed him was taken from Varashchagin's arithmetic book.

From here, Jabotinsky went on to attack, first, the textbook in question, and next, the Russian school system for its pedantry and regimentation. Whether or not the twelve-year-old Volodya was actually doing his arithmetic lessons when he fell suddenly ill, the passage is typical of Jabotinsky's *Odesskaya Novosti* pieces, which jump swiftly from the incidental to the essential as if to make the point that incidentality itself is an illusion. By starting anywhere, such writing implies, one can soon get to the heart of anything.

Jabotinsky had a light, quick touch and a flair for the provocative and unconventional that were ideal for the feuilleton form. His following grew. Newsboys hawked *Odesskaya Novosti* in the streets with the cry, "Extra! Read Altalena today!" No older than a university student, he was now a local celebrity. At the theater, he had a reserved reviewer's seat with his name written on it in bronze letters. People pointed him out in the street, sought introductions to him. He was lively company. Chaim Weizmann, who first met him in 1903, found him an "immensely attractive" if "rather ugly" person, and the few photographs of him from this period show a short, young man with a tower of dense wavy hair, a broad, wide forehead, thick lips, heavy brows, and nearsighted, slightly froggy eyes. He liked to dress well. In one photograph he stands, hands clasped behind his back, in a striped jacket, vest, necktie, and fashionable cardboard collar, the pince-nez on his nose attached to his lapel by a gold or silver chain.

Although he had the reputation of being a lady's man, his memoirs are reticent on the subject. (In the preface to his "Story of My Life," Jabotinsky wrote that he had in reality told only half the story and omitted its more intimate side, whose many "friends, relationships, experience, and memories" were "far deeper and more momentous" than the things he wrote about.) The one female figure from his bachelor years to appear in them is Yoanna or Ania Gelperin.[2] Jabotinsky and Ania met when he was fifteen and she was ten; he was visiting her brother and she was playing the piano in the living room; although he called her "Mademoiselle," which flattered her, she had to stifle a laugh at his funny looks. When he returned from Rome, she was sixteen. One day at the home of a mutual friend, he teasingly handed her a gold coin from his pocket and declared in rabbinical language, "Behold thou art sanctified to me by this coin according to the religion of Moses and Israel." All present laughed except the friend's religiously observant father, who sternly warned Jabotinsky that he was now Ania's husband and would need a divorce if he wished to marry again.

Odesskaya Novosti's offices were in the "Passage," a magnificent Parisian-style shopping arcade at the top of Deribasovskaya Street, near Cathedral Square. Built in the 1890s with a modern glass roof over its central mall, its two facing, block-long buildings, each with a row of classical nude sculptures

2. Ania, the Russian name that is more commonly spelled Anna or Anya in English, was the spelling Jabotinsky used and the one therefore used in this book.

holding up the third and top floor, housed many of Odessa's fanciest shops. In *The Five*, Jabotinsky describes his daily walk to it. This started along Bazarnaya Street, crossed the "majestically sleepy" Pushkinskaya, came to Richelevskaya with its tables of moneychangers on which lay "banknotes from all the planets in the solar system," and turned into Yekaterinskaya, amid whose "tall houses in yesterday's styles" stood the Cafés Robin and Fanconi, "noisy as the seas at a massif." (Menachem-Mendl wrote his wife about doing business at Fanconi's, the favorite hangout of the stock exchange traders, while eating ice cream ordered from a waiter in a frock coat.) Yekaterinskaya led to Deribasovskaya, "the queen of streets in the whole world." Though architecturally undistinguished, it was the promenade on which anyone who was anyone in Odessa had to be seen—so much so, the narrator says, that he felt privileged each time his foot touched its "sacred ground" and instinctively checked to see if his necktie was in place.

Fanconi's is now a sushi bar, but Odessans promenade on Deribasovskaya to this day. At its other, seaward end, back toward the Londonskaya and the municipal theater, stands the grand old municipal library, converted to an archaeological museum, its broad steps ascending to a colonnaded Greek facade. Joined to it is a humbler building, today housing a museum too, that once belonged to the city's Literary and Artistic Society. Here, in an ornate room, its ceiling and walls goldtinted, the Writers' Club frequented by Jabotinsky met once a week. Odessa's liveliest intellectual salon, it was, the narrator of *The Five* remarks, "the focus of our spiritual ferment."

It was at this club that Jabotinsky caused a furor in the winter of 1901-2 by delivering an address upholding the supreme importance of the individual over that of the masses as maintained by Marxism. Midway through his remarks—in which he cited the Russian anarchist Mikhail Bakunin's prediction that the Marxist "dictatorship of the proletariat" would pose a greater threat to human freedom than any preceding it in human history—he was shouted down by the pro-Marxist audience with cries of "Reactionary!" and "Anarchist!" The ensuing melee was so great that the police had to be called to restore order.

The voluntarism of anarchist theory was indeed more congenial to his spirit than the coercive socialism of Marxism. Already in Bern, his nonconformist nature had taken a dislike to the doctrinaireness of Marxist thought. His years in Italy, so much more undisciplined in its way of life than northern Europe, had influenced him, too; so also, perhaps, had his friend Roberto Lombardo, eventually to become prominent in the Italian anarcho-syndicalist movement. An acquaintance who visited Jabotinsky at the time of his Writers' Club address was struck by the presence on his bookshelves not only of Bakunin, but of such other Russian anarchists and populists as Kropotkin, Lavrov, and Mikhailovsky.

The Tsarist police were struck by it, too. Besides keeping track of the anti-establishment tone of Jabotinsky's feuilletons, they were aware of his having written for the Italian radical journal *Avanti* and of his connections with revolutionaries like Lebedentsev. In April 1902, they raided his mother's apartment, went through his books and belongings, and arrested him. He was held in detention for nearly two months before being released, pending a decision on his case.

Jabotinsky was to remember these months with an insouciance probably greater than what he felt at the time. Given a cell of his own in the political wing of Odessa's prison, he took part in a life that was intensely social even though its participants never saw each other. Shouted conversations were held from cell to cell; notes and letters, tied to lengths of twirled rope, passed back and forth between the prisoners. At night, when the din of prison life died down, educational lectures were given. Jabotinsky spoke about the Italian independence struggle; unable to refrain from his theme of "individualism," he was not asked by his Marxist neighbors to address them again. And yet, he wrote in his memoirs, he had been listened to more tolerantly by them than he had been at the Writers' Club. Most were awaiting trial and possible deportation to Siberia. He had no intention of joining them there. After his release, he wrote to Arrigo Razzini:

> I'm under special surveillance following a period of imprisonment. I spent seven weeks in jail in the best and merriest company, and was given fine treatment and even worse food than [we students used to eat] on Via Cappucini. Now I'm awaiting a verdict from a secret court in St. Petersburg. If I'm not acquitted, you'll see me soon, because I'll take to my heels. . . .

In the end, the charges were dropped, though recently discovered documents in Soviet archives have revealed that the police kept an active file on Jabotinsky until 1911. In it appears the information that he served briefly in 1903 as a neighborhood representative of the anti-Bolshevik Odessa section of the Social-Democratic party, and that he was arrested again in 1904 for a supposedly seditious speech delivered at an anti-regime banquet. This time he was freed immediately.

Jabotinsky's prison experience influenced a poem he wrote later that year about the historical figure of Charlotte Corday, a young woman from the French provinces whose assassination of the Jacobin leader Jean-Paul Marat, stabbed by her with a kitchen knife as he lay in his bathtub, was a dramatic episode of the French Revolution. Charlotte, who sided with the Girondists, the more moderate revolutionary faction, killed Marat for his part in the revolutionary terror of 1793 and was guillotined herself four days later. In an address left behind to the

French people, she voiced the hope that she had demonstrated how much even "the most feeble hand" could accomplish by an act of "total devotion."

Jabotinsky's poem took the form of an imaginary letter written by Charlotte on the night before her execution to a fellow Girondist named Charles. It was Charles who, stopping by the garden of her village home for a drink of water one day, had first aroused her enthusiasm for the revolution, which her female sex prevented her, to her frustration, from playing an active role in. Bees were buzzing in the garden; she told Charles not to fear them because, since they lost their sting and died when they used it, they rarely did so; he replied that he would rather die "by plunging home my sting" than from illness or old age. Now, from her prison cell, Charlotte writes:

> Ah, Charles! Without a tear
> I could have given up all of life's pleasures.
> The roof above my head, my hopes and dreams,
> A kindred soul's bright, shining star of love —
> I could have learned to live without them,
> Though life were hard as stone.
> Only when I lost my pride,
> And with it the last spark of self-respect,
> Did living come to be impossible,
> Since there was nothing standing any more
> Between me and the chasm of despair. . . .
> . . . .
> And then [in prison] I thought of you. A long-forgotten
>   light
> Shone in my heart, and in my thoughts
> I traveled back to when, as though it happened now,
> I stood and listened to you speak
> Beneath the shady tree where I rebelled
> Against my fate for the first time.
> There was a murmur in my ears:

A merry swarm of bees flew by, and in a flash
I dimly heard the echo of your words,
"I'd rather die by plunging home my sting."
Silent, I glanced up—and there, quite close to me,
Two bees gleamed golden in the sun,
Catching the rays sent from its goodly hoard
Like two glints of fire.
"Yes, you are nature's gold," I said to them,
"And I am but dull lead.
Roaming far and laboring for your hive,
You have better things to do
Than seek a bitter end by stinging.
Not from gold are the best bullets made.
That is the fate of lead—the fate that's mine."

Charlotte kills Marat both to save her countrymen from a revolution that is devouring its own and to give meaning to the "dull lead" of a life that, so she fears, will otherwise leave no mark. Jabotinsky, who had shared a cell block with revolutionaries, was clearly occupied with the question of revolutionary idealism, its excesses, and the restraining force of moral conscience—and also, it would seem, with the fear that his own young life was being squandered like Charlotte's.

He had begun to think of journalism as a futile profession. To Razzini he wrote that it was "ruining my nerves" and that, though it paid well and had made him "cheaply popular," he would have to abandon it. In April 1902, shortly before his arrest, he had published a feuilleton entitled "Clowns" in which he compared himself and his fellow journalists to circus performers, using every possible trick to entertain a bored public. In another piece, called "Helplessness" and published in September of that year, he related a conversation with an eighteen-year-old girl who had turned to him because she had no money for the operation needed to save her mother's life. "I'm sorry, miss, there's nothing I can do," he apologized to her before telling his readers: "How gladly I would trade all the words I know and all the fire I can breathe into them for one true act! Let it be modest, let it be unnoticed—but let it be true."

He was looking, like Charlotte, for something worthy of his devotion. Had Razzini, his good friend from Rome, been told this was about to be Zionism, it would have seemed hard to credit. Yet that same September, Jabotinsky published an article in *Odesskaya Novosti* in which his childhood belief in a Jewish *mlukhe* and his adolescent romanticism about Zion, all but forgotten during his years in Italy, resurfaced in new form, shaped by inner developments and outer events into a mature conviction.

He had been introduced to Zionist literature after his return from Rome by a young Odessan businessman and Zionist activist named Shlomo Saltzman. The two met during an intermission at the opera, where Saltzman was chatting with Vsevolod Lebedentsev. The subject of Zionist thought came up and Saltzman offered to lend Jabotinsky writings by Lilienblum, Pinsker, and Herzl. It was his first encounter with Zionism, not as a visceral sentiment, but as a serious analysis of the Jewish condition and plan for changing it, and the impression made on him was great.

Since its founding congress in Basel five years earlier, Herzl's Zionist Organization had grown rapidly. The number of its followers had swelled; in Russia alone they now amounted to seventy thousand dues-paying members in more than five hundred chapters. Noted European writers and intellectuals like Max Nordau, Bernard Lazare, and Israel Zangwill had joined its ranks; four more international congresses had been held; a Jewish Colonial Trust had been established; and a high-level Zionist weekly edited by the young Martin Buber, the German-language *Die Welt*, had begun to appear in Vienna.

Yet in spite of all this, efforts to obtain a Palestine charter from the Sultan in return for a Zionist-backed loan to pay off

Turkey's massive international debt had gone nowhere. Herzl had been several times to Constantinople; had met with international financiers; had sought the support of Germany, which maintained close economic and diplomatic ties with the Turks; had traveled to Palestine for an audience with the Kaiser—and had nothing to show for it.

In his hectic courting of Jewish bankers, alternately wooed with promises of lucrative profits and lectures on their responsibilities to their people, and of European statesmen and monarchs, before whom he dangled the bait of a mass exodus of unwanted Jews from their countries, Herzl was like a juggler rushing to put a new ball into play each time an old one fell to the ground. A semi-organized opposition to him called "the democratic faction," composed mainly of young Eastern European Zionists like Weizmann under the intellectual leadership of Ahad Ha'am, had arisen within his own movement. In his fixation on high diplomacy and grand publicity coups, it claimed, he was neglecting the practical work of expanding the already existing Zionist presence in Palestine and fostering Jewish national consciousness in the Diaspora. Exhausted and suffering from a serious heart condition though only in his early forties, Herzl was more than once close to despair.

Moreover, the Jewish situation was worsening. In Russia, a regime threatened by a revolutionary movement in which Jews were disproportionately represented was seeking to divert public anger into anti-Semitic channels with the help of the pulpit and the press. Russian Jewry was targeted as the subversive root of all evil; *bey zhidov, spasai Rossiyu*, "beat the Jews and save Russia," became a popular slogan. Pogroms resulting in widespread damage to Jewish property had taken place in the Ukraine in 1897 and 1899, and in Russian-ruled Poland in 1902. In Vilna, in 1900, a Jew was indicted for the ritual blood murder of a Christian girl. Legal restrictions on Jewish residence rights were tightened; Jewish educational and occupational quotas were lowered still further. Even in Odessa, things had taken a turn for the worse. "In general," says the narrator of *The Five*,

> it became uncomfortable in Odessa. I had trouble recognizing our city, which only a short while ago had been so free and easy and good-natured. Now it was swept by a malice that, they say, had never previously affected our mild southern metropolis, created over the centuries through the loving and harmonious efforts of peaceful races. They'd always quarreled and cursed each other as rogues and idiots, and sometimes even fought; but in all my memory, there'd never been any ferocious, authentic hostility. Now all this had changed. . . .

Things were even grimmer in Rumania, which shared a border with Russia not far from Odessa. Never granted full citizenship rights, a quarter million Rumanian Jews were now declared alien residents, expelled from all public educational institutions, and forbidden to engage in a wide range of professions or to work for the government. Jewish communal leaders were arrested and deported.

Eastern European Jewry was fleeing westward by the hundreds of thousands. Western skies, however, were darkening, too. In Austria and Germany, anti-Semitism had long been a staple of political discourse; in the wake of the Dreyfus Affair, it had become so in France as well. The only sure havens were America and England, for which most of the emigrants headed—yet their numbers were stoking prejudice against them there, too. In both countries there was talk of legislation to curb or bar Jewish immigration. The prospect of millions of desperate Jews with nowhere to turn loomed large.

Never had the hope of a reestablished Jewish homeland been more relevant—yet its realization seemed no closer than before Herzl's appearance on the scene. Zionism's critics had multiplied alongside its supporters. For the European Left, it was a bourgeois movement distracting the Jewish masses from the revolutionary struggle; for the Right, a subversive force fostering disloyalty to the countries Jews lived in. Left and Right alike considered it a pipe dream, and Herzl a spent illusionist with little left up his sleeve.

Zionism's fiercest critics, because they were the most threatened by an ideology that branded them unwanted by European society, were Jews. One such opponent in Russia was the St. Petersburg journalist and intellectual Ossip Bikerman, a leading member of the Society for the Promotion of Culture Among Russian Jews, an organization dedicated to Russian Jewry's full integration into Russian life. In the summer of 1902, Bikerman published an attack on Zionism in the magazine *Russkoye Bogatsvo* that consisted of three main arguments: that Zionism was historically retrograde; that it was politically reactionary; and that it was, practically speaking, unworkable. Jabotinsky read Bikerman's article and responded to it in *Odesskaya Novosti*. He did so dismissively, reserving his greatest scorn for its second point. "One can argue," he wrote,

> whether Zionism is a desirable or practical solution, but to call it reactionary is grossly to defame a dream sprung from the Jewish people's sea of tears and suffering. . . . Defame it if you must! The dream is greater than its slanderers. It need not fear their calumny.

Jabotinsky's first published remarks on Zionism, these show him not yet fully identified with it, more a sympathizer than an adherent. Perhaps he, too, still needed to be convinced that it was a practical solution to a Jewish problem that had begun to concern him. Of the validity of the Zionist dream, however, he needed no convincing. He had been exposed to it as a boy. It angered him to see it maligned.

Perhaps he was also struggling to combine a commitment to a national struggle with his philosophy of "individualism," two things that did not easily go together. The conflict between them is hinted at in a play he wrote in the same crucial year of 1902. Called *Ladno*, Russian for "all right," it is one of his most intriguing works.

It was not his first theater piece. That was an effort called "Minister Gamm," the text of which, long believed to be lost, was rediscovered in a St. Petersburg library after the fall of the Soviet Union. Composed while Jabotinsky was still in Rome, it was a reworking of a drama called *Il Sangue*, "Blood," written by his roommate Roberto Lombardo under the impact of the Boer War. Jabotinsky took "Blood," which tells the story of the foreign minister of an imaginary European country who starts a pointless imperialist war and then kills himself in remorse when a young man dear to a lady friend of his dies in the fighting, and put it into verse in the tradition of such nineteenth-century Russian plays as Pushkin's *Boris Godunov* and Lermontov's *Masquerade*. Conventional in its anti-war sentiments, it was staged by the Odessa theater in 1901, starring the well-known actress Anna Paskhalovna. Jabotinsky's memoirs relate:

> The theater was empty. Perhaps 300 seats were taken, perhaps less, half of them by friends and acquaintances. Naturally, they applauded, and I was even asked to take a curtain call, though when I came out to bow in the new frock coat I had bought for the occasion, I tripped on the curtain cord and would have fallen flat on my face if Paskhalovna hadn't grabbed me. . . . At the crack of dawn I ran out to buy the newspapers—all of them, even the *Police Gazette*. The critics were merciful, the *Police Gazette*'s too, and didn't spoil the occasion, but the play closed after two performances. A year later, my second play ["All Right"] was performed. Also in rhyme, it had only one act. Paskhalovna appeared in it again, but this time the critics had no pity. As though by prior agreement, all joked about the play's name, calling it "All Wrong," "Nothing Right," etc.

The main protagonist of "All Right," Korolkov, is a young Russian student who, in a more extreme version of Jabotinsky's Writers' Club address, espouses a philosophy of self-fulfillment that repudiates all notions of social duty. Halfway through the play, he formulates it clearly:

> A single right is all I know:
> The right to my own self. That's all—and yet
> It's great and has no bounds. No one can owe
> A thing to anyone. . . .
> . . . .
> Be content, a passionate believer
> In yourself. Suspect all sacrifice,
> From which no good can ever come. Never
> Did the slightest seed of happiness
> Sprout from it. Burn your sacred incense
> To your will alone! By it be led
> To love or knowledge, art or idleness,
> To silence like a stone's on the sea's bed,
> Or else to follow the ancient path
> Of service to one's nation. Yet then, too,
> Imbue it with your spirit. Proclaim anew:
> "There is no struggle that obliges me.
> I celebrate my own will's sovereignty!"

Korolkov's credo clashes with his love for Marusya, a young woman who loves him back but rebuffs him in favor of a dull but reliable suitor whom she can count on to support her poor family. Refusing to accept her decision, Korolkov composes a romantic ballad about a brave young nobleman who rebels against his country's king in order to rescue his beloved princess from her imprisonment in a fortress—a symbol of Marusya's impending marriage. The play climaxes with a confrontation between the two. Going down on his knees, Korolkov exclaims bitterly, "Why must I give you up when I'm the one who waited for you and believed for so long? I don't agree!"

Marusya, her defenses overwhelmed, gives in. "All right," she replies. "Then *I* agree. Do you hear me? I'm ready for anything. All right? I'm yours. Take me, seize me, overpower me, ravish me! Just decide! Just decide! Just decide!" And the play concludes:

> Korolkov: All right. *(He exits without looking back. Marusya goes on sitting there, her eyes shut. He can be heard in the vestibule, putting on his coat and boots before walking away.)*

It's a puzzling ending. "All right" to *what?* Eloping with Marusya? But why, then, hasn't Korolkov swept his beloved up in his arms as does the young nobleman in his poem? Why his cruelly nonchalant departure, leaving Marusya alone and uncertain of his intentions just when she has offered to stake her life on him? What was Jabotinsky trying to convey?

Perhaps that Korolkov, like Goffredo in "Diana," is not the Nietzschean man of will he has pretended to be. At the crucial moment, indeed, he seems to have no will at all. Whether "All right" means "Yes," "I'll think about it," "It's too late," or "Whatever" hardly matters. Korolkov turns out to be a sham. Marusya, who has mustered the resolve that her lover only pretends to have, learns the difference between words and deeds the hard way.

But it is Korolkov's betrayal of his belief, not the belief itself, that is condemned in "All Right." Although Jabotinsky never saved the text of the play, which was found together with "Blood," he quite remarkably still remembered parts of it by heart three decades later. Sitting in 1935 in a hotel room in St. Louis in the middle of an exhausting speaking tour of America, he wrote in a letter to his sister Tania:

> I'm a believer in "individualism" to this day. If I were a philosopher, I'd try to harmonize this with my sense of service [to the Jewish people] as follows: I serve not because I'm

"required" to—no one is required to do anything for anyone—but because I will to. This is the education given by
Betar [the Zionist youth movement founded by Jabotinsky in
1923]. If something isn't to your liking, don't commit yourself to it, but if you do, make your commitment one hundred percent as a matter of self-respect. If you'd like, I can
quote you [lines] from "All Right" that expressed this idea
33 years ago.

The lines that Jabotinsky proceeded to quote to his sister
with only a few inaccuracies were from Korolkov's "A single
right is all I know" speech. The letter from St. Louis was thus
not only a statement of Jabotinsky's own credo; it was also a
gloss on the play's ending. What Korolkov lacks, this tells us, is
not the right values. It is the self-respect of commitment.

Whether there was someone like Marusya in Jabotinsky's
life in these years is unknown. (Can it be only a coincidence
that the tragic heroine of *The Five*, also loved but never possessed by the narrator, is named Marusya too?) But although
"All Right" was a minor event in a season that saw productions
of operas like *Tosca*, *Tannhaüser*, and Tchaikovsky's *Mazeppe*,
and plays like *Cyrano de Bergerac*, Ibsen's *The Wild Duck*, and
Sergei Alekseyev's *Vanyushin's Children*, it was a major turning
point for Jabotinsky, who was already then debating whether to
follow "the ancient path of service to one's nation."

This is a line that doesn't ring quite true. Why should
Korolkov mention a possible course of action that nothing in
his life or outlook predisposes him to? The words seem put in
his mouth by a playwright who has stepped momentarily outside the mind of his own character—which is exactly what Jabotinsky was doing. Ever since his return to Odessa, he had
been laboring to reconcile a belief in the radical freedom of the
self with the increasingly powerful pull of Jewish nationalism.
The solution hit upon by him was given, though in a context of

dramatic irony, to Korolkov to enunciate. If one *wills* to serve a cause or set of principles, service, too, is freedom.

In the history of Western thought this is a commonplace, whether expressed religiously by a statement like Thomas à Kempis's that men "shall never get liberty of mind till they with all their heart subdue themselves for God," or philosophically by Kant's "freedom and self-legislation of the will are both autonomy and consequently interchangeable concepts." Yet for Jabotinsky, it had the excitement of an intellectual discovery that addressed the central paradox of his life—that of a partisan of the right, even the obligation, to be one's own self who nevertheless chose to dedicate this self to a people and ultimately to create a political movement that demanded from its followers an iron discipline in the name of a common goal. Whether his life was ultimately coherent—whether it had a deep inner consistency or was at bottom a tragic contradiction—depends on whether this paradox makes sense to us or whether, like the Columbia University historian Michael Stanislawski in *Zionism and the Fin de Siècle: Cosmopolitanism and Nationalism from Nordau to Jabotinsky*, we regard it as a rationalization, "at best a non sequitur, at worst nonsensical." The deeper debate about Jabotinsky starts here.

On April 6, 1903, a day on which Easter Sunday coincided with the seventh day of Passover, a pogrom broke out in Kishinev, a heavily Jewish town in the largely Rumanian-speaking province of Moldavia, a hundred miles northwest of Odessa. When the Russian army and police finally stepped in to quell the mayhem two days later, forty-five Jews had been killed, more than six hundred had been wounded or raped, and about fifteen hundred Jewish homes and stores had been sacked and looted. Some of the victims sought to fight back; on the whole, though, resistance was sporadic. Although there had been intermittent pogroms in Russia since 1881, the slaughter in Kishinev had a savagery not experienced by Jews anywhere since the seventeenth century. It came as a shock, not only to Russian and world Jewry, but to all who had thought that the worst barbarism of European anti-Semitism was a thing of the past.

It did not, however, come out of the blue. Throughout the early months of 1903, hostility toward Jews had grown in the Russian south after a Christian boy was found dead in the Moldovan town of Dubossary and Jews were accused of his ritual murder. (The boy, it later turned out, had been killed by his own uncle.) Local riots erupted, and the widely circulated Kishinev newspaper *Bessarabets* conducted an incendiary anti-Jewish campaign. As was often the case with such agitation, it peaked toward Easter time. One circular making the rounds in the days before the holiday read:

> Our great festival of the Resurrection of Christ draws near.
> . . . The vile Jews are not content with having shed the blood
> of our Savior, whom they crucified. Every year they shed
> the innocent blood of Christians and use it in their religious
> rites. . . . They aspire to seize our beloved Russia. They issue
> proclamations inciting the people against the authorities,
> even against our Little Father, the Tsar. . . . Brothers, we
> need your help: let us massacre the vile Jews!

Odessa was not far away; tensions mounted there, too. Yet the organized Jewish community remained passive, and Jabotinsky, who had his ear to the ground as a journalist, wrote letters to its leaders urging the establishment of a Jewish self-defense force. None of them replied—not surprisingly, perhaps, considering that he was calling for clandestine action. Yet some knew that such a force, the first in Russian Jewish history, was already being organized in Odessa by a Zionist student group called Jerusalem. Jabotinsky's letter was passed on to it and he was contacted and invited to join.

He responded at once. As recalled by a member of the group, Yisra'el Trivosch, there was a knock one night on the door of its underground office, where a flyer was being run off on a hectograph. Certain it was a police raid, the apprehensive young Zionists opened the door. Standing there was Jabotinsky with two companions. He took in the scene at a glance, said, "You look dead tired; let us spell you for a while," and stayed up until six in the morning, working the hectograph while the students slept. The flyer ended with the call: "Let there be an end to the shameful heritage of centuries in which we went like sheep to the slaughter. . . . All for one and one for all! To arms in our own defense!"

Jabotinsky threw himself into the self-defense force's activities. He helped to compose and print proclamations, raise money from wealthy Jews, negotiate with arms dealers for the purchase of revolvers, distribute them to volunteers taught to shoot, plan their deployment, and patrol the city to check for signs of impending trouble. He was remembered by his comrades as being everywhere, always cheerfully ready to lend a hand.

What impelled him to do it? In part, no doubt, the same instinct that had caused him as a boy to lunge at a Russian officer twice his size. It was his nature to fight back when attacked, and if attacked as a Jew, to fight back as one.

But it was more than that. As part of the self-defense force's fund-raising drive, Jabotinsky spoke one night to a group of Odessan Jewish intellectuals convened at the home of Meir Dizengoff. As quoted by Trivosch, he declared:

> We are a people [and] you may as well be angry with your parents for having brought you into the world as wish to be excused from belonging to your people. . . . Life is always a war. The weak are treated with contempt. The bug squashed beneath someone's foot does not feel insulted; [but] men are

sovereign, even if exaggerated egotism can drive them to suicidal extremes.

In theory, every man was—echoing Korolkov's language—"sovereign"; in practice, living one's sovereignty in isolation from others only led to being trampled on. With this formulation, the intellectual foundations of Jabotinsky's conversion to Zionism were completed. These were based on a belief in Jewish activism in Russia no less than in Palestine, since Zionism, as Leo Pinsker had written in his "Auto-Emancipation," called on Jews to take their destiny into their own hands in the Diaspora as well. Indeed, when Jabotinsky first heard of the Kishinev pogrom, he had just finished delivering a lecture on Pinsker at the Beseda Club. Though it was already the evening of the pogrom's second day, news of it had yet to reach Odessa, the city's newspapers and their telegraph services having been shut down for the Easter holiday. Present at the lecture was the historian Simon Dubnov, a non-Zionist Jewish nationalist who advocated Jewish autonomy in Eastern Europe. As he later wrote:

> That night the Jewish audience assembled to listen to the talk of a young Zionist, the Odessa *Wunderkind* V. Jabotinsky. . . . The young propagandist [*sic*] had great success with his audience [though] as for my own impression, his one-sided treatment of our historical problem depressed me. . . . During the [refreshment] break, while pacing up and down in the neighboring room, I noticed a sudden unrest in the audience: the news had spread that fugitives had arrived in Odessa from nearby Kishinev and reported on a bloody pogrom in progress there.

The next morning, according to Korney Chukovsky, Jabotinsky stormed into an editorial meeting of *Odesskaya Novosti*, turned to the non-Jews on the staff, berated them and the entire Christian world for what had happened, and stormed back out, slamming the door behind him. It was an uncharacteristic tirade for a generally even-tempered person and probably a factor in the newspaper's sponsorship of a relief fund that collected money and supplies for the pogrom's victims. Sent to Kishinev to oversee their distribution, Jabotinsky toured the sites of devastation, spoke to survivors, and visited the injured in the hospital.

Although it would have been an obvious subject to write about, he published nothing about Kishinev in *Odesskaya Novosti*. Almost demonstratively, his columns in the days after the pogrom dealt with other topics, such as an Italian actor performing in Odessa and the sexual exploitation of female workers by their employers. Yet far from indicating—as he was to claim in his memoirs—that the pogrom made little impression on him and taught him nothing he didn't know about Jewish helplessness (the more damning word used by him was "cowardice") in the face of aggression, his silence at the time suggests the opposite. The fury and frustration described by Chukovsky were real. If Jabotinsky didn't write about Kishinev, this was because, as a journalist with a reputation for wit and urbanity, he didn't trust himself to control his emotions.

A description of Jabotinsky's true reaction to the pogrom can be found in his third and last play, "A Strange Land," written in 1907 but never produced. Composed largely in verse like "Blood" and "All Right," it is set in Odessa during the 1905 uprising. Each of its main characters is a representative type of Russian Jewish youth; one, Gonta, has just returned from two years in America, where he went, he says, "to forget." "To forget what?" he is asked and replies "Who I was" and continues:

> I was in Kishinev.
> The Relief Committee sent me with some money
> And a bundle of old clothes.
> I spent three days there,
> And on the evening of the third, I fled.

I couldn't breathe. I kept thinking
People in the street were pointing at me:
"There goes a kike! Look at that cringing yid!"
I ran and took a train and faced the window,
Not even getting up to stretch my legs at stations.
I forced myself to talk to no one,
Look at nothing,
Think of nothing—
Nothing but the need to get away.

Gonta has returned from America not as "who he was," a revolutionary confident that the socialism that would solve all of Russia's problems would solve its Jewish problem too, but as a Zionist convinced that the Jews have no future in an irredeemably anti-Semitic society. "I say to you," he proclaims in the play's final act:

> stop living lies!
> You're in a lion's den. Have no illusions.
> Your dreams are nothing but a fool's effusions.
> At the volcano's edge, you're fireflies.
>> The glowworm's tiny spark
>> Can't cause a mountain to erupt,
> But get this through your heads: when it blows up
> You'll vanish with the first discharge,
> You and all your work, the laboring of ants.
> That's something you had better understand.

"What for?" someone wants to know, and Gonta replies:

> So that, once and for all, we'll burn
> Our bridges to this murderous land
> That never can be ours; learn to demand
> Nothing from it, give nothing in return;
> Spurn its alien pomp and circumstance;
> Turn upon its riches scornful backs
> And like a badge of honor wear our rags;

> Walk away from its grand opulence
> And festal boards with their munificence;
> Forgo it all; display the proud disdain
> Of a vagabond who once was king!

Gonta is not given the last word in "A Strange Land." When he is done speaking, his appeal to Jewish pride is mocked by another character:

> Ah, Monsieur Gonta, a highly interesting specimen! We [Russian Jews] disgusted him: his closeness to us was like a chain around his legs—no, like a hump on his back that he couldn't get rid of. And so now he's made a virtue of necessity and shouts from every rooftop, "How proud I am of my hump!"

This was not an unjustified observation regarding either Gonta-Jabotinsky or Zionism. In both cases, the pride and shame of being Jewish were closely linked. Without pride, shame could not be aroused; without shame, pride could not be spurred into action. Kishinev called, not for breast-beating, but for an end to the powerlessness of exile. As if to remind himself of this, Jabotinsky carried around with him for years a scrap of parchment from which the title of his play was taken. Torn from a desecrated Torah and retrieved from the rubble near one of Kishinev's synagogues, it bore part of the verse in Exodus, "I have been a stranger in a strange land." Some lines of poetry he wrote about it went:

> In that town, I spied in the debris
> The torn fragment of a parchment scroll
> And gently brushed away the dirt to see
> What tale it told.
> Written on it was "In a strange land"—
> Just a few words from the Bible, but the sum
> Of all one needs to understand
> Of a pogrom.

These lines appeared in Jabotinsky's introduction to a Russian translation he made of Bialik's long Hebrew poem "In the City of Slaughter." Bialik had been in Kishinev with a Jewish commission of inquiry and was, like Jabotinsky, shocked by the failure of most of the town's Jews, who made up half its population, to defend themselves. Raging more at them and their unsuccessful efforts to hide under beds and in basements than at their assailants, his poem assumed the mock-prophetic form of a bitter tirade by God, who guides the poet through the streets of Kishinev with commentary like:

> And now go down to their dark cellar holes!
> There, on each daughter of your people, amid junk and
>   old tools,
> Seven uncircumcised savages piled,
> Despoiling child in front of mother, mother in front of
>   child,
> Before, and as, and after their throats were slit.
> Touch the red-stained pillow and the gory sheet,
> The satyr's cesspit and the wild pig's sty;
> See the bloodied ax, and then espy,
> Crouched behind barrels and moldy hides,
> The husbands, the brothers, the betrothed of young
>   brides,
> Peering through peepholes at bodies that writhe.

"In the City of Slaughter" had an electrifying effect on Russian Jewry. Even before its publication, which was delayed by problems with the censor, it circulated widely in handwritten copies read aloud to audiences that gathered to hear it. Suffused with biblical language and allusions, it was nevertheless something new in Hebrew literature — not another lamentation for Jewish victimhood permitted by an all-powerful God, but self-castigation for what a powerless God could not have prevented, though a determined and organized Jewish populace might have. Jabotinsky's translation reached a larger audience than did the Hebrew original and helped make him known far beyond the confines of Odessa.

Jabotinsky's emergence as a Zionist voice led to his being asked to serve as a delegate from Odessa to the sixth Zionist Congress that convened in Basel in August 1903. The congress came after a period in which Herzl, having gotten nowhere with the Turks, had turned to England, whose colonial secretary Joseph Chamberlain had expressed sympathy for Zionism and a willingness to grant it a territory from Great Britain's imperial holdings. The most promising possibility raised by Chamberlain was of the arid, sparsely inhabited Mediterranean coast of the Sinai Peninsula near El-Arish, on British-controlled Egypt's side of its frontier with Turkish Palestine — a location, Herzl hoped, that Zionists could regard as a stepping stone to Palestine. Throughout the winter and spring of 1902–3 he worked on the project, conferring with Chamberlain in London, sending a fact-finding mission to Sinai, and traveling to Cairo for talks. Yet the mission's findings were unfavorable; British officials in Egypt opposed Herzl's idea of irrigating El-Arish's sands with Nile water; and by the summer of 1903, the scheme had collapsed.

This failure, however, remained a secret. As the congress's 592 delegates gathered from all over Europe for the informal caucuses preceding the opening session on August 23, the El-Arish plan was expected to be on the agenda. It threatened to divide the delegates into two warring factions — one, largely Western European, that did not object to launching the Zionist project next door to Zion, and the other, grouped around the "democratic faction," insisting on Zion itself. A fight also loomed over a second issue, a recent visit of Herzl's to St. Petersburg, where he had met with the openly anti-Semitic

Russian interior minister Vyacheslav von Plehve and extracted from him an endorsement of Zionism in return for a promise to restrict its activities to Jewish emigration and not to interfere in internal Russian affairs. Although Herzl sought to present this agreement as a significant achievement, it was seized on by his opponents as a capitulation to dark forces by which he was being manipulated. Zionism, they maintained, could only succeed by remaining an idealistic movement for which worthy ends did not justify squalid means.

Despite Jabotinsky's assertion in his memoirs that he arrived in Basel a total unknown in the Zionist world, this was not exactly the case. At the very least, his reputation merited being asked by Martin Buber to write the lead article for *Die Welt*'s pre-congress issue of August 6. Published in German under the byline "W. Schabotinsky" and the title "Kadima," Hebrew for both "eastward" and "onward," the article took issue with Jews who called Zionism an escapist fantasy. The real Jewish escapism, Jabotinsky argued, was assimilation, to which Zionism was the only effective alternative. "We Zionists," he concluded, "are summoning our people to an act of historic creation. We do not point to the east, saying: 'Run, find a cave you can hide in from your persecutors.' We point to it and say: *'Kadima!'*" In writing these words, he was surely thinking of the evening in Bern five years previously when he was mocked for urging Jews to "run away" to Palestine. Now, he was no longer a young student blurting out his raw impressions but a spokesman for a movement to which he fully belonged.

Jabotinsky also covered the congress for *Odesskaya Novosti*, in which he published four long dispatches. The first two dealt with caucuses he attended. One was held by the Mizrachi, the religiously Orthodox Zionist party; struck by its moderateness, he deemed it capable of collaborating with secular Zionists. The other was convened by a Hebraist faction that demanded

Hebrew's adoption as the official language of the Zionist movement and of a future Jewish state. (The congress itself was conducted in German, with delegates free to use Yiddish, Russian,
or Hebrew if they wished.) While confessing that he did not
understand spoken Hebrew well enough to follow the proceedings, Jabotinsky was impressed by the speakers' fluency and
predicted that their goal would be accomplished in Palestine
because Hebrew alone could serve as a lingua franca there; he
was also struck by the Sephardic diction used by some of them,
which he judged more exact and pleasing than the Ashkenazi
pronunciation he was familiar with. The experience spurred
him to take up the study of Hebrew again.

Jabotinsky's third dispatch—written, he told his readers, in
the middle of the night, on time stolen from his sleep—was an
account of the congress's gala opening session held earlier that
evening. After a brief description of the delegates, he moved
on to Herzl, who gave the keynote address and was "the most
interesting-looking man I have ever seen," with a manner "sub-
limely courageous."

> Unbending and magnificent, he has a profile like an Assyrian
> king's in an old bas-relief. He is self-confident [though] it's
> hard to say precisely wherein his power lies. He can't be
> called a great writer, despite having a fine style. . . . His ora-
> tory is not particularly emphatic—yet he outperforms all
> others. Many claim to be hypnotized by him. All this adds
> up to a man of mediocre abilities who is nonetheless a great
> figure—a genius of no special talents.

It was an oddly ambivalent form of adulation at first sight.
Having never put anyone on a pedestal before, Jabotinsky
appeared to be mystified by finding himself doing that now.
Thirty years later, a hero-worshiped politician himself, he was
still trying to understand the magical effect Herzl had had on
him. Nowadays, he wrote in a 1934 essay called "The Leader,"

European politics abounded in charismatic Duces and Führers who, if their true biographies were ever written, would prove to have been little more than "stuffed rag dolls." Yet in Herzl's day, the very concept of the charismatic politician did not exist; leaders were obeyed either by virtue of the authority invested in them by their office or because they were chosen by their electors. Herzl had no such objective power. He was able to lead because he spoke from and to a place of truth. Jews followed him not because of his personality, commanding though that was, but because they were carried away "as though by a gifted singer whose song is that of one's own deepest yearnings."

Yet at the sixth Zionist Congress, the melody was changed without warning. Herzl's keynote address, Jabotinsky informed his readers, dropped a bombshell. The El-Arish plan had fallen through. The British government, however, was now offering another territory, in the well-watered, temperate highlands of East Africa, where Jews would be allowed to enjoy home rule as a British protectorate. Given the urgent need to provide Eastern European Jewry with a reliable asylum, he, Herzl, favored accepting the proposal as long as Palestine, "the land of our forefathers," remained the ultimate goal. As a first step, he was asking the delegates to appoint a committee to investigate the prospects and report back.

The British offer—although apparently referring to an area in northwest Kenya near Lake Victoria, it immediately became known as the "Uganda plan"—was a sensational breakthrough for political Zionism: a mere six years after the movement's founding, it was being granted an opportunity to establish a semi-independent Jewish polity under the aegis of a major European power. Yet it was a breakthrough with agonizing implications, for Herzl's "Palestine proviso" could hardly be taken seriously. Unlike El-Arish, from which an expansion of Jewish settlement into nearby Palestine was imaginable, East Africa was thousands of miles away; the enormous investment of time, money, and human resources needed for developing an autonomous Jewish region there clearly precluded a similar effort elsewhere. Was it better, Jabotinsky asked in his dispatch, "to sacrifice an age-old tradition [of Jewish attachment to Palestine] for an immediately attainable success, or to reject a noble offer so as to carry on with the struggle for the Holy Land?"

It was an issue of profound historical and existential dimensions. Just who were the Jewish people that Zionism claimed to represent? What was their relation to their national and religious past? How much did or should this past define them? What role, if any, should a nation's founding myths play in its politics? A few days' debate culminating in a show of hands, if only to appoint a committee, was hardly an appropriate way to deal with such issues. Yet a show of hands, which he expected to win easily, was what Herzl wanted—and a bitter debate was what he got.

A majority of the Western Europeans again supported him. Most of them conceived of a Jewish state more as a place of refuge for their persecuted brethren than as an expression of Jewish national and cultural aspirations, and a well-disposed British protectorate in Africa seemed no worse an option than a hostile Turkish Palestine. The Eastern European vote was more divided—and more paradoxical. The Mizrachi voted with Herzl; under attack by the anti-Zionist Orthodox establishment for supporting a Jewish return to the Land of Israel without divine sanction, it sought to demonstrate that it was motivated solely by a desire to relieve Jewish suffering that was untainted by messianic fantasies. Nearly all of the secular Zionists of the "democratic faction," on the other hand, were fiercely opposed; products of the shtetl and its values even after having revolted against them, they could not imagine a Jewish homeland that was not the land Jews always had longed for. What could be the point of Jewish-owned plantations and haciendas in a country without roots in Jewish collective memory? What devotion could they inspire? By turning his back on Zion, it was argued, Herzl had betrayed the movement that bore its name.

The vote took place on the fourth day of the congress, in an atmosphere fraught with emotion. Two hundred ninety-five delegates voted in favor, 176 were against, and 143 abstained. For Herzl, it was a Pyrrhic victory. Sometimes grumbled about but always deferred to at Zionist Congresses until now, he was shocked by the size and intensity of the revolt against him. Worse yet, not only had he failed to command an absolute majority of the delegates, the "nay-sayers" spontaneously walked out of the hall as soon as the last vote was counted and adjourned to a nearby room, where they acted as though a disaster had befallen them. Some wept openly. Others sat on the floor and removed their shoes as Jews did on Tisha b'Av, the day of mourning for the destruction of the Temple.

Despite his admiration for Herzl, who seemed to him "without exaggeration, a giant," Jabotinsky voted with the opposition and joined the walkout—why, he later said, he wasn't sure. He had, he declared in his memoirs, "no romantic love for Palestine." The only explanation he could give was the same willful "because" that had made him leave school and Odessa for Rome.

Had he re-read his last dispatch to *Odesskaya Novosti*, he might have remembered things differently. There was, he wrote there, something genuinely tragic about what he had witnessed. "Think of what it is like," he told his readers, "to belong to a tribe that must weep over its first political victory in 1,800 years!" But although he could identify with both sides, it was the losing Easterners, he believed, "the mourners for Zion," who would prevail in the long run, since they were in touch with something in the Jewish psyche that the Westerners had lost contact with. The Russian delegates reflected the "natural and powerful will of the people." Even if Herzl were to get nowhere with the Sultan for the next twenty years, they still would say: "No matter. Maybe next time around we'll be luckier—and now let's get on with the work!" Although more of a "Westerner" in outlook himself, he felt in his heart that the "Easterners" were right.

In their breakaway quarters, the rebels debated whether to carry on with the fight or quit the congress and the Zionist Organization entirely. They were still arguing among themselves when Herzl, coming from the hotel room where he had adjourned, appeared at the door and asked to speak to them. Feelings were running so high that he was not immediately admitted—and when he was, Jabotinsky wrote, the nay-sayers signaled one another not to applaud his entrance as they always had done in the past. Yet Herzl spoke simply but eloquently,

> without oratorical flourishes and in full control of himself. Every word was self-assured, [even] patronizing. He spoke like a man who still expects to be listened to, as an adult speaks to a child. There were moments when I thought, "Here come the shouts of protest," but there were none. From his very first words, every face was rapt with attention.

Herzl defended himself. He had not given up on Palestine. But

> does that justify officially turning the British down without even looking at what they have suggested? . . . Forcing me to do so would put me in an untenable position. No one would ever want to negotiate with me again. I would be the man who lacked the power to get this congress even to consider a proposal I had received.

He ended on a recriminatory note:

> You can ask me to step down whenever you want. I won't argue. I'll go back to the private life that, believe me, I've been longing for. I only hope that afterwards no one will rightly be able to say that it was all because you didn't understand

me—that your ingratitude made you misconstrue my true intentions.

His words had their effect. The rebels decided to return to the congress for its closing session. A split had been avoided.

Jabotinsky's last dispatch ended with reflections on Zionism's future. The crucial question, he wrote, was whether the "Uganda plan" was simply a ploy on Herzl's part to extract concession from the Turks by convincing them he had other alternatives. Even the nay-sayers wondered whether he mightn't be "playing the game" now, too, with East Africa as one more ball to juggle with. If Herzl had the will to go on working for Palestine, Jabotinsky thought, he could still obtain it. Yet at the same time,

> I myself don't believe that Herzl is as indispensable to the movement called Zionism as he is commonly thought to be. . . . Although he may be a figure of unparalleled importance, I am sure that, were he to fall by the wayside, Zionism is too deeply grounded in the Jewish soul for the "game" not to go on. And Zionism leads only to Palestine. I have no doubt that that's where Herzl wishes to lead it to, too. The day he ceases to do so will be the day it marches on, unstoppably, without him.

Jabotinsky himself spoke only once at the congress—and not about East Africa. Allotted a quarter hour like every delegate, he used it to defend Herzl's dealings with Von Plehve. His memoirs relate:

> I had barely begun to argue that morality and political tactics were two totally different things when the benches of the opposition sensed what I—an unknown fellow with a great shock of dark hair and high-flown Russian like a high school student's declaiming for an exam—was driving at and began to shout: "Enough! We don't need to hear that!" There was a commotion in the presidium. Herzl heard the racket, came

running from a nearby room, and asked one of the delegates, "What's going on? What is he saying?" The delegate, who happened to be Dr. Weizmann, answered "Nonsense," and Herzl stepped up behind me and said, "*Ihr Zeit ist um* [Your time is up]." It was the first and last time he ever addressed me.

As Michael Stanislawski has pointed out, this does not appear to be what actually happened, since the congress's records state that it was the session's chairman, the German delegate Max Bodenheimer, who told Jabotinsky his time had run out. Stanislawski cites this inaccuracy in support of his view that "Jabotinsky's various autobiographical writings . . . are a self-conscious and highly inventive literary creation that deliberately, if quite naturally, presents a selective and factually distorted portrait of their author, often omitting the most salient and revealing truths." Jabotinsky—who wrote in a preface to "Remembrances of a Contemporary" that he had no patience for fact-checking, that readers should not expect "the whole truth from him," and that memoirs are a form of belles-lettres in which (quoting Goethe) "reality and vision" are combined— would not have taken umbrage at this. Yet Stanislawski's calling a comic description of a minor incident "perhaps the most evocative case of Jabotinsky's retroactive creation of his own myth" testifies, if anything, to Jabotinsky's overall restraint in retouching historical fact, with which he took liberties, when he did, more to deflate himself humorously than to puff himself up.[3] And who is to say, for that matter, that Herzl was not

---

3. In all his non-fiction, there is only one case known to me, to which he himself cheerfully confessed, of Jabotinsky's engaging in an outright fabrication (see p. 90). For the most part, I believe, his memoirs are a sincere if artful attempt to describe times and episodes in his life as he recalled them, and I have treated them as essentially reliable accounts despite whatever inaccuracies in them are attributable either to the vagaries of memory or to literary and personal considerations.

unrecordedly present at that moment and did not indeed tell Bodenheimer to cut Jabotinsky short?

Herzl died of a heart attack less than a year later. By then, Jabotinsky had left Odessa a second time and was living in St. Petersburg, where he was engaged in full-time Zionist work. It was an adventure he never turned back from.

2

Jabotinsky the Zionist

THE YOUNG JABOTINSKY bowed out in Basel. Never again was there to be a period like 1902–3 in which clashing vectors within him collided and threw him on a new course. From now on, that course held steady. His Zionist activity dominated all else. Although his career as a Zionist politician was to have its dramas, some major ones by any historical standard, it also spanned long and less momentous years in which no single chapter stands out above the rest.

Such were the years between 1903 and 1914, which began with his moving to St. Petersburg to join the editorial staff of the new Zionist periodical *Yevreiskaya Zhizhn* ("Jewish Life") and ended with the outbreak of World War I. It was a period that started darkly for Russia, yielded to an interlude of optimism, and then took another turn for the worse. First came the Russo-Japanese War and its resounding Russian defeat, followed by the "Bloody Sunday" of January 1905, with its massacre of anti-government demonstrators, and in October of that year, the most violent pogroms ever. (Odessa, spared in 1903, was hit badly.) Between the two, in May, occurred a popular uprising that led to the first free elections for the Duma, the Russian parliament, and to a temporary liberalization of Tsarist rule—a process that was reversed in 1906–7 with a gradual return to autocracy and the launching of a brutal campaign of political repression and government-sponsored anti-Semitism aimed at breaking the revolutionary Left. Yet the revolutionaries only emerged stronger as ever larger sectors of the Russian public grew convinced that nothing but the overthrow of the old regime could bring about genuine change.

For Zionism, these years commenced with Herzl's sudden death in 1904. Once the shock of it had passed, the movement, its executive now located in Berlin, entered a new phase, less flamboyant and driven by a quest for quick success, and also less stormy and divisive. The "Uganda plan" was finally shelved when its remaining supporters, now called "Territorialists," formally seceded from the Zionist Organization after its seventh congress in 1905. With no one of Herzl's stature to woo the potentates of Europe—the most important of whom, the crafty but corrupt Sultan, was deposed by the reformist "Young Turk" officer coup of 1908—the dream of a formal Palestine charter was abandoned for the more modest practical work advocated by the "democratic faction." Reinforced by an influx of young socialist pioneers who began arriving from Russia after the failure of the 1905 revolution, the Yishuv, the Jewish community of Palestine, continued to expand, and the first agricultural communes, from which were to develop the kibbutzim and moshavim of the future, took their place alongside the older colonies of private farmers. In the Diaspora, organizational and educational work was stepped up. In contravention of Herzl's pledge to Von Plehve, the Zionist movement entered Eastern European Jewish politics and even ran and elected its own candidates to the first and second Dumas.

Jabotinsky's activities in these years were diverse. They included the numerous articles he wrote for *Yevreiskaya Zhizhn,* later to become *Razsviet,* "The Dawn"; the feuilletons he continued to contribute, although less regularly, to *Odesskaya Novosti;* his rise to prominence as a Zionist lecturer and organizer who crisscrossed Russia from town to town, as his father had gone from river port to river port; his part, in 1905, in the founding convention of the "Alliance for Full Jewish Rights in Russia," an umbrella organization of Russian Jewry, and in 1906, in the Helsinki Conference, a gathering of Russian Zionists that resolved to fight for Jewish cultural autonomy as part of the overall struggle for minority empowerment in the Tsarist empire; and less successfully, several losing election campaigns on the Zionist ticket for the Duma.

In 1907 he married Ania Gelperin. His long courtship of her had seen its ups-and-downs—and not a few other girlfriends. In 1919, during a difficult period in their marriage, he wrote to her:

> Do you remember Ania Gelperin from Lermontov Street? I fought for her for twelve years, from November, 1895, when I called her *mademoiselle,* until July, 1907, when this ceased to be an appropriate form of address. During those years, she sometimes hated me, and sometimes looked down on me, and sometimes just looked the other way. And all that time, I acted the libertine and played the field (*mon Dieu, vous savez que ce n'est pas grand-chose*)[1] while remaining loyal to my *Padishah.*[2] Everyone thought you were a light-headed little girl. I alone knew how capable you were of doing battle

1. French: "Dear God, you know not to make too much of it."
2. Persian: "Great king."

over every hook in your corset. I alone knew, or guessed, that hiding behind those hooks was a great, rock-ribbed soul that could always be counted on in a pinch.

The letter continued, perhaps referring to the moment when the last hook fell:

And then, later, I saw her at dawn in St. Petersburg. Do you know that I've never seen anything more beautiful anywhere, not even in paintings or in dreams?

The twenty-year-old Ania was in St. Petersburg for a while in 1905, when Jabotinsky found work for her in the editorial office of *Razsviet*. That summer, after attending the seventh Zionist Congress at Basel, he, she, and several friends crossed the Alps on foot all the way to Venice. He described such a hike in a 1911 essay humorously titled "A Description of Switzerland," the real subject of which was the pleasures of hiking with friends whose enjoyable company matters more than anything they see on their way—of which, indeed, there is no description at all.

Not long after their wedding, Ania left for France with the plan of studying agriculture at the University of Nancy in preparation for a future life with Jabotinsky in Palestine. It was the first of the many separations that were to mark their marriage, in which togetherness and apartness alternated rhythmically. While Ania was in Nancy, where she never finished her studies, Jabotinsky spent months in Vienna researching the European minority problem, at its most intense in the Austro-Hungarian empire, for what was to become his law degree dissertation. The passionately longing letters from this period that he and Ania exchanged, referred to nostalgically in their later correspondence, have not survived.

In 1908, he made his first visit to Palestine after going to Turkey as a journalist to cover the Young Turks' takeover. He spent several weeks there, traveling south from Beirut and stopping in Jewish agricultural settlements in the Galilee. In a piece later published in *Odesskaya Novosti*, he described a hike to the top of Mount Tabor with a thirteen-year-old boy named Itamar as his guide. They conversed in Hebrew, Itamar's native and fluent, his own halting but sufficient, and when they reached the top with its panoramic view, the boy proudly pointed out the biblical sites below: the Kishon River in the Valley of Jezreel where Ya'el and Barak defeated the Canaanite chariots, Mount Gilboa where Saul and Jonathan fell fighting the Philistines, the Carmel where Elijah slew the prophets of the Ba'al. Yet suddenly, wrote Jabotinsky,

> his expression changed. . . . "You see, sir [he said], the valley is beautiful, but we Jews don't own a single acre of it. All those houses down there are Arab villages. Not one acre, do you understand?"
>
> "I do," I said, and I really did grasp the strange look in my small companion's eyes. It was hunger—that sacred, unparalleled hunger that has been uprooted from the hearts of our vagabond tribe, which may still know what it is like to be hungry for freedom, and perhaps even hungry for power, but has forgotten the pure, wondrous hunger for land.

On top of the mountain is a French monastery that the two enter to ask for a cold drink. The head monk, obviously no admirer of Jews, orders them to wait outside in the hot sun until it is brought, and as they stand there, the narrator exclaims, "If I weren't so thirsty, I'd spit in his face and clear out."

> Itamar shrugged as if to say:
>
> "What's he to you?"
>
> That was when I understood another look of his, the one that had taken in the entrance hall, the courtyard, the officious monk, and the imposing foreign stonework rising on Mount Tabor. It, too, was a look I had never seen before.

It wasn't the look of cowardly, semi-obsequious hatred with which the outcast regards his casters-out, the possessors of what is denied him; nor was it a look of helpless anger or injured honor. It was a look of cold annoyance and confident contempt—of the builder who encounters an obstacle that has yet to be removed—of the lumberjack whose glance measures the tree he is about to cut down—of the conqueror—and above all, of the proprietor of all that he sees.

Looks call for interpretation, and Jabotinsky's tells us what, in 1908, he thought Palestinian Zionism should, and in its native-born youth would, become: proudly rooted in land and history, yet lucidly aware that the claims that were self-evident to itself would not be so to others, and certain, however unrealistic it might seem, that it would be able to enforce them when the time came. Since Jewish-Arab tensions were largely still latent in 1908, the conclusion, reached by Jabotinsky well ahead of most Zionists, that Palestine would not be given to the Jews by anyone, but would have to be taken by them, owed less to events there than to developments in Europe. The collapse of liberal reform in Russia, its Jews left to face their enemies alone, and the intensifying nationalism of Europe's many stateless ethnicities, who were as hostile toward one another—Poles and Ukrainians, Serbs and Croatians, Czechs and Sudeten Germans—as they were toward their imperial rulers, and most hostile toward the Jews in their midst, had convinced him that in the growing turmoil of the early twentieth century it was every people for itself.

Gone were the days of fin-de-siècle Odessa's "good-natured fraternization of nationalities" with its "Babylonian diversity" that was "a symbol of a splendid tomorrow." Writing in *Odesskaya Novosti* on New Year's Day, 1908, Jabotinsky, having despaired of the alliance of Russian liberals and national minorities that he had joined in promoting several years earlier, handed

Russia its divorce papers. "I have no season's greetings for you," he bitterly told the paper's readers, "because I no longer care about your future. The only tomorrow that matters to me is my own breaking dawn, which I believe in with every fiber of my being." In a 1910 essay called *Homo Homini Lupus*, occasioned by that year's race riots in America in which dozens of Negroes were lynched, he declared, referring to the essay's Latin title:

> Wise was the philosopher who said that men are wolves to men. Long years will not be enough to change this. Neither political reforms, nor cultural remedies, nor even the hard lessons of life will do the least good. He who puts his trust in a neighbor, be it the friendliest and most kind-hearted, is a fool. He who trusts in justice is one, too. Justice exists for those with the physical power and persistence to appropriate it for themselves. When I am accused of preaching [national] separateness, distrust, and other such things that are offensive to delicate minds, I am tempted to answer: "I plead guilty as charged. I indeed preach all this and will continue to. Separateness, distrust, vigilance at all times, a club in one's hands at all times—there is no other way to survive the wars of the wolves."

All the instincts of the modern European Jew, who had put his trust in the emergence of a new, liberal order by which he would be fully accepted, rebelled against such a view. Yet a people with a healthy national ego, like the one Jabotinsky believed was being forged in Palestine, understood the facts of life and did not shrink from them.

Gazing up at Mount Tabor several months before Jabotinsky gazed down from it, David Grien, a twenty-one-year-old socialist pioneer, thought it "proud in its loneliness, its round dome aloof from the mountains around it." Soon to rename himself Ben-Gurion, Grien was entranced by his new surroundings, having recently come to live and work in the little commune of Sejera in the Lower Galilee. The view, he wrote his father in Poland, was "sublime,"

> a vision of endless majesty. At my feet are green hills, valleys spread with young carpets of flowers . . . while facing me to the north, a two day's walk from here, looms a giant, the grand elder of the land's mountains, covered with gleaming, blinding snow—ever-white Mount Hermon. A land of wonders is the Land of Israel!

In Sejera, he had found the Palestine he had dreamed of in his native shtetl of Plonsk:

> There are no shopkeepers or jobbers, no hired hands, no idlers living off the work of others. All the members of the commune work and enjoy the fruits of their labors. The men plow and sow the earth. The women garden and milk the cows. The children herd the ducks on the threshing floor and ride out to the fields on horseback to greet their fathers. They're country boys and girls, smelling of wheat and manure, their faces sun-bronzed.

Jabotinsky, who did not meet Ben-Gurion on his 1908 trip, had a mixed opinion of the socialist pioneers he encountered. While admiring their commitment and tenacity, he found their proletarian airs pretentious and doubted whether the Zionist enterprise in Palestine was ripe for experiments in collective living. Many of the newcomers worked as hired hands in the older colonies, where they had a reputation for recalcitrance. "They have," Jabotinsky wrote in *Odesskaya Novosti*, "a chip on their shoulders from [the counterrevolution of] 1906 and bristle like porcupines even before the farmers make an employer's demands on them."

In 1909 he returned to Constantinople, which the new regime preferred to call by its Turkish name of Istanbul, at the request of the Zionist Executive, the administrative body chosen anew at each Zionist Organization congress, in order to edit three newly founded Zionist newspapers, one Hebrew, one French, and one Ladino. He also helped run the pro-Zionist, French-language *Le Jeune Turc*, which the Executive subsidized. He liked the Turks—an "honest, frugal, hospitable, gallant" people, as he called them—but not the city. Although the narrator of his 1912 short story "Edmée," a German-Jewish doctor living in the Levant, is not a simple alter ego like the narrator of "Diana" and was not necessarily speaking for the author in calling Istanbul "ugly" and its populace a "yelling rabble dressed in savage-painted rags," Jabotinsky did not have a high opinion of the culture of the Turkish capital. The Orientalism that appealed to Zionists like Martin Buber, with its rejection of a supposedly decadent West for the profounder spirituality of an East that Jews were now returning to, struck him as mawkish. Even in his greatest fury at European anti-Semitism, he regarded the Jews as an inalienably European people. Indeed, he was to write in a 1926 essay called "The Orient," without the Jews' messianic dreaming, persistent questioning, and restless discontent with the status quo, Europe would never have become the dynamic society it was, always "searching, improving, destroying, clawing its way upward."

Yet the Young Turks had come to power on a program of Europeanization and Jabotinsky's later, retrospective claim to have known all along that the Ottoman empire was doomed is not borne out by his journalism from Istanbul. In it, he reserved judgment on the Young Turks' prospects for success. The biggest obstacle in their way, he thought, was their discontented minorities. Even after losing most of its European possessions during the nineteenth century, the empire remained a mosaic of different nationalities. Over half its population consisted of Armenians, Greeks, Albanians, Kurds, Arabs, and Jews, and the Young Turks' stated goal of granting them all equality while Turkifying them culturally and linguistically—an ambition never shared by the Sultanate—was unrealistic. The more Turkification was forced on them, Jabotinsky wrote, the more fiercely they would resist it and cause the empire's disintegration. Zionism's hope lay in the Young Turks' realizing this. Although they were at the moment unfriendly to Zionism, once they understood that their minorities would have to be accommodated in a decentralized state that granted each autonomy while playing it off against the others, they would recognize the advantage of a strong Jewish presence in Palestine to offset Arab preponderance in the southern part of their territory. Zionism, they would then realize, was made to order for them.

This analysis, though unlikely to have proven accurate even had the Ottoman empire survived World War I, was consistent with the belief always held by Jabotinsky that, despite the temporary eclipse of Herzlian diplomacy, Zionism would always need great-power support. In a world in which might made right, mustering enough might depended on aligning Zionist interests with those of a major country that could control or influence events in Palestine. This set him apart from the Labor Zionists, as the adherents of the Zionist Left were called, who continued to argue after Herzl's death, on both moral and practical grounds, for Zionist self-sufficiency. It was enough, they contended, to create facts on the ground in Palestine that the world would have to take into account; what mattered was to cultivate, not close relations with this or that government, but "acre after acre and goat after goat" until the Arabs, seeing the material progress Zionism brought in its wake, made their peace with it. Jabotinsky disagreed. Arab nationalism was still at an early stage, but future conflict with it, he was convinced, was inevitable. Zionist and imperialist ambitions in Palestine might coincide. Zionist and Arab ambitions never could.

Although Jabotinsky worked hard at his job in Istanbul and

expanded his newspapers' circulation, he resigned after eight months, in March 1910, following a quarrel with the Zionist Executive in Berlin. Later that year, his only son, Eri, was born. In 1912, he received his law degree from the University of Yaroslavl, followed by a grueling, fifty-stop lecture tour on behalf of Hebrew-language Jewish education in Russia. In 1913, he was appointed to the planning committee of the newly projected Hebrew University in Jerusalem, a position that again led to friction with his colleagues, this time headed by Chaim Weizmann. Whereas Weizmann favored beginning with a modest research institute that might gradually be enlarged, Jabotinsky was for launching a full-scale institution of higher learning all at once; to the objection that this would lead to an academic fiasco, he replied that academic standards mattered less than providing a home for the Jewish students and scholars rejected by Europe while injecting a new intellectual and cultural stimulus into Palestinian Jewish life. It was the first but not the last time that found him unsuccessfully pushing, once more in a Herzlian vein, for the greater risks and possible rewards of a grand Zionist project versus a more cautious, step-by-step approach.

He had by now acquired a reputation as a maverick with a tendency to go it alone. He had also become known as a virtuoso public speaker with a repertoire of languages that eventually included, besides Russian and Italian, Yiddish, German, Hebrew, French, English, and Polish. After hearing him speak in these years, the Russian journalist and statesman V. D. Nabokov, the father of the famous novelist, called him the finest orator in all of Russia.

Watching and listening to Jabotinsky today on the bits of tape and film footage that exist of his public appearances, all from the 1930s, one feels challenged to explain such a reaction. His style is calm and deliberate, his body language restrained, almost stiff, his enunciation slow and careful; there are no theatrics, no waving of the hands or straining of the voice, which remains level despite a noticeably suppressed tension reproduced in the fists clenched and unclenched by his side. Rather, there is the sense of being taken into the confidence of a man of high intelligence who excels at organizing his thoughts, so that, while their reasoning may be complex, they are delivered with the clear and simple structure of a conversation. What Jabotinsky's audiences perhaps most came away with was the feeling that they *had* conversed with him—that although they themselves had said nothing, he had answered their questions, dealt fairly with their objections, and shown them the respect accorded by a superior mind to those whose time and intelligence it values as greatly as its own. Arthur Koestler, who heard Jabotinsky speak to a full house in the Kursaal, Vienna's largest concert hall, in 1924, wrote of the experience:

> It was an extraordinary event. Since then, I've had the opportunity to listen to many political speakers. None of them had [Jabotinsky's] ability to mesmerize an audience for three hours without once resorting to the orator's bag of tricks. There was nothing trite in anything he said. . . . Its power lay in its transparent clarity and the beauty of its logic.

In Jabotinsky's younger years, however, he resorted to the orator's tricks often. The best description of his use of them is his own. In a feuilleton written in 1910 and entitled "Three Arts," he had three friends argue about which art is the highest. The first makes the case for great poetry, whose transcendent accomplishment is such that "it will live on even though men forget it, even though the book it is written in is lost." The second friend scoffs at the idea of art for art's sake and argues on behalf of oratory. "I don't believe you can have art without an audience," he says—and who is more connected to his audience than the orator? With sufficient talent, he can do with it as he wishes. At first, to be sure, he ascends the tribune lazily, apathetically. His face is tired, his eye-lids lowered. He begins by speaking clumsily, un-evenly, stammeringly. Only little by little does he become animated; his grasp of the question grows firmer. He ana-lyses, criticizes. He is logical, correct, and dry. He cites facts, compares figures, throws out reminders. He is very circum-stantial and even somewhat dull.

So far, we could be reading a satirical self-portrait of the Jabotinsky of tape and film. Yet,

gradually, sarcastic undertones begin to leaven his speech. A harmless little joke is followed by another, perhaps a shade sharper than the first. The third is quite malicious, and sud-denly you see before you a different man. He no longer rea-sons; he ridicules. He pulls his opponent by the ear from one comic situation to another. He bares the contradictions hidden in his opponent's argument and, in a masterly phrase or two, reduces its weak points to absurdities and caps each phrase with the laughter of his audience. And then, suddenly, the ridicule stops—a momentary pause—and before you is a third man, the man of great ire. He no longer reasons, he no longer ridicules—he is out for blood. His low voice rolls out in a subdued rumble like a still-imprisoned torrent. Then—the torrent breaks forth in all its wild force, hurtling the rocks down upon the doomed multitude. . . . Long, for minutes on end, roars the mighty storm, heavy, far-echoing, explosions bursting at intervals over the crowd.

Joseph Schechtman, who attributed such virtuoso effects to the "Italian school" of oratory that Jabotinsky was exposed to in Rome, described hearing him speak on several occasions in Odessa. One was in 1905, when he denounced an audience of Russian liberals, many of them anti-Zionists, who had gathered to protest that year's pogroms. Reviewing case after case of Russian liberalism's past indifference to anti-Semitic discrimi-nation and violence, he summed up each with the rhetorical question, his voice louder and more scathing each time: "And where were you then, all you progressive Russian intellectuals?" The speech built up to a thundering crescendo.

The third participant in the conversation in "Three Arts" is dismissive of both his friends. "What is poetry?" he asks.

> Whereas a given thought can have but one perfect expression, the writer of verse has to compromise this ideal form for the sake of meter and weaken it still further for the sake of rhyme. And what is a public speech? It is quackery, playing the fool to entreat applause from the crowd. . . . For me, the highest art is the politician's. To sit locked in your study behind a broad table heaped with papers; to say simple words in a quiet tone of voice; to give brief orders—and to hold in your hands all the knots of a million strings. . . . You move a white pawn and know that in eight moves it will check the red king. You weave complicated webs and are aware who is destined to fall into them. . . . [The masses] think they act from their own volition, little knowing that the will in question is your own.

All three friends, clearly, were felt by Jabotinsky to be sides of himself. By 1910, though he was still writing an occasional short story, the poet of "Piazza di Spagna" and "Unhappy Charlotte" had been silenced by the orator and politician. That same year, the Russian author Alexander Kuprin, speaking to an audience of Odessan Jews about the Odessa-born Jewish novelist and short story writer Semyon Yushkevitch, said of Jabotinsky:

> As far as Yushkevitch is concerned, you can have him. But there's another Odessan, a God-given talent who could have been an eagle of Russian literature had you [Jews] not stolen him from us, quite simply whisked him away. . . . Good lord, what have you done to him, this young eagle? You've clipped his wings and dragged him off to your Jewish pale of settle-

ment, where he'll soon be just one more cackling hen. . . .
What a great loss to Russian literature, only a few of whose
writers have been blessed with his style, his wit, his insight
into our soul!

To many of his admirers, Jabotinsky's abandonment of
literature for Zionist politics and stump-speaking could only
have seemed a profanation of his talents. Others viewed it
as a noble sacrifice. The Jabotinsky of these years disagreed
with both judgments. Chaim Weizmann's wife Vera, who was
friendly with Jabotinsky when he and the Weizmanns lived in
London during World War I, recalled once admonishing him
that politics were not his true vocation. Jabotinsky, she related,
was stung. "But Vera Yasayevna, my dear," he replied, "politics
are my greatest gift and talent!" There is no reason to doubt
he was being sincere. The excitement of the public arena—the
gratification of seeing one's words take instant effect before
one's eyes—the thrill of making history: what was the poet's
lonely craft compared to these?

The views expressed in his speeches and writings from this
period do not fully reflect Jabotinsky's mature thought, but
they do foreshadow much of it. Although he had not yet moved
markedly rightward on economic issues and still considered
socialism the wave of the future, he was critical of Europe's
socialist parties, not so much for their opposition to capitalism as for their coolness, in the name of "proletarian interna-
tionalism," to the numerous independence movements of the
small peoples of the Tsarist, Austro-Hungarian, and Ottoman
empires. These, despite the danger of nationalistic excesses, he
strongly supported. Had Garibaldi, he wrote in a 1911 essay sar-
castically called "The Reactionary," conducted his campaign of
national liberation in the early years of the twentieth century,
he would have been pilloried by a European Left that

the more radical it is, the more negatively it regards [nationalist struggles] as absurd, unnecessary, and harmful for blurring class consciousness and distracting humanity from its true task. . . . Only a reactionary would [in its eyes] dream of creating new states when there are already too many old ones; only a reactionary would want governments to divide one people from another.

Jabotinsky's belief in the positive force of nationalism was characteristically nineteenth-century in its assumption that every nation was, not the artificial "construction" that later twentieth-century theorists like Eric Hobsbawm and Ernest Gellner argued it was, but a natural form of social organization mediating between the individual and the world—or, as he was to put in his memoirs, that "God first created the human being, then the nation, and only then humanity." Yet since Labor Zionism was openly nationalistic too, which had led to its ostracization by the European socialist movement, "The Reactionary" was not aimed at it. Neither was Jabotinsky's attack, in a 1906 essay, on the Algemayner Yiddisher Arbiter Bund, the General Jewish Workers' Alliance, founded in 1897 as an anti-Zionist Eastern European Jewish socialist party; nor his play "A Strange Land," which comically portrays a strike by a pitiful handful of Jewish workers in a pathetically small Jewish-owned factory. Although both essay and play ridicule the notion of class warfare in an Eastern European Jewish society whose small businessmen were often as destitute as their employees, Labor Zionism, too, maintained that Jews as Jews could meaningfully participate in the fight against capitalism only in a homeland of their own.

Nevertheless, while Jabotinsky was not yet the anti-socialist he was to become, he had an admiration for the Jewish commercial class, no doubt partly rooted in memories of his father, that Labor Zionism lacked. He himself had not followed in his father's footsteps; yet in his 1912 feuilleton "A Conversation," he called on Russian Jewish youth to do just that. "For generations," says this dialogue's main speaker, "doing business was the pillar of Jewish life—why abandon it now?" The desire of young Jews to be doctors, lawyers, professors, anything but businessmen, the speaker argues, stems from a delegitimization of commerce by anti-bourgeois ideologies and the desire to flee Jewish stereotypes; in both cases, it means exchanging the more interesting and adventurous life of economic entrepreneurship for the less productive one of the professions. Young Jews should be told: "Back to the shop counter! Back to the stores, the banks, the stock exchange—not only to buying and selling, but to industry, to manufacture, to everything 'practical.'"

Jabotinsky was not, even in those years, partial to "proletarian Zionism" and did not think that an organized Jewish working class indoctrinated in hostility to the Jewish businessman and to a private-property-oriented Jewish religious tradition could be Zionism's main driving force. It was, he wrote in a 1911 Passover piece called "The Four Sons," the Jewish artisan and tradesman, "the shoemaker, the tailor, the egg seller going from door to door, the rag dealer, the Torah scribe, the small shop owner," who were the backbone of their people and

> still pull what is left of the battered harness [of Jewish identity], moaning and groaning but filling the synagogues on Friday nights. . . . They are the bulwark of an eternal people and the bearers of its future destiny.

In itself, though, the "battered harness" of rabbinic Judaism held little intrinsic value for him. It had been, as he saw it, an indispensable but strictly functional tool, a way of life that had developed in the Diaspora over the centuries to enable the Jews to survive as a de-territorialized nation. A substitute for a land that had been lost, it would lose much of its relevance once that land was regained. Jabotinsky's ardent Hebraism did not contradict this belief. The revival of spoken Hebrew signified for him both an affirmation of Jewish historical continuity *and* a repudiation of Diaspora culture with its Judeo-German, Judeo-Spanish, and other hybrid Jewish languages. Hebrew alone could link Jews all over the world with one another and with their past, and restore them to the more authentic, unhyphenated existence of the pre-Exilic Jew.

This was a common secular Zionist position and close to that of Ahad Ha'am, who also regarded rabbinic Judaism as an outer form designed to preserve the inner core of Jewish nationhood under conditions of homelessness and dispersal. Ahad Ha'am and his followers, however, esteemed this form in its own right as an expression of a moral striving inherent in the Jewish "national spirit," worth preserving even when decoupled from religious faith. The pre–World War I Jabotinsky evinced little interest in either the "spirit" or the rituals of Judaism. Estranged from religion as a boy in Odessa, he believed that language and territory—Hebrew and the Land of Israel—would be enough to define Jews as Jews. The Jews, in his opinion, had no moral uniqueness or mission in the world—no mission of any kind except to take their rightful place among the nations. What Zionism had to offer them was the freedom, in a national framework of their own, to be whatever they chose to be without fearing the loss of national identity that came with assimilation. This aligned him with secular critics of Ahad Ha'am like Micha Yosef Berdichevsky and Jacob Klatzkin who denied essential qualities to Jewishness, which was simply what Jewish life made of it. What Jabotinsky himself wished to make of it was what he called in another essay a "Jewish humanism," whose values would be those of liberal European society.

Naturally, the Ahad Ha'amists could and did ask: why strive to return to an ancient homeland when Jews could live "humanistically" just as well or better in Europe? To this, Jabotinsky's twofold answer was: Jews could *not* live in Europe because European anti-Semitism would not let them—and even if it did, their pride and self-esteem enjoined them from living on the sufferance of others. Only in a country of their own *away* from Europe could they exist as Europeans with dignity.

And yet if they had no special role in the world, why should not the Jews, as the assimilationists proposed, quite simply disappear? One could not, after all, argue that anti-Semitism ruled out assimilation too, because most Jewish converts to Christianity in modern Europe had managed to blend with Gentile society—and in an increasingly secular age in which conversion was fast becoming unnecessary, such integration would prove even easier. Nor could one appeal to Jewish pride when the assimilationist had none. One could either accept assimilation as a valid alternative to Zionism, as many Zionists (including Herzl) did, or find some other reason not to.

The reason Jabotinsky found was first developed by him in a 1913 essay called "Race." It began with the proposition: "If we do not strive too hard for exactness of terminology, we can as a general rule say that every people has its own 'racial composition.'" No "race," the essay hastened to state, was ever pure; all were mixed, having interbred with others. Yet since interbreeding between "races" was never as great as inbreeding within them, every nation had its own physical composition—and just as "any two physiologically different individuals will react differently to the same psychological stimulus," so will any two nations.

This "racial psychology," Jabotinsky contended, is the ultimate determinant of nationhood; for while other group attributes, such as territory, language, and culture, characterize most but not all peoples, "the true selfhood of a people, the first and last bastion of its uniqueness, is its special physical traits." A people could lose its other characteristics to foreign conquest or influence, but as long as it retained its "racial constitution," it preserved its identity. Consequently, its individual members could never—barring the intermarriages that produced "intermediate types"—successfully cut their ties to it, since they would always, if only unconsciously, feel closer to their racial cohorts than to others. Since the wholesale assimilation of any people, the Jews included, was thus an objective impossibility, Zionism was an objective necessity.

Jabotinsky was writing in the context of a discourse about the role of race in human history and society that was prominent in the late nineteenth and early twentieth centuries and that ranged from the neo-Darwinism of serious thinkers like Herbert Spencer and Thomas Huxley to the toxic ideologies of racists like Arthur Gobineau and Houston Stewart Chamberlain. The Jews, because of their long record of endogamy, had a special place in this discourse quite apart from the preoccupations of the anti-Semites and were often regarded as a test case. If, after all, Europe had such a thing as a true "race" whose behavior and characteristics were at least partly determined by heredity, what better place to look for it than a people that had so stubbornly refused to mix biologically with others?

Whether the Jews were indeed innately distinct was much debated by Jews themselves. Two of the leading figures in the controversy were the Polish-born artist and writer Alfred Nossig, who founded the Bureau for Jewish Statistics in Berlin in 1904, and the Russian-born American physician and physical anthropologist Maurice Fishberg, whose *Jews, Race, and Environment*, published in 1911, became a standard text in its field. Nossig held that such Jewish qualities as "a marked sense of family, a deeply rooted habituation to the virtuous life, an unusual intellectual dexterity, and an ideal spirituality" had been biologically passed on "undiminished from generation to generation." Fishberg argued that differences between Jews and Christians were due "not to anatomical or physiological pecu-

liarities, but solely to the result of the social and political environment."

Fishberg was an assimilationist. Nossig was a Zionist, as
were others who adduced Jewish racial unity as a justification
of Jewish nationalism, such as Arthur Ruppin, Nossig's successor at the Bureau for Jewish Statistics and later a senior figure
in the Zionist movement. The Jabotinsky of "Race" disagreed
with Fishberg and Nossig alike. Although he did not believe
that Jews differed from others only as a consequence of envi-
ronmental factors, neither did he did attribute to them heredi-
tary virtues not possessed by others. Inherited national traits,
as he conceived of them, were a matter of subtle dispositions
of temperament, not of the social mores that such dispositions
helped shape. "As far as I'm concerned," he had a Jew tell a Russian anti-Semite in a 1911 feuilleton,

> there are no superior and inferior races. Each race has its
> own qualities, its own physiognomy, its own gifts. If one
> could invent a barometer capable of measuring these exactly,
> one would discover that they are more or less of equal value.

If the illiterate Kalmucks of Siberia, the Jew declares, were
to live in conditions like those enjoyed by the ancient Greeks,
they would produce a culture as great as, though not the same
as, the Greeks did. Cultural differences, in any case, never justify prejudice or oppression. "In the United States, the freest
republic in the world," Jabotinsky wrote in *Homo Homini Lupus*,

> tens of millions of citizens live shockingly without rights just
> because of the color of their skin, [even though] it is no secret
> that the Negroes are a talented, intellectually quick, and re-
> tentive people, who have produced first-rate writers, preach-
> ers, and professors. True, none of these have been "geniuses"
> by the standards of white taste, but . . . no people can be bur-
> dened with having to live up to another's expectations. What
> geniuses have been produced by the Bulgarians or the Turks?

It is debatable, in fact, whether the great American republic itself has yet to produce a single genius worthy of the name. The Americans know this, know that "lack of genius" is no reason to deprive a race of its rights, and yet they go on resorting to such an argument.

This is a far cry from the "racism" that Jabotinsky was sometimes accused of inculcating. Like others of his age who thought race mattered, he had no way of foreseeing the murderous use to which racial theories would soon be put. In 1913, the discovery of the biological mechanism by which genetic differences are produced and transmitted was forty years in the future; most of the populations of Europe were still relatively homogeneous; and there was little intermarriage between them and their Jewish minorities. It was far less obvious then than it is today that the psychological and cultural differences between the physical subdivisions of mankind owe more to nurture than to nature, and that the descendants of such groups do not as a rule continue to feel an instinctive affinity for them once removed from them and are not necessarily more attracted to those they are genetically closer to.

Nor was Jabotinsky a neo-Darwinist for whom human history chronicles the survival of the eugenically fittest. His 1913 essay concludes with a utopian vision of all "races" living side-by side in a world in which, the need for war having been eliminated by the end of capitalist competition, there is an unprecedented flowering of civilization, every people remaining itself while engaged in "mutual exchanges of the fruits of its independent and original creativity" in an atmosphere of peace and harmony. "Fortunate will be the nations," declares the essay's concluding sentence, "who live to see such blessed times."

So rosy an outlook was less opposed to the grim view of *Homo Homini Lupus* than might appear at first glance. The political thinker that Jabotinsky emerged as in the years before

World War I might be termed a Hobbesian democrat. Despite *Homo Homini Lupus*'s pessimism, he did not take an overly dim view of humanity. If nations, like individuals, were cruel and exploitative, this was because men were, not naturally evil, but naturally selfish in the promotion of their interests—and while human nature could not be changed, human interests could be. Within the framework of the state, this was achievable by the rule of law and a political system of checks and balances; between states, by an international order of free and independent peoples, each serving as a brake on the others. The wolf in man could be leashed by other men; the wolf in nations, by other nations. In adding one more state to the constellation of states, therefore, Zionism would not just be solving the Jewish problem. It would also be contributing to a multiplicity that, like the multiplicity of institutions in a society, prevented the overconcentration and abuse of power. Whichever "came first," the individual, the nation, or humanity, all three needed each other.

Meanwhile, however, the Europe of the decade before World War I was a Hobbesian jungle in which nation stalked nation, imperial powers roamed in search of prey, and international alliances formed, dissolved, and reformed, with countries switching sides in an atmosphere of intrigue and distrust. The Japanese drove the Russians from Manchuria; the French and Spanish were allowed to carve up Morocco in return for granting Germany a slice of the Congo and the British a free hand in Egypt; Italy snatched Libya from the Turks and invaded Ethiopia; Austria-Hungary grabbed Bosnia and Herzegovina. In the first and second Balkan Wars of 1912–13, Serbia, Bulgaria, Rumania, Albania, Greece, and Macedonia fought Turkey and one another while Russia and Austria-Hungary meddled from the sidelines and the Germans backed the Turks as part of their economic and diplomatic penetration of the Middle East.

A global arms race was under way. The newly invented airplane was adapted for military use. Germany and England beefed up their navies, building new battleships and submarines. The French prepared for a possible German attack. The Three Emperors' League of Russia, Germany, and Austria-Hungary became the "Triple Alliance" of Germany, Austria-Hungary, and Italy, deserted by Russia for a "Triple Entente" with France and Great Britain. Everywhere the ground was trembling. The century of relative peace and stability that Europe had known since the downfall of Napoleon had, so it seemed, run its course.

On January 1, 1912, Jabotinsky published another of his New Year's pieces in *Odesskaya Novosti*. In it he proposed doing something new: rather than review, as was the custom, the events of the previous year, he would write "a horoscope of the newly born *annus Domini* MCMXII." This would be confined to one prediction, which concerned

> the war of which the world is so frightened, and which, at the same time, it expects with such morbid, painful curiosity: a war in the center of Europe, between two (or more) first-rate, civilized powers, fully armed to the teeth with all the grandiose madness of present-day technical equipment, with the participation of ground, sea, underwater, and aerial forces, and with an incredible number of human casualties and financial losses.

Jabotinsky predicted that such a war would indeed break out. It would begin, he said, between England and Germany. The reason was simple. England was the world's greatest empire by virtue of one thing alone: its hitherto invincible navy, which controlled global shipping routes and had enabled a tiny island to maintain its grip on overseas possessions a hundred times its size. Although never in the nineteenth century had England's supremacy at sea been challenged by a continental power, Germany was doing so now. The English would have to

strike soon to keep their advantage. The only question, Jabotinsky wrote, was "whether the storm will break in 1912 or be
postponed until some months later," and whether other countries would be drawn into it. Although they would seek not to
be, "one thing only is known about such conflagrations: where
they start. Who knows where this one will end?"

The war broke out two and a half years later, in the mid-
summer of 1914. Within days the German army unexpectedly
swept through southern Belgium in an end-run into northern France. The British declared war on Germany a day later.
By then Russia and Austria-Hungary were involved too, the
former on the side of Great Britain and France, the latter allied
with the Germans. No one indeed knew where it would end.

Jabotinsky was in St. Petersburg at the war's onset. Although the Russian army, mauled by the Germans and Austri-
ans, was soon in retreat in Poland and eastern Galicia, the front
was far away. With no threat to the safety of Ania and Eri, he
traveled to Moscow, obtained a job with the prominent newspaper *Russkaya Vyedomosti* as a war correspondent in Western
Europe, and set out at once. The paper was pleased to have a
journalist of Jabotinsky's caliber covering the war in the West
and he was glad to have the income. In the preceding years, he
had cut back on journalism in favor of Zionist lecturing and his
work at *Razsviet*. Now, with the Zionist Executive stationed in
an enemy capital, both *Razsviet* (which was shut down by the
authorities a year later) and Russian Zionism were in a precarious position. Neither could be counted on for a livelihood.

It was not, however, just a matter of a job. The conflagra-
tion Jabotinsky had predicted was raging across Europe. Although there was no saying what would be left standing when
it had burned itself out, much would not be. For Zionism, this
meant old thinking to be discarded and new opportunities to be
seized. Jabotinsky was eager to form his own first-hand opin-

ion of what these were, and there was no better way of doing so than as a journalist. If one wanted to know what was happening anywhere, he once wrote, the people to talk to were the correspondents. They were better informed than the intellectuals, more forthcoming than the politicians, and less blinded by prejudgments than either.

His first stop was Stockholm, which he reached via Finland before proceeding to Norway. Even neutral Scandinavia, he observed in his first dispatches to *Russkaya Vyedomosti*, was stricken with war fever. All talk was of the fighting; there was a sense of being left out, almost a longing to be part of it. From Norway, he sailed to Holland and made his way to Belgium, reaching it in mid-September. The country's northern half was still in government hands. In France, the battle of the Marne had just ended with frightful casualties. Reinforced by a British expeditionary force, the French had stemmed the Germans' advance and even pushed them back, dashing their hopes for a quick march on Paris and setting the stage for the years of trench warfare that were to follow.

Jabotinsky visited towns damaged by German air and artillery strikes and telegraphed *Russkaya Vyedomosti* from Antwerp, describing a calm city proud of the stiff resistance Belgium had put up. Yet despite his anti-German bias, which he would have been expected to display for his Russian readers even had it not come naturally to him, his secret wish in the war's early days, as he was afterwards to confess, was for a speedy German victory on the Eastern front that would topple the Tsarist regime. In this, his sentiments did not differ from those of millions of other Jews.

Though poorly preserved, Jabotinsky's *Russkaya Vyedomosti* dispatches chart his movements in the next several months. After a week in Belgium, he moved on to England. A week later he was back in Belgium, where he witnessed a German air raid from his hotel in Ostend. From there he continued to Bruges and managed, with frequent changes of trains, to reach Paris.

The French capital struck him as semi-deserted. Its government offices had been evacuated to Bordeaux, its able-bodied men were at the front, and those who remained preferred to stay at home—not from fright, Jabotinsky told his readers, but from shame at not being in uniform. Yet the city brimmed with foreign reporters, and in search of a scoop he headed for Reims, reports of artillery damage to whose medieval cathedral had shocked the world. ("For some reason," he later wrote, "it was still clear to us in those days that shooting at human beings was permissible, but not at historic buildings.") Since the town was near the front and barred to foreign journalists, he traveled as far as Épernay and walked the last fifteen miles on back roads. In *Russkaya Vyedomosti* he gave an account of the bombed-out cathedral; wrote about the ongoing artillery barrages, a shell from which fell outside a barbershop in which he was being shaved; and praised the British forces fighting north of the town for their courage. Flares and explosions lit the horizon at night.

Unable to get any closer to the front, Jabotinsky spent the next two weeks reporting on life behind it and on French civilian and military morale—which, with the stabilization of the battle lines, had risen. Yet the large numbers of wounded, encountered everywhere, were a stark reminder of the war's ferocity. One dispatch described being made to vacate a first-class train carriage for a group of them, still dressed in the bright colors of nineteenth-century warfare. (The Germans had already switched to camouflage gray.)

> We left the car. By the half blacked-out lights of the station, we saw a row of stretchers, and further back, the dim outlines of the wounded who could stand, their blue tunics and red trousers barely visible in the darkness, which made their

bandages stand out more brightly. These white medals of injury gleamed on the dark silhouettes: heads in white, arms in white, legs in white—a veritable exhibition of the art of wound-dressing. . . . Each had his own injury and his own face. Two things alone were shared in common: the feverish look in their eyes and the smudge at the knees of their red pants. Although some had been in the hospital for weeks, a stain of yellow clay, the true badge of the combat soldier, was still there, a souvenir from long hours of kneeling behind earthworks or fallen trees. Ground into the red fabric, it could no longer be expunged, and perhaps no one had tried very hard to do so. Whenever you passed a company of soldiers marching down a road, you could tell from this one sign whether it had already been under fire.

As a war correspondent restricted to the rear, he was engaged, as he put it, in "dull work"; the temptation of imaginative embellishment was great. On at least one occasion, a November 1 report of a conversation with a German prisoner-of-war, he succumbed. Meeting on a train from Paris to Bordeaux, *Russkaya Vyedomosti*'s readers were told, Jabotinsky, a French officer, and the prisoner, a lecturer in linguistics from the University of Frankfurt, discussed French dialects and vied in quoting Provençal poetry. The piece portrayed the intellectual absurdity of a war in which cultured soldiers on either side had more in common with each other than with their comrades in the trenches—and was, as Jabotinsky later admitted, pure invention, occasioned by a translation he had begun of Fréderic Mistral's long Provençal poem *Miréio*. Having worked on it to while away the boredom of his Paris hotel room, he decided to put it to journalistic use.

Yet even this, the sole documentable instance in his writing of a total fiction being passed off as the truth, had a basis in reality. The train ride itself did take place, Jabotinsky having gone to Bordeaux to write about the relocated French government. He never published the piece, however, and probably never wrote it, for upon arriving in the city, he heard dramatic news: the Turks had joined the war on Germany's side and had already taken part in a German bombardment of Russian Black Sea ports. On November 2, Russia declared war on Turkey, and three days later, Britain and France followed suit. Overnight, the Middle East had become a military theater. If defeated together with Germany and Austria-Hungary, the Turks stood to lose their empire, Palestine included. For Zionism, everything had changed.

Jabotinsky, who had been feeling at loose ends, was re-energized. From Bordeaux he cabled Moscow, asking *Russkaya Vyedomosti*'s approval for a trip through North Africa, on whose Arab population, rumored to be on the verge of a Turkish-instigated pan-Islamist uprising against French colonial rule, he proposed to report. The paper agreed, and he returned to Paris, packed his bags, and was in Spain, on his way to Gibraltar, by late November. North Africa was little more than a pretext. His real destination was Egypt, along whose frontier with Palestine hostilities between the British and Turks were about to break out.

In Madrid, Jabotinsky met with the aging Max Nordau—who, as an Austro-Hungarian citizen, had been expelled from his residence in France. Asked what he thought Zionism's wartime policies should be, Nordau, the Zionist leader who had been closest personally to Herzl, counseled neutrality. It would be a grave mistake, he thought, to place one's bets on an Entente victory and risk being on the losing side. The two men argued. For Jabotinsky, the outcome of the war, at least in the West, was not in doubt; the little he had seen of it had convinced him that the French and British had the determination, endurance, and strategic supremacy needed to prevail. It was only a matter of time, he had assured the readers of *Russkaya*

Vyedomosti, before they crossed the Rhine and carried the fight to German territory. After meeting with Nordau, he wrote a letter to Yisra'el Rozov, a colleague at *Razsviet*, suggesting two possible courses of action. The minimal one would be to open an office in London or Paris to lobby for Zionist goals, circumventing the Executive in Berlin. The maximal one was

> to propose to England, or to England and France, the formation of a military corps of [Jewish] volunteers that would mainly assist in the conquest of Palestine in return for certain promises that I won't elaborate on here. . . . Although I have no idea how many volunteers we could raise, now is the right time for it, when every single individual is important [for the war effort].

The second plan—a military force that would stake the Jewish claim to Palestine by fighting for it—was clearly the one Jabotinsky favored. An idea that had not the slightest currency in Zionist circles at the time, it may have been first suggested to him as a student in Italy by the would-be Jewish Garibaldi, Marcou-Baruch. Once he reached Egypt, there was hardly a day in the next four years that was not at least partly devoted to it. It was to become his personal obsession—his *idée fixe*—an overriding ambition that catapulted him from being a Zionist writer and intellectual known to few outside Russia to the front ranks of world Jewish prominence.

Jabotinsky spent barely two weeks in North Africa, traveling eastward from Tangiers, on the Moroccan side of the Straits of Gibraltar, as far as Tunis. Warned by the French police not to interview people in the street, he spoke mainly to colonial administrators, French settlers, educated Arabs, and Jewish merchants, and his dispatches to *Russkaya Vyedomosti* had more padding in them than substance. The Arab population of the Maghreb, he explained, as though in justification of his failure to talk to it, was "sphinxlike." No outsider could know what it thought, or even if it had thoughts at all.

Yet on the subject of the mooted pan-Islamic revolt, his assessment was accurate. It would not take place, he told his readers, because the religion of the North African masses was a matter of local traditions and allegiances involving no wider Islamic identity, while the educated Muslim elite was as anti-Turkish as it was anti-French. It dreamed of an independent Morocco, Algeria, and Tunisia, not of the restored caliphate of Turkish war propaganda. It would not leave its coffeehouses for political activity, and the average Muslim was too fatalistic to try to change anything.

Jabotinsky thought even less of Arab culture than he did of Turkish. In his memoirs, he wrote of his North African trip:

> Tangiers, Algiers, Tunis: a geographical West that was cul-turally "the East." . . . The Middle East and all that is im-plied by that concept are foreign to me. I don't appreciate its beauty. I don't understand its traditions. Its music makes me wince and its thought fails to interest me. I would feel more at home with a tribe of Eskimos at the far end of Labrador. People tell me the fault is mine, not the Middle East's—and in fact, I appear to suffer from a congenital defect that pre-vents me from fathoming the region's subtleties, just as I suf-fer from one that makes Stravinsky's music leave me cold.

Most of all, he disliked what struck him as the passivity of Arab society. In a 1926 essay, he was to write of it:

> The Orient, if Europe does not prod or irritate it, exists in a state of equilibrium. There, too, there is an enormous gap between rich and poor; there is exploitation worse than any Europe has seen for a century; yet nowhere is there an active movement of the poorer against the richer classes; nowhere is there a moral protest, taking the form of public pres-sure, against the inequitable division of material goods. The

ability of the Orient's masses to make do, like the Stoics, with a minimum is legendary, just as the principled, uncompromising dissatisfaction of the impoverished classes of Europe is a basic feature of European life.

Yet "East" and "West," he wrote, were not immutable concepts. In the early Middle Ages, the Arab world was more "western" than Europe, and as Europeanization took place in it in the twentieth century, it would "westernize" again. "The harem, the veil, the patriarchal sheikh, the obeisance to fate" — all, Jabotinsky wrote, would be swept away, leaving "not a single 'Oriental' trait." But even though Moroccan, Tunisian, and Algerian nationalism, inspired by European models and ideologies, would eventually pose a greater threat to French colonialism than did traditional Islam, that day was still far off. Meanwhile, North Africa would slumber on through the war.

Jabotinsky reached Alexandria in late December, after a detour to Rome. A first clash between the British and Turkish forces in Sinai had already taken place near Kantara, at the northern end of the Suez Canal, and a larger Turkish attack was anticipated. Yet the British were confident. The Ottoman empire, Jabotinsky wrote in a letter to the Zionist Executive's vice-president Yechiel Tshlenov on January 1, 1915, was seeing its last days. What he feared was not a British defeat, but Anglo-French collusion whereby France would be given Palestine and Syria as its share of the spoils. (The British and French were in fact to arrive at a secret understanding, the "Sykes-Picot agreement" of 1916, but it gave Syria alone to France while calling for a joint and never implemented French-English condominium in Palestine.) This worried him because while the French were, as he put it, "a hundred times better" than the Turks as administrators, they were far inferior to the British, and a British-ruled Palestine would be better for Zionism.

The expected Turkish offensive was launched in early February when two Ottoman divisions attempted to cross the Suez Canal on rafts and pontoons north of the Great Bitter Lake. Dug-in Indian machine gunners mowed most of them down before they reached the far bank and the rest were repulsed with light British casualties and retreated back across Sinai. Touring the scene of the battle a week later, Jabotinsky reported in *Russkaya Vyedomosti*, he saw the corpses of Turkish soldiers still floating in the water. "On a 30-kilometer boat ride," he wrote with the studied blaséness of the veteran war correspondent that he was far from being,

> I counted nine of them. . . . When I mentioned this to the manager of one of the docking basins along the way, he told me: "Two or three more turn up every day—and those are the ones who managed to ditch their rifles. Many more must have been dragged to the bottom by their arms and ammunition."
>
> "Then how can you know how many you killed?" I asked.
>
> "We'll have to send down divers to count them."
>
> He laughed. I laughed. The Greek pilot laughed. Very funny.

In the weeks before the Turkish attack, Jabotinsky had been occupied with other things. At the time of his arrival in Alexandria, close to six thousand Jewish refugees from Palestine were housed there in Australian military barracks known as "Camp Gabari." Nearly half of Palestine's eighty thousand Jews were non-Ottoman nationals who had been issued an ultimatum by the Turks to either accept Ottoman citizenship or face possible deportation; many had left at once, a large number for Egypt, where they formed a microcosm of Palestinian Jewry—Ashkenazim and Sephardim, religious Jews and freethinkers, Orthodox and ultra-Orthodox, patriarchal Jews from

Georgia and the Caucasus and young socialist pioneers from Russia. Asked to join a relief committee, probably because of his experience in Kishinev, Jabotinsky was put in charge of the camp's daily regimen.

One of the pioneers, Yosef Trumpeldor, was older than the others. The same age as Jabotinsky, he had an unusual background for a Russian Jew. His father had been a "Cantonist," a Jew impressed into the army as a child during the reign of Nicholas I. Despite forcible baptism and long, harsh years of military service, he had clung to his Jewish identity, and as it was punishable for men like him to reembrace Judaism once discharged, he had settled in a remote region of the Caucasus where he could raise his children freely as Jews. Yosef, influenced equally as a boy by his father's Jewish loyalty and the ideals of a nearby Tolstoyan commune, studied dentistry, was drafted at the time of the war with Japan, fought heroically in it, and lost an arm in the battle of Port Arthur, for his role in which he was decorated several times and promoted to the rank of captain. He left the army as its highest-ranking Jewish officer, studied law in St. Petersburg, and in 1912 emigrated to Palestine, where lived in communal settlements in the Galilee until joining the exiles in Alexandria.

Jabotinsky's memoirs describe his first impressions of Trumpeldor, whom he sought out:

> He was in when I called, a northern-looking type whom I would have taken for a Scot or Swede had I passed him in the street. . . . To this day, I can't say whether he was "clever" in our Jew-sense [*sic!*] of the word. Perhaps not. So much is involved in that notion, such a mishmash of sugar-and-spice, horseradish, onions, and balm of Gilead—skepticism, and suspiciousness, and shrewdness, and the ability to make the straightest line so crooked that its tail ends up in its mouth. He had none of that. What he had was the clarity of vision to

tell white from black and a gentle, gracious sense of humor that never confused what was essential with what wasn't.

The two men struck up an immediate rapport. They shared much in common, from a deeply Russian side of themselves to a tough-minded Jewish patriotism, and already at their first meeting Jabotinsky broached his plan for a "Jewish legion." No one, he must have felt, could have understood him better than this former Jewish officer with four Orders of St. George. Unaffected by the war fever that had gripped many of their co-religionists in the West, most Russian Jews continued to associate armies with all the worst features of Gentile society—its empty pomp, brutality, contempt for the intellect, and disregard for human life. This was the traditional Jewish attitude toward the military. Even Herzl, in his utopian Zionist novel *Altneuland*, gave an army no place in a Jewish state.

Trumpeldor was won over immediately. As a first step, the two men set out to organize a group of volunteers from Camp Gabari to form the kernel of their legion. Close to a hundred of the refugees declared their willingness to join. The next day, they began to drill in the camp's central square. As Jabotinsky recalled:

> Just then, Trumpeldor appeared. Three platoons fell in and began proudly to parade (or so they thought they were doing) in front of him. He watched for a while and nodded his approval. "But they look like a flock of sheep!" I whispered. "Never mind," he said.

A meeting was held with General John Maxwell, commander of the British forces in Egypt. Maxwell put a damper on the volunteers' enthusiasm. No British attack on Palestine was in the offing, he told them, nor was there any precedent for non-British subjects serving as combat soldiers in the British army. However, he had a counterproposal. Based on his knowledge of a plan for an Anglo-French amphibious landing at Gallipoli, along the Dardanelles near Istanbul, he suggested the volunteers might form a transportation battalion in the army's mule corps and be sent to another front. England's gratitude, he assured them, would be earned by such a gesture just as well and would stand the Jewish people in good stead.

Mules and draft horses were in extensive use with the British Expeditionary Force in France, nearly half a million being employed by the war's end to pull artillery, troop wagons, and ambulances, and to haul supplies and ammunition. Handling them under fire demanded skill and courage, and Trumpeldor, who felt no need to prove his mettle in combat, was for accepting Maxwell's offer. Jabotinsky was opposed. He had conceived of his legion, above all, as a way of mobilizing Jewish and world public opinion for the Zionist cause, and a contingent of Jewish "donkey drivers" elsewhere than Palestine was worth little in his opinion. Moreover, he was thinking ahead. In a letter to Zionist Executive member Viktor Jacobson, he wrote:

> The newspapers and various rumors have misconstrued me as calling for a Jewish army that will conquer Palestine all by itself, etc. All that is ridiculous. What I'm thinking of is this: when one day a peace conference is convened, an item on the agenda will be the dismemberment of Turkey. (My whole plan is based on that.) The parts of Turkey to be divided up, including Palestine, will already be under military occupation. In Palestine, I imagine, some 20,000 soldiers will be needed. (That's for garrisoning the country during peace negotiations, not for conquering it.) My goal is to have a reasonably large Jewish unit form a third to half of this number.

Such a contingent, Jabotinsky thought, would be the quickest way to exert an immediate Zionist influence on British policy and a valuable card in the chaotic situation that was sure to prevail in occupied Palestine until a British administration was firmly in place. Eager to demobilize after a long war, the British would welcome Jewish troops to help guarantee public order against the Arab nationalist emotions aroused by the casting off of four hundred years of Turkish rule. A Jewish transportation unit disbanded at the war's end could accomplish none of this.

At the same time, however, there was no point in standing in Trumpeldor's way. Leaving him in Egypt to work out the details of what was to become the Zion Mule Corps, whose soldiers served with distinction in the failed Gallipoli campaign of 1915, Jabotinsky sailed for England to promote his legion there.

Ironically, his future political opponent, David Ben-Gurion, was then engaged in a similar effort—on the opposite side. The question of Ottomanization had not gone undebated in the Yishuv. Forty years of Zionist construction, it was argued by some, could not simply be abandoned by fleeing the country, especially when there was no certainty that the Turks would lose their empire or that, if they retained it, the refugees would be allowed to return. Ben-Gurion, now a leader of the small Po'alei Tsiyon or "Workers of Zion" party, was one of those who took this line. Having recently returned from studies in Turkey, he knew the Turks well and thought them capable of holding their own in the fighting. Rather than court their wrath by joining their enemies, he argued, Turkish-ruled Jews should behave patriotically. If Turkey retained its grip on Palestine, the wisdom of this would be self-evident; if it didn't, no one could be blamed for having been loyal to his government. Together with his friend Yitzhak Ben-Tsvi, one day to become the second president of the state of Israel, Ben-Gurion sought to encourage Palestinian Jews to become Ottoman citizens and fight for Turkey under the Zionist flag.

The Turks, though, had even less interest in a Jewish combat unit than did General Maxwell's staff in Egypt. Aware that most Palestinian Jews were pro-English, they commenced a crackdown on Zionist activity. Ben-Gurion and Ben-Tsvi were arrested and deported, arriving in Egypt in the spring of 1915 before continuing to the United States. By then, Jabotinsky was gone, too. Had he and Ben-Gurion had their way at the time, they might have begun their long rivalry by shooting at each other from the trenches, as did hundreds of thousands of other Jews who took part in the war's slaughter, killing one another in opposing armies as if they were just so many more of the foe.

Jabotinsky sailed to Brindisi, spent several days in Rome and Paris, and continued to London. His months in Egypt had convinced him that the formation of a Jewish legion depended, not on the generals in Cairo, but on a British government persuaded of its political value. Yet he had few contacts in England apart from Chaim Weizmann, then engaged in war-related research on explosives at the University of Manchester while lobbying for the Zionist cause with the British officials his work gave him access to—and though Weizmann was cooperative, his attempts to arrange a meeting between Jabotinsky and postmaster-general Herbert Samuel, a Zionist sympathizer and the highest-ranking Jew in the Liberal government of Prime Minister Herbert Asquith, fell through. Temporarily thwarted, Jabotinsky traveled that summer to Stockholm to meet Ania and Eri and went on to Copenhagen, to which the Zionist Executive had moved to be in a neutral country.

Copenhagen was more discouraging still. The Executive's members were opposed to the idea of a legion. Some hoped for a German victory, whether because they were German Jews or because they were Russian ones eager to see the end of Tsardom. Others felt, like Nordau, that siding militarily with the Entente was too great a risk. Even if Germany eventually went down to defeat, they held, it should not be antagonized in the meantime, since it alone could restrain the Turks from loosing their fury on Palestine's Jews as they had done on the Armenians. In vain Jabotinsky argued that an Anglo-French victory was inevitable and that neutral America, which had successfully intervened more than once with the Turks on the Yishuv's behalf, was a better guarantor of its safety than Germany. Nor was that safety an end in itself. The Yishuv, he declared, was an outpost of the entire Jewish people, whose needs came first. This was a theme he was often to return to in his later disputes with the Zionist Left.

Someone less stubborn might have given up. But by autumn, Jabotinsky was back in England, prepared to carry on. Weizmann had moved to London at the behest of the War Ministry, leaving his wife Vera temporarily in Manchester, and the two men shared rented rooms on Justice Walk, a small street of redbrick houses in Chelsea, a block from the Thames. From there, while the war continued to take a horrendous toll in Europe and the British pushed cautiously across Sinai toward Palestine, where they were to reach the outskirts of Gaza by early 1917, Jabotinsky pressed his initiative.

It was a one-man campaign, launched and conducted without an organization, without financial resources, without prior access to the corridors of power, without at first any fluency in spoken English. Apart from his personal charm and determination, Jabotinsky's sole initial asset was a unique streak of philo-Semitism in British society. Deriving from the Puritans' identification with the biblical Israelites, and transmitted by seventeenth- and eighteenth-century Protestant dissenters, this had penetrated nineteenth-century Anglicanism as well, particularly in evangelical, "Low Church" circles. Pro-Jewish sentiment, while far from characterizing most Englishmen, ran more strongly in some than anywhere else in Europe. Gentile Zionism, composed of equal parts Christian millenarianism and imperial *realpolitik*, actually preceded Jewish Zionism in England by several decades. Jabotinsky had potential backers in high places before they had even heard of him.

Still, quite apart from the opposition of the Zionist Executive, he had far more going against him: the widespread prejudice that Jews could not make good or loyal soldiers; a British government and army that did not see the relevance of a small Jewish force to the war effort; an English Zionist organization which, under the influence of Ahad Ha'am, now living in London too, opposed Zionism's "militarization"; an old, well-integrated Anglo-Jewish establishment that objected to Zionism as such; and a new, Eastern European immigrant community, most of it still holding Russian citizenship, whose youth had little desire to fight in a distant Middle Eastern country. In 1915, compulsory military service had yet to be introduced in England, whose millions of soldiers were mostly volunteers—a situation that prevailed until the passage of the Military Service Act in January 1916. The immigrants' fear of being conscripted, ahead of other Englishmen, into an all-Jewish legion was great.

At first, in addition to Weizmann and the Russian Zionist journalist Meir Grossman, who had met Jabotinsky in Copenhagen and now came to London to work with him, the plan had but a handful of active supporters. One was the colorful figure of Lieutenant-Colonel John Henry Patterson, an Irish Protestant veteran of the Boer War, renowned African big game hunter, and commander of the Zion Mule Corps at Gallipoli. Patterson, a lover of the Bible with a "sympathy for the Jewish race," as he put it in his book *With the Zionists in Gallipoli*, had been struck by the courage of his 540 volunteers, led by Trumpeldor; returning to England on sick leave in December 1915, he introduced Jabotinsky to his friend Leopold Amery, a Conservative member of Parliament soon to be promoted to assistant secretary in the war cabinet. Other political contacts followed, some facilitated by the Russian embassy in London.

Only with the passage of the Military Service Act, however, from which non-British subjects were exempt, did the plan gain traction. Overnight, an estimated thirty to forty thousand draft-age Jewish immigrants, mostly concentrated in London's East End, had become the largest body of young men in England not called upon to serve. Worse yet, they spoke Yiddish, a language like German; were hostile to Russia, England's ally; and were reputed to harbor pro-Bolshevik sentiments. Word spread of an "unseen hand," a code phrase for a partially Jewish conspiracy to sabotage the British war effort. When Lord Horatio Kitchener, Great Britain's secretary of state for war, went down in June 1916 aboard a British cruiser hit by a German mine, rumors circulated of a German-Jewish-Bolshevik cabal behind his death.

The old Anglo-Jewish establishment, whose sons were fighting in the front lines, feared the tide of hostility would wash over it, too. There was talk of anti-Jewish riots. (A year later, indeed, these were to break out in both London and Leeds.) Approached by East End Jews about organizing an Odessa-like self-defense group, Jabotinsky wrote a letter to Herbert Samuel, now serving as home secretary. In it he appealed for police protection for the immigrants and argued for a legion that would fight in Palestine as the only solution to the problem posed by them, since they could not fairly be expected to aid England's anti-Semitic Russian ally by fighting against Germany in Europe.

Samuel ignored Jabotinsky's letter and proposed changing the law so as to subject the immigrants to the draft, then relented but threatened to deport them unless they volunteered for military service on their own. In response, Jabotinsky composed and circulated a petition in the East End affirming the desire of young Russian-born Jews to serve only on the Palestine front. Yet after several months of rallies and assemblies that encountered frequent disruptions, in one of which his eyeglasses were smashed by hostile demonstrators, barely three hundred signatures had been amassed. Stung by charges that he wished to send the immigrants off to war while remaining securely in London, Jabotinsky applied for special permission to enroll in an officers training course of the London Regiment, also known as the Royal Fusiliers. (The largest regiment in the British army, the Fusiliers had eighty-eight infantry battalions fighting in different theaters by the end of World War I.)

By then, however, events had taken two unexpected turns. The first was Trumpeldor's arrival from Alexandria, followed by 120 reenlisted members of the Zion Mule Corps, now upgraded to an infantry unit and transferred as a separate company, the 5th, to the Royal Fusiliers's 20th Battalion. The second was the resignation of Lord Asquith, under heavy criticism for his conduct of the war, in December 1915 and his replacement as prime minister by David Lloyd George, who chose Arthur Balfour as his foreign secretary. Unlike Asquith, both Lloyd George and Balfour came from Bible-reading Low Church families and were sympathetic to Zionism; moreover, whereas Asquith had lost interest in the eastern Mediterranean following the British defeat at Gallipoli, both men believed that a victory over Turkey would hasten the war's end in Europe, too, and facilitate the long-term British presence in Palestine that was needed to guard Suez, England's link to India, from the east.

And yet in the new world order that would emerge from the war—a first harbinger of which was the fall of the Tsarist regime in February 1917 and the establishment of a provisional revolutionary Russian government—a British-ruled Palestine would call for greater justification than naked imperialist ambition. An internationally recognized Jewish state-in-progress under English tutelage, Lloyd George and Balfour calculated, could provide this. They also hoped British support for Zionism would inspire a wave of pro-English sentiment in the world's two largest Jewish communities, America's and Russia's, each of which they were eager to win over: the first to help sway the U.S. government to enter the war on England's side, the second to combat left-wing agitation in Russia to sign a separate peace with Germany and drop out of the fighting. Zionism thus seemed to them a practical no less than a moral desideratum, and its official endorsement became the subject of intensive negotiations between the British government and a Zionist movement mainly represented by Weizmann, now president of the British Zionist Organization.

Jabotinsky took no part in these negotiations, which culminated in the Balfour Declaration's promise, in November 1917, to establish a Jewish "national home" in Palestine. The new attitude toward Zionism prevailing in government circles, however, favorably affected attitudes toward a Jewish legion, too. Canceling his officers training course application, Jabotinsky enlisted in Trumpeldor's 5th Company, the obvious nucleus around which to build such a force.

Even then, the slow workings of government and military bureaucracy, the hostility of Anglo-Jewish leaders, the continued opposition of the Zionist Executive, and the negativity of the Jewish immigrant community kept raising new obstacles. Trumpeldor, denied an infantry commission because of his foreign citizenship, left for Russia to marshal volunteers there. In February 1917, the 5th Company was sent for training to Winchester, sixty miles southwest of London. Given the noncommissioned rank of lance sergeant, Jabotinsky was in an unusual, even comical position. While in principle an ordinary soldier, he was at the same time, under orders from above, given liberty to travel to London for whatever meetings he deemed necessary. Bawled out one day by an officer during barracks inspection as a "bloody fool," he might be holding discussions the next day with Henry Wickham Steed, foreign editor of the *Times* of London, South African president Jan Smuts, or war secretary Lord Derby.

The pace of progress was frustrating. Only in July 1917 was the final go-ahead given for a Jewish battalion to fight in Palestine, and three more months went by before it was fully mustered. Designated the London Regiment's 38th, it had eight hundred soldiers (most, according to Patterson, who was given its command, "East End tailors"), a rabbi for its chaplain, Saturday as its day of rest, and kosher food served in its mess hall.

Four days later the Balfour Declaration was issued; the day after that, Ania and the six-year-old Eri arrived from Norway. The Jabotinskys rented rooms in a small hotel near Hyde Park before moving to a furnished flat in Maida Hill, where they stayed while the 38th Battalion finished basic training in Plymouth and awaited orders. Given leave by Patterson to remain in London, Jabotinsky spent his days with his family. It was, Eri recalled in his reminiscences, a highly social time, full of visits to friends and the theater, including two movies for his seventh birthday. (Not that Jabotinsky needed excuses to go to the movies. The cinema was a lifelong enthusiasm rivaled only by his love of detective stories.)

The family was not together for long. On February 2, 1918, the 38th Battalion embarked for Alexandria. Jabotinsky, now promoted to second lieutenant, sailed with it, one of two non-British subjects, thanks to Patterson, ever commissioned as a British officer. (The other was Kaiser Wilhelm, who was cashiered when the war broke out.) First, though, the battalion paraded through the streets of London in full battle gear, carrying the Zionist flag with its Star of David alongside the Union Jack. Starting from the Tower of London, the Jewish troops marched down Mile End Road into an East End that was, according to Patterson, "fairly rocking" with excitement.

On the whole, however, the balance sheet of accomplishment was not spectacular. Though two more battalions, the 39th and 40th, were added in the coming year, all three were considerably smaller than the force Jabotinsky had envisioned, and none arrived in time to take part in the British invasion of Palestine. In November 1917, while the 38th Battalion was still organizing in Plymouth, three British divisions commanded by General Edmond Allenby had broken through Turkish defenses in Gaza. Jerusalem fell in early December, and the Turks formed a new defensive line running from north of Jaffa's Jewish suburb of Tel Aviv, now in British hands too, to the Jordan Valley.

Already while waiting in Plymouth, a junior officer in the force he had created, Jabotinsky experienced the bittersweetness of his triumph. Standing there one snowy, moonlit night, so he wrote,

> I looked around me with an odd feeling. Everywhere were low barracks, a hundred or so young men in each—the Jewish legion I had dreamed of and sacrificed so much for. And yet I was a stranger here, no longer constructing or directing a thing. It was like the fairytale in which Aladdin's work is done by invisible spirits. Who was Aladdin? A nobody. He found a rusty old lamp that he wanted to clean and he rubbed it with a rag, and suddenly the djinns appeared and built him a palace. The palace will go on standing, but Aladdin and his lamp are no longer needed. Perhaps this is what true victory consists of: the victor's becoming irrelevant.

The 38th Battalion of the Royal Fusiliers reached Alexandria on March 1, 1918. After several months of advanced infantry training in Egypt, it proceeded to Palestine and took up a position in the Samarian hills north of Jerusalem on June 27. Jabotinsky, who had spent most of June attached to British headquarters near Jaffa, asked for and received permission to rejoin his unit at the front.

In the half year since Jerusalem's conquest, despite two unsuccessful British attacks across the Jordan, this hadn't changed. The 38th Battalion held a northward-looking hill dropping along terraces planted with olive trees to a deep wadi; across from it, a southward-looking hill was held by the Turks. Though exchanging occasional machine gun and artillery fire, neither side attempted to dislodge the other. The British sent out nightly patrols and Jabotinsky took his turn commanding them. His platoon would descend to the wadi, comb it in either direction, and sometimes venture halfway up the opposite hill until met by Turkish barbed wire. As he recalled in his memoirs:

> You were just a few hundred meters from the Turkish trenches, but you weren't there to do anything about it. Sometimes, a weary foot would kick a loose stone. Then a shot would ring out and ricochet off the rocks not far from the last man in your column. (Although you were supposed to be in the middle of your single file of men, it was considered more "sporting" to lead from in front.) You whispered as loud as you could, "Hit the ground," and the patrol threw itself down. Three hundred feet away up the hill a spark flared, soared, and turned into a red rocket that flooded the valley with its glare, lighting up the thorn bushes, the dry watercourse, the rocks and crevices. It would have been a fine sight if we could have paid it any attention.

From the British side would come covering fire and perhaps an artillery barrage. "It would last half an hour. Then all quieted down and you crawled back to your base, where a vat of sweet, boiling-hot tea awaited you."

Jabotinsky was not at the front the entire time. He made frequent trips to Jerusalem to confer with British officials, attending the laying of the cornerstone of the Hebrew University on July 24, and was out of commission for several weeks with a knee infection caused by an encounter with barbed wire. On August 9, the 38th Battalion was transferred to the Jordan Valley, marching on foot from Jerusalem to the Auja, a stream emptying into the Jordan River some twelve hundred feet below sea level. It was the most brutally hot time of the year in a desolate region, situated north of the Dead Sea between the highlands of Palestine and Transjordan, that was notorious for its heat in all seasons. The valley was ridden with flies and malarial mosquitoes, its air filled with dust, its waters brackish, its barren, chalk-white earth tasting of salt and sulfur. The battalion, moreover, was in a precarious position. Situated at the extreme eastern end of British lines, it faced a Turkish arc, part of the Ottoman 4th Army, that exposed it to attack from several directions. The nearest available reinforcements were the Anzacs, a division of Australian and New Zealand cavalry camped to the south. Were the Turks to seek to turn the British flank, or simply to pick off its most vulnerable segment, they would start with the 38th.

Fortunately, they had no such ambitions. Their deployment was defensive, designed to hold the fords on the Jordan and prevent the British from trying again to cross it, take the heights on its other side, link up with T. E. Lawrence's force of Bedouin guerrillas now advancing from the Arabian desert, and march on Damascus. The British, although planning their main breakthrough at the western, Mediterranean end of the front, encouraged the Turks to think this was their intention; they patrolled the Jordan Valley aggressively and filled it with dummy artillery batteries and cavalry camps while lighting large bonfires at night to make it look, in Patterson's words, "as if a mighty army were bivouacked all around." The 38th Battalion took part in this deception, probing Turkish positions and engaging in brief firefights.

On September 15, it was joined by the 39th, which had arrived from America with Ben-Gurion and Ben-Tsvi in its ranks. On September 19, the British launched their offensive. Five infantry and two mounted divisions, supported by French and

Australian cavalry and the Royal Fusiliers's 40th Battalion, composed largely of Palestinian Jewish volunteers, smashed through the 7th and 8th Ottoman Armies near the coast. The Turkish retreat quickly became a rout. On September 23, the British took Haifa. By the 25th, they were in Tiberias. Damascus fell with no resistance on October 1, followed by Aleppo. On October 30, Turkey officially laid down its arms. Two and a half weeks later, Germany surrendered, and the war was over.

The three Jewish battalions played a minor role in all this. The task assigned the 38th was to seize a ford on the Jordan, for which the Turks were expected to put up a stiff fight. When Jabotinsky's lead platoon reached the river, however, the Turkish position had been abandoned. The 38th and 39th Battalions made the steep ascent to the Transjordanian town of es-Salt, trudging through flames and smoke from fields set afire by the retreating forces. Halfway to the top, the 38th was ordered to march back down and escort a group of Turkish prisoners to Jericho. A Turk in the column guarded by Jabotinsky's platoon collapsed on the way. His comrades, at the end of their strength, refused to carry him. Jabotinsky conferred with the battalion's chaplain, a London rabbi. If left by the roadside, the fallen prisoner would be eaten alive by jackals before he could die. The decision was to shoot him.

All told, the three battalions lost eighty-seven men in the war, most victims of malaria. For Jabotinsky, it was a chance to test himself in new circumstances. It was one thing to head a campaign for a Jewish legion, quite another to command men under Turkish fire, even if—as he wrote wryly in a letter to Ania—his greatest act of heroism was commandeering a horse from its angry Bedouin owner on the way to es-Salt. Always confident of his abilities of leadership, he now had acquired the moral authority to demand of others what he had been willing to ask of himself.

Yet the war's worst moment for him was not facing death in combat. It was the killing of the Turkish prisoner, the memory of which haunted him long afterwards. (Although his memoirs do not say so, it was probably he, as the officer in charge, who pressed the trigger.) This did not, however, change his beliefs. "Today," he wrote years later,

> when I'm openly called a militarist, I think of that night and of that road in the Jordan Valley . . . and I refuse to say it wasn't worth it.
>
> It's an awful thing, the life of a nation. It's hard to keep going in the wilderness. You can't? Then lie down and die. Humanity is a battalion, too, and no one is going to carry you to Jericho. You either march on with all the cruelty to yourself and others that this calls for, or you give up and are swallowed by oblivion together with all your hopes.

On September 17, on the eve of the British offensive, Jabotinsky wrote a letter to Ania with instructions that it be forwarded to her should he be killed in action. "My Dearest," it began,

> I don't know how one goes about writing a letter like this.
>
> I've been unfair to you and Eri. Perhaps the right thing to do would have been to remain quietly [in British headquarters] in Jaffa, as I was asked to. But though you may have forgotten what you once said to me, I haven't. "I'm so glad," you said in London, "that you're not a coward." In matters like this, there's something *plus fort que nous mêmes*.[3] I swear to you, the world's opinion of me doesn't matter, but that you or Eri might think less of me—that settled things. Forgive me, my darling, for having crossed your path in life, and

3. French: "stronger than we are."

taken you away from it, and left you all alone now with Eri. I would have given a great deal for it not to have happened this way . . .

I've put you through a great deal, Ania, but all my life you've been my great love. For years now, I've watched my dreams slowly fade. I've worked to no purpose, partly from a sense of duty and partly because I couldn't say no to my own abilities, but my heart was never in it. The one dream that remained was of a warm retreat somewhere with you and Eri, if only for a few years, where I might make up for everything. It didn't work out. If you receive this letter, at least I'll have left you and Eri a name to be proud of, one that will one day cause hats to be doffed to you in the street. Believe me, that's the only thing I really value in all this. I want Eri to master Hebrew. As for the rest, I won't give you any advice. You've always known better and acted more wisely than I have. I believe in you and know that *got un layt veln dir mekaney zayn af dayn zun.*[4]

Forgive me for everything, Annalee: it was all for my love, which I don't have to give you proof of. I often go over our story in my mind, from that first evening on Dogtyirnaya Street [in Odessa] to that [last] day in Southhampton. That's 23 years. If I could have them back, I'd make better use of them. And yet there isn't and never could be anything more wonderful to remember. I kiss your hands, my love. I don't want to write in a different vein now—but re-read my old letters to you from Vienna and know that I could still write each one of them today.

Show Eri this letter some day. It's meant for him too. God watch over you.

Volodya

Despondent and ridden by a sense of failure in his life and marriage, the figure revealed by this letter is so at odds with Ja-

4. Yiddish: "God and man will envy you your son."

botinsky's public persona and the conventional image of him that one is jolted by it even after remembering his warning that his memoirs dealt only with "the writer and politician, not the man." Was the man, then, so unhappy with the life that the politician had chosen? Was his heart really "never in" the national struggle he had taken part in since 1903? Or are we, the letter's readers, unintended witnesses to what was merely a dark but passing shadow cast on a soldier's mind by the thought of going into battle?

The doubt and self-recrimination were real. Men live with consciences lightened by the belief that there is still time for what they have neglected to do; the realization that time may have suddenly run out is thus doubly crushing, adding anguish for a miscalculated life to fear of death. Jabotinsky was nearly thirty-eight; his career as a journalist and Zionist leader had caused him to spend much of his marriage away from his wife and son; he had comforted himself with the thought of all the years they still had ahead of them; now, these stood to be snatched away all at once.

The same was true of his literary talents. They were great; he knew they were, knew he had in him an inner world that was entirely his own as no collective cause, however noble, could be; he had devoted himself to such a cause in the confidence that he would one day be able to give this world shape and form; he hadn't counted on its perishing at a ford of the Jordan.

The ford fell without a shot. The shadow passed.

This is one way of reading Jabotinsky's letter of September 17. Yet judging from other mail to Ania that same summer and autumn, he was also experiencing a more general malaise. For example:

March 27:

I'm here [in Palestine] as a spokesman for a non-existent state and as a commander in a non-existent army.

April 3:

Over and over I have to start from the beginning (with the British, not with the Palestinian youngsters). The young people are eager to fight, but they're being turned away [as volunteers]. They [the British], it seems, are waiting for their enthusiasm to wane. . . . Outwardly, everyone [in the British command] is for us, but the atmosphere is chilly.

April 10:

I sit in my tent with nothing to do. Our mood isn't good. . . . The Arabs are apprehensive about Zionism, and the more afraid of it they are, the more afraid the [British] authorities are of them.

May 16:

Today I received your letter of April 9 in which you complain about not getting mail from me and of how "dry" the letter [that you did receive] was. . . . From you, I don't even get "dry" mail. If you must write only once in a century, don't just write about how bad I am.

May 29:

Everything is fine, but I'm sick and tired of it all. Nothing can make me either happy or sad. I hope you've begun to receive my [army] salary—but what good is it when it's only a few pennies? . . . No one is having a fine time of it these days, but it seems to me that you and Eri are having a worse time than others and that I'm to blame.

July 9:

I remember everything. The letters we sent from Vienna and Nancy: what didn't we write in them! . . . [Yet] I'm afraid, my dearest, that if I were to come to you [in London] now, you'd throw me out, so [before you do] I'm giving you another kiss.

August 11:

I just received your letters written after [Eri's] operation [for a harelip]. . . . Oh, my love, may this be the last time you and Eri have to suffer!

September 12:

Psychologically, I'm exhausted. . . . The impossibility of grand or sweeping action, on the one hand—the impossibility, on the other, of simply walking away from it all—the constant uncertainty of everything—it's no good.

He was now the Aladdin of his reverie in Plymouth, pushed from the center of things to their periphery. His work at British headquarters had left him with time on his hands and an enfeebling sense of superfluity. He was, despite the Balfour Declaration, distrustful of British intentions and worried about the effect of anti-Zionist Arab agitation. He missed Ania and felt guilty for the financial straits she was in; for the first time in their marriage, he was unable to support her and Eri properly. Army mail was slow and they weren't hearing from each other regularly.

The lack of mail was even harder for Ania. She was full of fears. On September 17, two days before the British offensive, she wrote Jabotinsky a letter that he received over a month later, long after the fighting was over. It began:

Darling,
    What can be the meaning of this, that there is no word from you two posts [i.e., army mail deliveries] in a row? I imagine you wounded, dead. I think I'm losing my mind.

She was "terrible lonely" and "a bundle of nerves." She had put on weight and grown grayer; it would not make him happy to see her. She suspected he was hiding their true financial situation from her. She had heard rumors that he was planning to travel to Russia or America and was furious that he hadn't told her. She couldn't understand how he could think of going elsewhere than London, to her and Eri, let alone to a Russia in the throes of a civil war.

> Why must I hear about everything from others? I've told you before and I'll say it again: if you go to Russia, you'll never see me or Eri again. You must remember that I've never stood in your way, and if I'm so strongly against it now, it's no mere whim of mine. . . . Please treat me as an adult, a friend, and write me everything. I'm a grown-up woman now and no longer want to be the figurehead queen. I love you very much, and the deeper and more serious my love becomes, the more serious are its demands.

She fretted that he was being unfaithful. Gossip had reached her, she wrote in August, that "you are womanizing and that my biggest rival is a Mademoiselle Berlin (about whom, by the way, you've never said a word). Why don't you amuse me a bit by telling me about all my rivals?" Two weeks later, she issued the veiled threat: "I hear you're fine and not living a dull life. Well, I don't intend to live one, either."

Jabotinsky did not receive these letters until late October, when he answered Ania's accusations one by one. He was not, he protested, concealing money matters. He had no travel plans. As for "Mademoiselle Berlin," she was one of two sisters, volunteer army nurses, who had helped care for his infected knee. "They're both quite lovely," he wrote.

> The older is an interesting young redhead of twenty-five. The youngest is twenty-two and more of a domestic type. I'm very friendly with both, and neither gets in the way of the other, because one lives in Jerusalem and one in Jaffa. (I wish there were a third in Haifa, because now that the Galilee has been liberated, I'll have to be there sometimes, too.) You needn't worry about our flirtation—it's all per-

fectly proper. Since I'm being truthful, though, I should confess that what's holding me back isn't me but rather—as I've complained to you in the past—my accursed position as a "public figure" who has to be totally aboveboard.

The two sisters were Bella and Nina Berligne, the daughters of a Palestinian olive oil manufacturer. It was Jabotinsky's typical way of dealing in his correspondence with the issue of fidelity, which could not but concern a couple that was apart so often: to acknowledge the reality of temptation, speak of himself and Ania as worldly people who were not shocked by such a thing, and poke fun at the possibility that anything untoward might actually have happened. Yet in the case of Nina Berligne (the younger and "more dangerous" of the two sisters, as he teasingly wrote Ania in another letter), he did not, it would seem, "hold back" for long. He had first met Nina the previous spring in Cairo, while his battalion was still in Egypt, and though his first letters to her were within the bounds of ordinary friendship, their tone changed in the winter of 1918-19. On January 23, for instance, he wrote in reply to a hurt letter from her (like her other mail to him, it has been lost):

> Ninochka more precious than gold,
>   Don't take seriously anything in my letters that might be upsetting to you. Be like me—I never believe you when you hurt me. I know that in your heart is a barrel of sweet oranges, all meant for me. . . .
>   Señorita, I kiss your feet. (I swear to God, I'm not being cheeky. That's what they say in Spain. You know perfectly well that what interests me at the moment is not your feet.)
>   V. [Volodya]

This was no longer the language of mere "flirtation." A month before that, apparently responding to Nina's concern that their relationship could not last because of the difference in years between them, he had written her:

Don't be sad, my little one. Everything will be fine. You're still at the beginning of your life. Despite my advanced age, I have no intention of growing old right now. . . . I want you to love me all you can and all the time, as I love you.

V.Z.

The relationship gradually lost its intensity toward the summer of 1919, when Nina left with Bella for Switzerland. Perhaps she did so because she had learned from Jabotinsky that Ania was planning to come with Eri to Palestine in late July, the army having relaxed its restrictions on officers' families joining them abroad. In early July, when Nina was already in Lausanne, Jabotinsky wrote in reply to a letter from her: "You're quite right, my dear child whom I adore: it's not worth loving anyone if you have to end up missing them badly afterwards."

The Berligne sisters were the only women ever to have their names linked romantically to the married Jabotinsky. If he had other, passing involvements while away from Ania, they were conducted discreetly and perhaps even with her consent. (Writing to her from Chicago in 1926, he described, in his usual bantering tone, an attractive young lady assigned to shepherd him around between lectures and added, "I've had no successes, despite the permit you've given me.") As for the possibility of other men in Ania's life, this was alluded to by Jabotinsky in the 1919 letter in which he recalled his stubborn courtship of her. Still referring to her in the third person, he had continued in a humorous but not unserious tone:

> Sometimes she resorted to extravagant, 12-horsepower fits. She still does. She also takes offense quickly, bears grudges, and complains incessantly. She never appears in my dreams at night, so that I can't even remember what she looks or sounds like. I take this to be a deliberate slight on her part. Sometimes she tells me about her betrayals. Even though I pretend

not to, I tend to believe her and respect her. If she ever leaves me, I'll fight for her twelve more years. *Voilà!*

Some or all of these "betrayals," of course, may have been mere verbal provocations like Jabotinsky's. That Ania complained a lot is confirmed by Eri, who wrote of feeling when young that his mother's constant criticism was a hindrance to his father's ambitions. (As he grew older, Eri said, he came to understand Ania's side of it better.) Her discontent had its reasons. She was married to a man who could have supported her handsomely as a journalist but didn't, so that they were constantly in need of money, and even in the 1920s and '30s, when their separations were shorter, Jabotinsky traveled constantly and was sometimes away for weeks or months at a time. "The next time I marry," Ania was reported once to have remarked, "it won't be to a Zionist—they're never at home." Many of these trips were necessary; some could have been avoided. (All were undertaken with a "Nansen passport," a travel document for stateless persons issued by the League of Nations, since Jabotinsky insisted on becoming a citizen only of a Jewish state when there was one.) As much as he assured Ania that he longed for nothing more than a life of quiet domesticity, Jabotinsky resisted domestic enclosure.

Yet their marriage was a strong one whose love, mutual commitment, and joint devotion to Eri overcame the difficulties. For all her misgivings, Ania understood from the start that she had married a man who needed to follow his own star and that it was wiser to regard this as a privilege not easily borne than as a misfortune to be combated. She was ultimately supportive of Jabotinsky's decisions, even when she carped about them, and did her best to play the role, which she did not like, of a politician's wife. A good housekeeper, dresser, and entertainer, she combined, as recalled by Eizik Remba, Jabotinsky's secretary in Paris in the 1930s, "aristocracy with simplicity."

She much preferred social evenings, friends, and theater to discussions of Zionism, but Remba remembered her sitting silently by Jabotinsky's side in their apartment through night-long sessions of the Revisionist leadership, determined to keep him company and serve snacks and drinks even if she would rather be in bed.

Jabotinsky trusted and honored her. Never one to believe that women needed men to be responsible for them, he let her manage their joint affairs. Already in prewar Russia, he had considered himself a feminist. Women, he was persuaded, were better organizers than men, more practical and more self-disciplined. Invited to give an after-dinner address to an all-female audience in London in 1923, he chose as his subject a historical comparison of Europe's kings and queens and argued that the queens had a higher percentage of successful rulers. Although Russia's Peter the Great, by way of illustration, was a "genius," he was a ham-handed administrator, whereas his successor Catherine ran a well-managed kingdom. As "conquerors and overthrowers" men were superior to woman, but "insofar as governing means organizing and building," women did it better. And indeed, in the early 1930s, when the Tel-Hai Fund, the Revisionist movement's cultural and educational wing, lapsed into financial disarray under a series of male directors, Jabotinsky asked Ania to step in and straighten things out.

By temperament a romantic who kept his romanticism in check, he did not, in writing to Ania, ever repeat the newly-wed passion of his letters from Vienna—nor, perhaps, did he ever feel it again in quite the same way. Still, his deepest sense of their marriage remained romantic. The only poem he ever wrote to her, composed in 1926 in Detroit while on one of his speaking tours, began:

> Once you said, "You sing for other people
> And for me alone your muse is mute."

But what if my whole life's a sonnet cycle,
And the only theme of it is you?

A few days later, he wrote her from Chicago:

Did you get my madrigal from Detroit? . . . The main thing,
madame, is that I'm incurably in love with you. I believe it
started the moment I put on the wedding ring.

The day he said "the nine Hebrew words" beneath the wedding canopy was "the best day of his life," he wrote in 1939 in a congratulatory note to the young head of Betar, Menachem Begin, on occasion of the latter's marriage in Poland. These words were *harey at mekudeshet li b'taba'at zu k'dat Moshe v'Yisra'el*, and Jabotinsky had already uttered them to Ania, substituting a ritually valid coin for a ring, when she was sixteen. It may have been only a jest, but as in a fairy tale, she was his from then on.

One of his favorite poems was Edgar Allan Poe's "Annabel Lee," which he translated into a Hebrew as mellifluously haunting as Poe's English. The poem begins:

It was many and many a year ago,
    In a kingdom by the sea,
That a maiden there lived whom you may know
    By the name of Annabel Lee;
And this maiden she lived with no other thought
    Than to love and be loved by me.

I was a child and she was a child,
    In this kingdom by the sea;
But we loved with a love that was more than love—
    I and my Annabel Lee . . .

Jabotinsky's "Annabel Lee," like his Hebrew version of Poe's "The Raven," remains a high-water mark of Hebrew translation to this day. Yet there is an apparent error in it that is puzzling, for the third and fourth lines of its first stanza are *sham dara yalda, shma lo teda, karati la Annabel Lee*—"a maiden there lived whose name you know not, I called her Annabel Lee." This was the opposite of what Poe wrote.

The puzzle is cleared up when one recalls that Jabotinsky's pet name for Ania, used by him alone, was "Annalee."

Where could it have been, this kingdom by the sea, if not in Odessa?

3

Between Palestine and Europe

THE PALESTINE THAT emerged from World War I, war-weary but not badly war-damaged, was a new country in more ways than one. During the long centuries of Ottoman rule, there had been no administrative region of Palestine and nothing corresponding on Turkish maps to either the Jewish *eretz-yisra'el* or "Land of Israel," the Christian "Holy Land," or the Arab "Filastin"—none of which were in themselves precisely delineated territories or entirely congruent with one another. The area east of Sinai and the Mediterranean and south of the mountains of Lebanon had never been governed by the Turks as a discrete entity. During the last decades of their empire it was divided, west of the Jordan River, into the northern province of Nablus, which belonged to the department of Beirut, and the southern province of Jerusalem, part of the department of Damascus until 1887. To the east of the Jordan were the provinces of Hauran and el-Kerak, both governed from Damascus, too.

The single land called Palestine established by the British military occupation did away with this division. To the south and west, its borders followed the prewar Turkish-Egyptian frontier from the Mediterranean to the head of the Gulf of Aqaba. To the east, they extended far beyond the Jordan into the northern reaches of Arabia. In the north, pending the conclusion of negotiations with France, now in control of Syria and Lebanon, they ran eastward along a line that started midway between Acre and Tyre, looped to include the Golan Heights, and cut back through the middle of the Sea of Galilee. (An Anglo-French agreement in 1923 reassigned the Golan to Syria and all of the "sea"—in reality, a moderately sized lake—to Palestine.) Jerusalem, where the British established their administrative headquarters, was the country's capital.

Within this area of some 45,000 square miles, three-quarters of it across the Jordan, lived approximately a million people. Two hundred thousand of them, mostly tent-dwelling Bedouin, resided to the river's east; to the west were 750,000 Arabs and 57,000 Jews. (Another 18,000 Jews had left during the war.) Heavily rural, the Arab population was nine-tenths Muslim with a minority of Christians and Druze. Mostly urban, the Jewish population was divided equally between an old, anti-Zionist, ultra-Orthodox community and a newer Zionist one that was, following the British conquest, organized in the form of a "Provisional Council" in which different religious, ethnic, and ideological factions were represented. This became the "National Council" when reappointed by an "Assembly of Representatives" chosen in general elections in 1920.

It may not have seemed the most promising foundation on which to build the Jewish "national home" spoken of in the Balfour Declaration. Yet Zionist hopes that massive Jewish immigration would redress the demographic imbalance were not unfounded. During the four years of the world war, the Jewish situation in Europe had changed as dramatically as had the situation in Palestine. Tsarist Russia, the home of half the world's population of 13 million Jews, had vanished, its place taken by an independent Poland, Lithuania, Latvia, and Estonia, on the one hand, and a Russia and Ukraine torn by civil war on the other. Revolutionary "Red" and counterrevolutionary "White" armies marched back and forth, battling each other while wreaking—the Whites especially—havoc on the Jews in their path. The shtetls of Eastern Poland, Belarus, Galicia, and Ukraine, many already devastated by the fighting between German, Austrian, and Russian troops and the anti-Semitic atrocities of the latter, now fell victim to a slaughter unprecedented in European Jewish history. Between 1917 and 1921, 75,000 or more Jews were murdered in a multitude of massacres that dwarfed pogroms like Kishinev's. Eastern European Jewry was eager to resume its large-scale emigration of the prewar years. A recognized Jewish homeland under British law and protection could, Zionism's supporters believed, compete favorably with other options, especially after the Aliens Act of 1919 in Great Britain, and the restrictive U.S. immigration laws of 1921 and 1924, effectively shut down these two destinations.

For the British, too, Palestine was something new. Acquiring and administering overseas colonies was a task they were accustomed to, as was attracting and assisting English colonists to settle in them. But governing a country promised over the heads of its native population to colonists who were not English, or even entirely European, had no precedent. Moreover, the terms of the promise were ambiguous. Not only had the Balfour Declaration—written in the form of a brief letter to Lord Lionel Rothschild, a prominent Anglo-Jew and friend of Chaim Weizmann—not spoken explicitly of a Jewish state, it had qualified its support for Zionism with the proviso that "nothing shall be done [in Palestine] which may prejudice the civil and religious rights of existing non-Jewish communities."

How could a country that was overwhelmingly Arab be turned into a national home for Jews without prejudice to Arab rights?

To complicate matters further, promises, though of a less public nature, had been made to the Arabs as well. In a wartime effort to win their backing and encourage the revolt of the Bedouin loyal to Hussein ibn Ali, the Sherif of Mecca, who fought with Lawrence, the British government had committed itself—most clearly in a series of letters to Hussein from Henry McMahon, the British high commissioner of Egypt—to support Arab independence in the liberated areas after the war. Now, it was faced with having to honor contradictory pledges while safeguarding its own imperial interests.

From the very outset, then, the thirty years of British rule in Palestine, which received the international authorization of a League of Nations mandate in 1922, were plagued by inconsistency, indecisiveness, and a vacillating pattern of seeking to placate now this and now that side while ultimately antagonizing both. Again and again, the Zionist movement felt betrayed by England's failure to work wholeheartedly for the national home it had vowed to establish; again and again, Palestine's Arabs felt confirmed in their belief that they were faced with a British-sponsored Jewish invasion and takeover of their country. Nor were the British, despite the dilemma they were in, totally displeased with it. Although their desire to keep the peace in Palestine was genuine, they were well aware that their role as its keepers was a strong justification for their presence there. They could not turn the country over to the Jews because there were too few of them; they could not turn it over to the Arabs because of what might happen to the Jews; what choice had they but to remain?

This was the view from London, which did its best to steer a middle course on Palestine at the Versailles Peace Conference in 1919. The concerns of the British military occupation in Jerusalem, however, were different. General Allenby and his staff were not politicians or diplomats. They had a country to run and its inhabitants were preponderantly Arab. In most matters, therefore, they not unnaturally gave Arab demands priority and tended to be dismissive of Jewish ones. Angry Arabs could make more trouble than angry Jews.

Most of the prominently involved figures on the Jewish side, such as Weizmann, now president of the Zionist Organization and chairman of the "Zionist Commission," an ad hoc body of Zionist leaders from abroad that worked alongside the Provisional Council, shrugged this off. Once the army made way for a civilian regime, they held, the latter would be more responsive to Zionist wishes. Jabotinsky did not share their optimism. The danger of an erosion of British support, already feared by him during the war, struck him as real. In a lengthy communication to Weizmann in November 1918, he listed a series of British slights to Zionism (Hebrew had not been recognized like Arabic as an official language; Jews were underrepresented in appointed municipal councils; Arabs had gone unpunished for attacking peaceful Jewish demonstrations, and so on) before going on to what he considered the gravest: the marginalization of the three battalions of the Jewish legion. Far from forming an integral part of the occupation force as he had assumed they would do, the 40th Battalion had been stationed in Egypt, the 39th was being kept in its barracks, and his own, the 38th, had been sent to man the Egyptian-Palestinian frontier at Rafah. "I'm beginning to worry about the coming civil administration," he wrote Weizmann. "Will there really be such a difference between British military and civilian governors? I deem it likely they'll have much in common—an aversion to problems, for instance, and a tendency to favor the dark-skinned native over the ambitious *babu*[1] with his pretensions of European culture even though he isn't an Englishman."

---

1. A term sometimes used disparagingly in India for natives who put on British airs.

The soldiers of the three battalions were demoralized. In July 1919, a revolt broke out in the 38th. Declaring they had not enlisted in order to serve in a sleepy border post, fifty of its men went on strike to demand their discharge and were court-martialed. Soon after, several dozen soldiers of the 39th Battalion were also tried for disobeying orders while protesting the mistreatment of a comrade. As the possessor of a law degree, Jabotinsky was assigned by the army to defend both groups and managed to obtain an acquittal for a part of them and a relatively mild sentence for the rest. His first courtroom appearance, it encouraged him to think (British military courts rarely acquitted anyone) that he might make a good lawyer.

In the midst of all this, Ania and Eri arrived in Palestine. Jabotinsky had barely enough time to meet their ship in Port Said, accompany them to the apartment he had rented in Tel Aviv, and dash back to the trials in Egypt. At the summer's end, the family moved to Jerusalem, where it was joined by Jabotinsky's mother and sister from Odessa. All lived together in a large flat in a new Jewish neighborhood outside the old walled city, facing the Tower of David and the Jaffa Gate. By now, demobilized like many of the legionnaires, Jabotinsky was again a civilian. Eri, who was nine, remembered long walks with him in the city and its surrounding hills. On one of these, he wrote, his father decided to stalk a jackal with his army pistol, lost his way, and came home hours later to a furious and frantic Ania.

In April 1920, during an annual Muslim festival in honor of the prophet Moses, riots broke out in Jerusalem. Events had been building up to them. Postwar Jewish immigration, still very low in 1919, had begun to rise, stoking Arab fears for the future. Anti-Zionist emotions had mounted, whipped up by the fiery Arab nationalist Haj Amin el-Husseini, soon to become Grand Mufti of Jerusalem. Lacking confidence in British protection, the Yishuv had organized a force of several hundred young men, many of them former legionnaires, known as *ha-haganah*, "the defense." As an officer with combat experience and a reputation for resolve, Jabotinsky was put in command of it.

The British response to the disturbances confirmed Jewish fears. Loath to turn its guns on the rioters, the army was slow to order its troops into action; it was only Jabotinsky's well-deployed though poorly armed men, most carrying little more than sticks and clubs, who kept the Arabs out of the Jewish neighborhoods of the new city. When a detachment of them was dispatched to the old city's Jewish Quarter, however, it was turned back by soldiers guarding the gates, with the result that the quarter's population of largely ultra-Orthodox Jews suffered dead and wounded. To add insult to injury, the British then sought to demonstrate their even-handedness by arresting nineteen of the Jewish defenders for the illegal possession of three rifles, two pistols, and 250 rounds of ammunition. Jabotinsky, hearing of this, went to the police, declared himself responsible for the weaponry, and demanded to be arrested too.

The British obliged him. After a week's detention, the group went before a military court. The nineteen were convicted and sentenced to three years at hard labor. Jabotinsky was tried separately and served as his own counsel. Acquitted on two counts, he was convicted on three others and sentenced to fifteen years in prison—as many as were given, in absentia, to Haj Amin el-Husseini, who had meanwhile gone into hiding.

The convicted men were incarcerated in an old Turkish prison in Acre. They spent three months there while an outraged Yishuv protested, backed by Zionist supporters in England and America. Early in the summer of 1920, the military regime in Palestine was disbanded and a civilian administration took its place. To the delight of the Zionists, the Lloyd George government appointed Herbert Samuel as the country's first high commissioner. One of his initial acts was to pardon and free the Acre prisoners.

Jabotinsky, lionized by the Jewish press the world over, emerged from the episode a national hero. He had not suffered unduly. The authorities had treated him leniently, housing him in a comfortable private cell in which visitors came and went freely. Ania and Eri were among them, and when Jabotinsky wasn't working on a Hebrew translation of Dante's *Inferno* that he had begun, he gave his son daily lessons. One was in the art of writing poetry, in illustration of which he composed a simple anthem that became known as "The Song of the Prisoners of Acre."

> From Dan down to Beersheba,
> From the mountains to the flood,
> Not a square inch of our country
> Is not paid for with our blood.
>
> Hebrew blood on plain and highland,
> Everywhere beneath the sky;
> Yet none ever has been purer
> Than the blood spilled at Tel-Hai.
>
> Between Ayelet and Metula,
> A lone tombstone does embalm
> A guardian of our homeland,
> A brave man with but one arm.
>
> We're in prison, but our spirits
> Are up north now, at Tel-Hai.
> It is ours and always will be,
> Ours forever and for aye.

The one-armed "guardian of the homeland" was Yosef Trumpeldor, killed a month before the Jerusalem riots at Tel-Hai, a tiny Jewish agricultural commune in the far northeast of the Upper Galilee, beyond the swampland of the Hula Valley. Together with the farming village of Metula and two other communes, Ayelet ha-Shahar and Hamara, Tel-Hai was situated in a sparsely populated area claimed by France but controlled by warlike Bedouin. In the course of 1919, relations between the Bedouin and the Jewish colonists had deteriorated until the four settlements were threatened with attack. Trumpeldor was then in Palestine, preparing to leave for Russia on a recruiting campaign for Zionist pioneers. Asked to take charge of the settlements' defense, he dropped his travel plans and went north.

Trumpeldor was a man of the Left. He believed in the commune as a social and economic model and undertook his mission at the behest of Palestine's two socialist parties, Ben-Gurion's Po'alei Tsiyon and its less Marxist rival, Ha-Po'el ha-Tsa'ir, "The Young Worker." (Together, the two made up the Yishuv's best-organized political force. Following Po'alei Tsiyon's merger later that year with several smaller left-wing groups to form Achdut ha-Avodah, "Labor Unity," they won a third of the seats in elections for the Assembly of Representatives and formed its largest bloc.) When Trumpeldor reached the Upper Galilee, the situation was grave. Ordering the evacuation of Hamara as indefensible, he appealed urgently for reinforcements. Po'alei Tsiyon and Ha-Po'el ha-Tsa'ir promised to send them but didn't. Jabotinsky, who believed that not even reinforcements could save the settlements, proposed evacuating the other three as well.

Trumpeldor was not prepared to do this without an explicit order. At an emergency meeting of the Provisional Council, a socialist-led majority refused to issue it. The settlements, it insisted, had to hold out; any relinquishment of Jewish land would set a dangerous precedent. Jabotinsky's plea for a withdrawal was rejected and it was resolved to send an immediate relief force. By the time this arrived, however, the settlements were empty. Two had been abandoned. The third, Tel-Hai, was overrun. Seven of the pioneers and Trumpeldor had died in the fighting.

Although Jabotinsky fully took part in the subsequent glorification of Tel-Hai that turned it into a saga of Zionist courage, he never publicly acknowledged the emotional impact that Trumpeldor's death must have had. The two men, to be sure, were not intimate friends; they never had an opportunity to become that and might not have done so if they had, since each guarded his deeper self behind a shield of privacy. Yet apart from Herzl, whom he venerated, no one in Jewish or Zionist life was ever admired as much by Jabotinsky, or felt as instinctively close, as Trumpeldor. Jabotinsky was always careful to celebrate him, not as a martyr cut down by unjust bullets, but as a soldier fallen in the line of duty. "Among those who most sing his praises," he declared in 1928, alluding to anti-militarists on the Zionist Left, "are the most bitter opponents of anything having to do with the sword and the gun." But Trumpeldor was above all, he insisted, a man of the gun:

> To this he owes his renown with the Jewish masses. . . . The ordinary Jew knows that he himself can't give [his enemies] a good box on the ear, but only an armchair intellectual could think he's proud of this. Far from it: he knows it's a scourge of the exile like all its other scourges, and his heart leaps when he sees one of his own give as good as he gets.

The rancor Jabotinsky felt toward the Zionist Left for, as he saw it, abandoning Trumpeldor to his death was to remain with him. When he openly broke with the Left several years later by founding his own anti-leftist Zionist youth movement, the name chosen for it, Betar, was a Hebrew acronym for B'rit Trumpeldor, "the Trumpeldor League." (The name had a double resonance, since Betar was also the name of a village near Jerusalem where the Jewish fighters of the Bar-Kokhba revolt made their last, heroic stand against the Romans.) An act of homage, this was also one of appropriation, a statement of the political direction that Jabotinsky believed Trumpeldor would have moved in had he lived. Although in a letter to Max Nordau from Acre prison, Jabotinsky praised the Left for being the only element in the Yishuv to possess an "ardor for sacrifice," Trumpeldor's own understanding of sacrifice, he repeatedly emphasized, was far more radical. "We need to create a generation," he quoted Trumpeldor as having said to him about the *halutz*, the Zionist pioneer,

> that can be hammered into whatever is needed for the machine of the nation. Is it missing a wheel? I'm that wheel. A nail, a screwdriver, a crankshaft? That's me. . . . I have no face. I have no psychology. I have no sentiments. I don't even have a name. I am the idea of pure service, ready for everything, attached to nothing.

These words were paraphrased in a never-produced film script written by Jabotinsky in 1926, in which Trumpeldor appears in a cameo role. Asked what he, a new arrival in Palestine, wants to be there, he replies: "A worker—or a teacher—or a lawyer—or a soldier. . . . It's all the same to me. I'm nothing but pure will."

This script was the weakest of Jabotinsky's dramatic works, far inferior to "A Strange Land" and "All Right." Yet Trumpeldor's lines in it make one think of "All Right" and of Korolkov. Though exalting the will, Korolkov had none. Trumpeldor had and laid down his life with it.

Of course, the concept of "pure will" is an idealized one. This does not, however, make it less problematic. It demands the reduction of individuality to action. It constitutes a rebellion against individuality—its crystallization into a single point excluding all else. It reflects a weariness with it, and a desire to pare down its inner complexity into something interchangeable with the similarly pared-down. Such a desire can lead to many things, one being the fascism that Jabotinsky was eventually to be accused of. When he was, the accusations focused on Betar.

Between the events of 1920 and the founding of Betar stretched a period in which Jabotinsky again felt directionless. He, Ania, and Eri lived in Jerusalem with his mother and sister for barely a year. He had trouble making ends meet. Although he was working for the new Hebrew newspaper *Haaretz*, published by his Odessa friend Shlomo Saltzman, now a Jerusalemite too, the pay was not enough to support five people comfortably or even to furnish their apartment. Ania disliked life in Palestine. So did Jabotinsky—or at least, its Zionist immigrants. "The atmosphere is oppressive," he wrote to Bella Berligne. "Everyone is envious, suspicious, and resentful. Everyone was a [Zionist] celebrity in his home town and is disappointed not to be treated like one here." If offered a decent job elsewhere, he asserted, "I swear, I'd drop everything and clear out." The country inspired no deep sentiments. Jerusalem was "without warmth." The sand dunes of Tel Aviv put him in "a melancholy and irritable mood. They make me think of vanished hopes."

The job elsewhere soon materialized. Now based in London, the Zionist Executive had established a body called Keren Hayesod, the Jewish National Fund, whose purpose was to raise money for Zionist projects, and Jabotinsky was asked by Weizmann to head its public relations bureau. Although he lacked the ingratiating disposition of a fund raiser, it was a chance for him to earn a good living while remaining at the center of Zionist activity—and in any event, he thought of the position as temporary. His commitment to making a home in Palestine, as provincial as life in it might be, remained firm. He just needed to guarantee his economic future there. He was thinking of starting a Hebrew publishing company with Saltzman, or perhaps of opening his own law firm.

The Jabotinskys were in London in May 1921 when new anti-Zionist riots erupted in Palestine. Starting this time in Jaffa, they were more severe than those of the year before; at their end, 46 Jews were dead and 146 were wounded. Arab casualties at the hands of the British were also high, but the army had taken its time to intervene again. For Jabotinsky, this proved how right he had been to insist on a postwar role for the now fully disbanded legion. "As long as there were 5,000 Jewish soldiers in Palestine, there were no anti-Jewish disturbances there," he wrote Winston Churchill, then serving as Secretary of State for Colonies. "When their number dropped to 400 [in 1920], six Jews were killed in Jerusalem. Now that they have been demobilized entirely, over 30 Jews have been killed in Jaffa [alone]." Unless the legion was revived, he warned, the Yishuv would have to train and maintain a paramilitary force of its own.

A commission of inquiry headed by Sir Thomas Haycraft, chief justice of Palestine's supreme court, was appointed by Herbert Samuel. While holding the Arabs responsible for the violence, the Haycraft Commission sympathized with their grievances and recommended putting an end to unrestricted Jewish immigration, which henceforth should not exceed Palestine's "economic absorptive capacity." Seconded by Samuel, in whom the Yishuv had become deeply disappointed, this policy was officially adopted by the British government in a White Paper issued by Churchill in 1922. While reaffirming the Balfour Declaration, the new approach called for an elected Palestinian legislature, the composition of which would be heavily Arab, and for detaching the area east of the Jordan from the territory of the League of Nations mandate. (A year later, a separate Kingdom of Transjordan was officially established, with Hussein ibn Ali's son Abdullah as its monarch.)

Both the National Council in Palestine and the Zionist Executive in London, on which Jabotinsky had been chosen to serve by the twelfth Zionist Congress in Karlsbad in 1921, accepted the White Paper with only mild objections. Transjordan was mostly desert and had no Jews living in it, while Jewish immigration, then averaging about ten thousand arrivals a year, was well below any economic ceiling that might be set for it. Moreover, neither the Weizmann-dominated Executive nor the Labor Zionist–controlled Council wished to see a large influx of European Jews who were not interested in agricultural pioneering. Their first priority was not maximally increasing the Jewish population of Palestine, which could be done only by the rapid growth of cities like Tel Aviv. Rather, as Weizmann stated, it was "converting into peasant farmers an urbanized people" as part of the transformation of values in Jewish life that Zionism stood for. This demanded a selective processing of immigrants—a task that the Zionist Executive and British government now agreed to collaborate in, with the British setting annual quotas for immigrants and Zionist bodies apportioning the available visas to applicants who did not have assured jobs or independent financial means. A new type of urban Jew was envisioned, too, and when Achdut ha-Avodah and Ha-Po'el ha-Tsa'ir joined hands in 1920 to establish the Histadrut ha-Ovdim ha-Ivri'im b'Eretz-Yisra'el, "the Hebrew Workers Organization of the Land of Israel," with Ben-Gurion as its head, they did it to create not a conventional labor union, but a comprehensive framework of interlocking cooperatives in which city workers would live by the same socialist ideals that guided members of rural communes like Tel-Hai.

Jabotinsky had all along been opposed to linking Zionism either to Jewish agrarianization or to socialism, of which he had been led to take a dimmer view by the brutality of the Bolshevik Revolution—a revolution that Ben-Gurion and Achdut ha-Avodah identified with; eventually, he was to formulate this as his creed of "Zionist monism," the belief that the goal of a Jewish state must not be compromised or adulterated by admixture with other ideologies. He also differed on the question of immigration. Like Max Nordau, who had proposed a world Jewish campaign to bring half a million Jews to Palestine immediately after the war, he believed that reaching a Jewish majority there as quickly as possible was crucial, since without one Palestine's Jews, no matter how model a society they created, were doomed to be crushed by the superior forces of Arab nationalism. Yet he was not against the idea of "economic absorptive capacity"— Zionism, he agreed, had no right to encourage immigrants who could not find gainful employment—and pressured by Weizmann, who wished to present a united Zionist Executive front, he issued a qualified endorsement of the White Paper, too.

Jabotinsky's qualifications were spelled out in a memorandum sent to the Executive in December 1922. In it, he demanded the restoration to the Mandate of Transjordan—which alone, he maintained, had sufficient empty space for the speedy settlement of millions of European Jews—and the creation of a semi-independent Palestinian state administered by a calibrated system of Jewish-Arab power sharing heavily weighted in the Jews' favor. It was a plan that stood no chance of winning Arab acceptance, and Jabotinsky himself may not have intended it seriously. His true convictions had been set forth half a year previously in a letter from America to the German Zionist Richard Lichtheim. Commenting on the accusations of "militarism" made against him, he wrote:

> I would like to see military training become as common among Jews as lighting Sabbath candles once was. It's needed because the danger zone is rapidly spreading over the globe. Just a few months ago there were fears of a pogrom in Vienna. I've read of attacks on Jews in Berlin. And recently, when I was in Texas [for the Jewish National Fund], I witnessed a parade of the Ku Klux Klan. . . . My Jewish friends

looked out the window and spoke in the frightened tones of the Russian Jews in Odessa years ago as they watched the pogromists march by.

Frankly, though, this goal—local self-defense—is not my only or even my main one. Even our vegetarian friends [in the Zionist movement] must realize by now that we are faced with only two possibilities: either to forget about Palestine—or to fight a war for it. . . . Today we number a mere 12 percent of the population and aspire to reach 20 percent. That's why so few Arabs realize the threat to them. The real battle will begin when we reach 30 percent and set our sights on 51 percent. We have to prepare for that day. It would be foolish to ask at this point how military training for a Jew in Austria might some day prove useful in Palestine. Those responsible when the time comes will find ways and means [of answering this]—provided there are trained Jews in every country from which it is possible to sail for Palestine.

Even if Jabotinsky's memorandum was a sincere plan for getting to the "30-plus percent" that would trigger an Arab-Jewish war, he was certain that no Jewish state could be established without one. This was publicly stated by him in his 1923 essay "An Iron Wall," in which he wrote that "the Arabs have the same instinctive love and inbred zeal for Palestine that the Aztecs had for Mexico and the Sioux had for the prairies," and that "every native people fights foreign settlers as long as it can hope to get rid of them." It was a form of disdain for the Arabs of Palestine, he held, to think they would be less willing than others to shed their blood for their country. Palestine would have to be seized from them by force. He had already concluded as much in 1908, looking down from the top of Mount Tabor.

Armed Jewish self-defense in the Diaspora and a military role for Diaspora-trained Jews in Palestine's conquest were hardly new ideas for him, either. The second of these had inspired the legion. The first had occupied him since Kishinev. In 1921–22, it surfaced in what came to be known as the Slavinsky affair.

Maxim Slavinsky was a pro-Zionist Ukrainian journalist and supporter of the anti-Communist Ukrainian nationalist leader Semyon Petliura, whose troops had been responsible for most of the post–World War I killings of Jews on Ukrainian soil. Jabotinsky knew Slavinsky from Odessa and met him again in the summer of 1921 in Czechoslovakia, where he had gone for the Zionist Congress. By then the Ukrainian forces, defeated by the Red Army, had retreated to Poland, hoping to regroup and counterattack, and Jabotinsky suggested to Slavinsky that when they did, armed Jewish units accompany them to protect the Jewish population of the areas they retook. The suggestion was passed on to Petliura—who, seeing a chance to disassociate himself from his troops' rapacity, responded positively. Slavinsky and Jabotinsky then formulated and signed an understanding that was never put to the test, since the Ukrainian government-in-exile collapsed soon afterwards. When word of the document got out, however, there was furor in the Jewish world, particularly on the pro-Bolshevik Zionist Left. How, it was asked, could someone like Jabotinsky make common cause with the murderers of Jews? And who had authorized him to sign agreements on behalf of the Jewish people without consulting its representative organizations?

At the time the storm broke, Jabotinsky was on his way to the United States for the Jewish National Fund mission that took him as far as Texas. In a letter to the Zionist Executive from New York, he claimed that the understanding with Slavinsky was a private one in which he had spoken only for himself. As for its contents, he wrote, "It's entirely irrelevant whether the [Ukrainian] government is composed of anti-Semites or not. . . . I would just as unhesitatingly support such a [Jewish] force operating under Bolsheviks fighting against Petliura.

Alle beide stinken,[2] but Jews need to be protected, whether with God's help or the Devil's."

The furor over the Slavinsky affair died down slowly and only after straining still further Jabotinsky's tense relations with the Zionist Executive and the Yishuv's socialist parties. Once again, though, he was being consistent. His defense of his dealings with the Petliura government was no different from his support at the 1903 Zionist Congress for Herzl's negotiations with Von Plehve. In the world of real alternatives, he held, moral appearances were a not always affordable luxury.

He spent over half a year in America, much of it in the company of John Henry Patterson, with whom he spoke to Jewish audiences in over two dozen cities. He was not enamored with what he saw. America, he wrote to Vera Weizmann from Kansas City, was "a boring place. I haven't seen a thing here that was worth crossing the ocean for." The Americans, he conceded, were a friendly people, but the insularity and ignorance of the immigrant Jewish community depressed him. "The thing that frightens me most is that I'm becoming a snob," he confessed in a letter from Pittsburgh. "My whole cultivated being rebels against everything here and wants only to get away. And the worst of it is that I don't always (or is it ever?) manage to hide it."

Nor did he manage to raise much money. Although things went well in New York, elsewhere the tour was poorly promoted and audiences were small. After two months, he was exhausted and ready to return to London. Yet he soldiered on for four more, sometimes even enjoying himself. Toward the end of his stay, so he wrote Ania from New York, he was "up half the night dancing with two Christian young ladies at Rutenberg's." (The former Russian revolutionary Pinchas Ruten-

2. German: "Both stink." The allusion is to Heine's poem *Disputation,* in which a rabbi and a monk debate their respective religions before a king and his queen—who, when asked by her husband which of the two she thinks is right, answers that she doesn't know but that "alle beide stinken."

berg, a flamboyant figure in the Zionist movement, was a man Jabotinsky was fond of despite their political differences.) The young ladies, he related, "taught us to dance. (I have talent but no intelligence.)" This not only leaves us, but may well have left Ania, as accustomed as she was to such a style, wondering.

Although he was to visit the United States several more times and even to die there, it was a country he never warmed up to. He was too European, too much a man of formal manners, social reserve, and cosmopolitan tastes, to feel at home with America's brashness, and while he shared the belief in free enterprise of such patrician American Jews as Louis Brandeis, Louis Marshall, Julius Mack, and Felix Frankfurter, all Zionist sympathizers, he did not think well of their grasp of Palestinian realities or of their demand that they be given a say on Zionist policies in return for their economic support. (In the course of the 1920s, this became an increasingly divisive issue in the Zionist movement, in which a majority led by Weizmann sought to encourage the participation of wealthy Jewish philanthropists by including them on the board of the planned Jewish Agency, an organization that would supervise all aspects of the Yishuv's development.)

All in all, Jabotinsky was slow to appreciate America's importance for Zionism or to cultivate a political base there. Its Jews, he felt, had no visceral attachment to Zionism; it was a movement, as they saw it, not for them but for their less fortunate brethren in Europe, whom they were at most under an obligation to help. Thoroughly Eurocentric in his outlook, he would come to understand only late in the day how badly America was needed.

In January 1923, half a year after returning from America, Jabotinsky quit both the Zionist Executive and his Jewish National Fund position and canceled his membership in the Zionist Organization. (Along with voting rights for delegates to Zionist Congresses, this was acquired by the purchase of a Zionist "shekel," pegged to the rate of a single French franc.) Repeatedly outvoted in his demand that the Executive react more militantly to the pro-Arab tilt of the Samuel administration in Jerusalem, he had been asked by his colleagues either to cease criticizing them in public or to resign. He did not think any more than they did that England would necessarily renege on its promises. Although he had none of the deep love for England that he had for Italy, he admired the British people for what he took to be their ingrained sense of principle, which would cause them, he believed, to hold their leaders accountable for their country's commitments. To appeal to this sense, however, Zionism had to speak out vocally. Weizmann, though also unhappy with Samuel's policies, was unwilling to do so. More could be accomplished, he thought, by a discreet use of the channels of diplomacy.

Jabotinsky, relieved of his official responsibilities, returned to the world of writing. He set to work on a historical novel about the biblical figure of Samson first conceived of several years previously, rejoined the editorial board of *Razsviet*, now located in Berlin, and founded with Saltzman the Hebrew publishing house, called Hasefer, "The Book," that they had been thinking of. As Berlin was a major center of Hebrew publishing, it was decided to establish the company in the German capital with the intention of eventually transferring it to Palestine, and the Jabotinskys moved there in the summer of 1923. Hasefer's business plan was to concentrate on text and reference books, with a Hebrew atlas as its first major project. An ambitious undertaking involving extensive research and painstaking graphic design, this took two years and a large investment of Jabotinsky's time to complete.

One of Hasefer's first volumes, issued in 1923, was a slim collection of Jabotinsky's Hebrew poetry translations. In it were selections from Poe and D'Annunzio, the whole of Fitzgerald's *Rubaiyat*, and sections of Edmond Rostan's *Cyrano de Bergerac*. What made it noteworthy, however, was not its content but its use of the Sephardic diction that Jabotinsky had first heard in Basel in 1903, together with the Sephardic system of poetic scansion. Although the Hebrew spoken in twentieth-century Palestine had adopted the Sephardic pronunciation, nearly all prominent Hebrew poets of the day were still adhering to the Ashkenazi rules of composition. Jabotinsky's translations had an impact on the younger generation of Hebrew poets and helped speed the transition to a Sephardic prosody that took in the 1920s.

A second, more radical change that he promoted never attracted many followers. This was the Latinization of the Hebrew alphabet for purposes of phonetic clarity, an idea in keeping with similar spelling reforms undertaken at the time, such as the simplification of Russian and Yiddish orthography in the Soviet Union and the Latinization under Atatürk of Turkish's Arabic script. It was a symptom of Jabotinsky's ambivalent attitude toward Jewish tradition that he, the ardent lover and proponent of Hebrew, had an almost dyslexic difficulty with its written characters—"those damned square letters," he once called them—and wished to exchange them for an alien system that would have severed the language from its ancient roots. Happily, few of its users agreed with him.

He was unable to remain aloof from the political arena for long. In November 1923, he traveled to the Baltic states to drum up subscriptions for *Razsviet*. The trip was to prove a fateful one. While in Riga he delivered a lecture on the need for a more "activist" Zionism, after which he was approached by some students in the audience, members of a German-style Jewish dueling fraternity named the Hasmonean. He sat up with them till late at night, drinking beer and singing student and Zionist songs, and they proposed launching a movement to be headed by him that would put "activist" Zionism into practice.

The young Hasmoneans caught Jabotinsky's fancy. Even in their carousing, they seemed different from other young Zionists he knew—less argumentative, less concerned with ideology and its fine points, more prepared to act as a cohesive body. Mutual aid was a supreme value for them. At the railroad station as he prepared to leave Riga, he witnessed a fraternity member, recognizable by his cap, struggling with two heavy suitcases. At once a fellow Hasmonean left the girl he was talking to and hurried across the platform to help. A simple, even trivial incident, it struck Jabotinsky as something he would never have seen in his own student years.

He returned to Berlin full of enthusiasm. He had met, he wrote in a letter, a new Jewish youth,

> one thirsting for discipline and strong leadership—something that didn't exist in my own generation or in the generation of the war. It's had a decisive effect on me. I've made up my mind to return to [the sphere of] action rather than [limit myself to] writing—that is, to do whatever is necessary to found a movement that will encompass [Zionist] activists from all over the world.

A Yosef Trumpeldor Organization for Activist Zionist Youth was established in Riga, and Jabotinsky founded a League of Zionist Activists in Berlin. This was the beginning of Betar, which did not start out as a centralized or even single organization. At first it had a clear structure only in Latvia. Elsewhere, it evolved as a scattering of independent Zionist youth groups influenced by Jabotinsky's ideas but bearing different names in different places and often unaware of one another's existence. Strongest in the Baltic states and Poland, these were consolidated into a single movement in 1927.

Left-leaning Zionist youth movements like he-Halutz, "The Pioneer," and Ha-Shomer ha-Tsa'ir, "The Young Guard," were active in Eastern Europe before Betar and shared many of the characteristics of two distinct but related aspects of the youth culture of the 1920s. One of these took the form of loose associations like the German *Wandervögel* that emphasized the camaraderie of young people and their right and ability to regulate their own lives, with an emphasis on hiking, camping, and a love of nature. The other consisted of organizations linked to political parties and under their control, such as the Russian Komsomol, the French Jeunesse Communiste, and the German Freie Sozialistiche Jugend. The Zionist groups had something of both elements. While having political agendas, they operated independently of adult supervision. Their leaders were as young, or almost as young, as those they led.

Betar, too, though it was to become affiliated in time with the Revisionist Party, was an autonomous movement. Like its Zionist rivals, its goal, apart from sponsoring a wide range of social and cultural activities, was to prepare its members for life in Palestine by teaching them Hebrew, offering lectures and courses in Jewish history and Zionist thought, and providing vocational training. What distinguished it from them was its "Zionist monism" and paramilitary orientation. Its members practiced martial exercises, were taught calisthenics and techniques of self-defense, drilled at marching and parading, wore military-style uniforms on formal occasions, were organized by rank, company, and battalion, had their own special salute, and were expected to carry out the orders of their "commanders." No other Zionist youth movement had such features.

This was not the outcome of a preexistent design. It resulted from a number of factors, such as Betar's origins in the Jewish dueling fraternities of Latvia (Jabotinsky himself witnessed one of their ceremonial sword fights on a second visit to Riga in 1925), the influence of militarily-styled non-Jewish youth movements like the nationalistic Czech Sokol and the Italian fascist Avanguardisti, and Jabotinsky's own Jewish legion experience and developing thought. In Betar's early years, he followed it from afar without playing an active role; it stood in his mind for something momentous but still nebulous. In a Hebrew missive to the Latvian organization in 1928, he wrote:

> What was born in Riga five years ago was not a new organization, a new party, or a new program. . . . It was a new world, a new spiritual race, a new dimension to the inner soul of our nation.
>
> We mustn't exaggerate: it was born, but it hasn't yet crystallized or matured. Betar is but the seed from which the sapling may grow; a half-mute intimation of an idea still to come. Together we'll nurse this seed; together we'll search and make mistakes and lose our way until (perhaps?) we'll find what Herzl sought but couldn't find, what Ahad Ha'am sought but couldn't find, what Trumpeldor sought but couldn't find: the face of a Hebrew generation that not only yearns for national rejuvenation but is capable of it.
>
> I'm speaking dimly. If I had clear, simple words to express myself in, I'd be happier—but it's difficult to formulate with the precision of the multiplication table what you still can't see but can only feel. All of you are young and not every one of you may grasp what I'm trying to say. Never mind. Its time will come, and the world will understand that the years in the wilderness are over and the prince of Israel has re-ascended his throne.

He was liberally indulging in the very exaggeration he had cautioned against; certainly, there was nothing about Betar, then still a miniscule organization, remotely to justify so grandiose a vision. But it was an age of grandiose visions, whose prophecies of human and social transfiguration went back to those two radically opposed nineteenth-century seers Marx and Nietzsche. The *novy sovietsky chelovek* of the Russian Revolution, the *nuovo uomo* of Italian fascism, the *halutz* of Labor Zionism: everywhere Europe was dreaming of a new man, fashioned in the image of this or that ideology, who would lead humanity or the nation to the fulfillment of its hitherto unrealized potential. Jabotinsky was swept up in the current; perhaps he felt he had no choice if he was to compete with the Zionist Left. If Labor Zionism had its heroic ideal of the pioneer, so would he—and the Betarnik would be more noble, more iron-willed, more self-mastering and self-transcending than the Zionist prole of the socialist commune. The missive continued:

> Betar is also austereness; guard the purity and grandeur [*tif'eret*] of your lives like the Nazarites of old. Let this be your credo: grandeur in everything—in your speech and behavior, in your relations with friends and enemies, with Jews and Gentiles, with women and children and the elderly. Treat your work (whether behind a desk or outdoors, in a private or public capacity) as something sacred; be a weapon, strong and sharp, in times of danger; be exemplars of courtesy and honesty in your daily lives in society.

Eventually, Jabotinsky found the "clear, simple word" he was looking for. It was the Hebrew *hadar*, which replaced the *tif'eret* of his 1928 missive. *Hadar* has no exact equivalent in English. "Majesty," "dignity," "pride of bearing"—there is something in it of each. For Jabotinsky, it embraced a comprehensive code of behavior that would rehabilitate the new Jew from the maiming effects of Diaspora life. In his manifesto "The Idea of Betar," written in 1934 when the movement was nearly seventy thousand strong, he devoted a section to *hadar* that stated:

> Although it is important that everyone strive for *hadar*, it is particularly important for us Jews. The life of exile has greatly weakened in us the healthy instincts of a normal people, above all, in relation to the outer forms of our existence. We all know, and sometimes complain to ourselves, that the average Jew considers it superfluous to pay attention to his manners and appearance. . . . [Yet] Just as every-

one should attend to his personal hygiene, not because of what others will say if he doesn't but—even if he lives on a desert island—as a matter of self-respect, so every word he utters and every movement he makes should reflect a higher consciousness of his "lordliness." Every man must be a lord unto himself, the Jew especially. . . . We Jews are the most "aristocratic" people on earth. . . . Behind every one of us stand seventy generations of ancestors who could read and write, and who spoke about and inquired into God and history, peoples and kingdoms, ideas of justice and integrity, humanity and its future. Every Jew is in this sense a "prince." It is a bitter irony, the consequence of exile, that Jews are regarded everywhere, even by themselves, as lacking the social graces of a nursery school child.

Hadar meant acquiring such graces:

[It] consists of the thousands of "trifles" that make up our daily lives. Eat quietly and moderately; keep your elbows out of sight when you eat; don't slurp your soup so that you're heard a mile away. When you walk with your friends in the street, don't hog the sidewalk. If you climb the stairs of a house at night, don't be loud or wake the neighbors. Let women, old people, small children, everyone, go first; if someone is rude to you, don't you be, too. All this, and an infinite number of other "trifles," give a Betar member his *hadar*.

Such strictures might have been taken from a Victorian boys' etiquette manual. Their primness is difficult to square with the figure of the iconoclastic young Odessan journalist who mocked the regimentation of conventional education, let alone with the birth of a daring new "spiritual race." Laughable to Jabotinsky's detractors, they were embarrassing to some of his admirers as well.

They were not, however, so out of character. Jabotinsky had always been fastidious in dress and deportment. He had also always had a strong sense of boundaries; contemporaries remarked on his touchy reaction to being addressed familiarly by non-intimates, to being backslapped, to having his personal space infringed on. He was at once easily approachable and standoffish. Yet his formality, as described by those who knew him, had no superior airs. Meticulously egalitarian, it projected a respect-and-be-respected attitude toward all, from his political colleagues to the secretaries in his office. One of his idiosyncrasies was his insistence on addressing children, not by the familiar personal pronoun (Russian *ty*, German *du*, French *tu*) with which they were commonly spoken to, but by the polite form (*vy*, *Sie*, *vous*) used with adults. As a child himself, he explained, he had felt belittled by being treated familiarly and had sworn to relate to children as his equals when he grew up.

Jabotinsky's emphasis on ordinary manners as intrinsic to *hadar* can be traced at least as far back as his journey through Galicia as an eighteen-year-old. The unruly appearance and behavior of the Jews he saw there—such had been his impression of them—came as a shock to him. The polished product of an Odessan *lycée*, he had reacted like a typical Western European Jew to his first encounter with the *Ostjuden* of the shtetl. *Hadar* was meant as a corrective to this. Learning not to slurp one's soup was indeed trivial. Unlearning a way of life that disdained all concern for the aesthetics of the everyday—that held the very category of the aesthetic to be a Gentile overvaluation, unbefitting a Jew, of mere appearances—was for Jabotinsky as indispensable a part of the Zionist revolution as returning to the soil and to a healthy physical existence were for Labor Zionism.

Nor was this just, to his mind, a task for the Jews of Eastern Europe. Zionist immigration to Palestine had been largely Eastern European, and despite its rebellion against the shtetl, the Yishuv had retained many of the shtetl's characteristics: its abruptness of manners, its indifference to ideals of beauty and good taste, its scorn for all that failed to serve immediate utilitarian ends. Reinforced by the socialist Left's rejection of all formalistic and sentimental "bourgeois values," this had led, particularly among the *halutzim*, to a functional bareness far from the refined Mediterranean-type society that Jabotinsky envisioned for Palestine. The *halutz*'s ragged clothes, his drab tents and shacks, his workers' kitchens with their monotonous fare, his ideological bickering with his comrades, the shouting and interruptions at his meetings and assemblies—such things might be explainable by economic exigency or political ardor, but Jabotinsky found it absurd to make a virtue of them.

All this was expressed in an obliquely fictional form in a long story entitled "The Truth About the Isle of Tristan de Runha," first published by him in Russian in 1930. The story purports to be a two-part report by a British journalist on his visit to an experimental colony on a remote island in the South Atlantic populated by "fifteen different nationalities" of convicted criminals and their descendants, who have been left alone to their own devices with no contact with the outside world apart from periodic transports of new convicts to their shores. Remarkably, the journalist relates, the inhabitants of the island have not only managed to survive in their desolate surroundings, they have succeeded in creating a functioning society, with its own lingua franca, in which life and property are respected. Still, he goes on,

> my impressions of Tristan de Runha are by no means undilutedly pleasant. I wish I could describe a Utopia; but it is no Utopia. It is an interesting microcosm, but whether one would like to live in it is another question. It is a land of brusque and harsh ways, of a stern simplicity of outlook which often jars on civilized nerves as a bad kind of rudeness. Yet I think it is a land of great promise.

Tristan de Runha (the model for which was Fernando de Noronha, a small Atlantic archipelago that was the site of a nineteenth-century Portuguese penal colony) indeed bears a resemblance to the Palestinian Yishuv as Jabotinsky perceived it. *Hadar* was conceived as a standard for a new Jewish society that would be more elevated, more cultivated, more ceremonial, and more gracious than the one created by Labor Zionism.

But if the section on *hadar* in "The Idea of Betar" might have made some readers squirm, the section on "Discipline" would have made others cringe. It began with a Trumpeldorian image:

> Our goal (which is still far from having been reached) is to turn Betar into a worldwide organism that will be able, at a single command from its center, to execute instantly, with many tens of thousands of hands, the exact same thing in every town and country. Our opponents claim that this is "beneath the dignity of free men" and means "becoming a machine." I propose that we answer proudly, without being the least ashamed of it: Yes, a machine!

What, "The Idea of Betar" asked, was a successful choir or orchestra if not a finely tuned "machine" for the making of music that unthinkingly obeyed every movement of its conductor's baton? Such an "orchestra" needed to be forged of the Jewish people, and Betar was the first step toward forging it. There was no more compulsion in this than there was in being a symphony violinist.

> Discipline involves the masses yielding to a higher authority, and this authority to an even higher one, and so on. No one's will is enslaved in the process. The commander is the vehicle of your own will, your representative, whom you willingly delegate to conduct your "orchestra"—if you didn't, you would not have joined or remained in Betar. . . . We all share a single will, we are all constructing the same building, and so we all defer to the same architect whose blueprint has won our approval. As long as he is faithful to it, we lay the bricks and wield our hammers at his bidding.

"The Idea of Betar" hastened to qualify this seemingly fascistic philosophy in its next paragraph, which proposed as a political model the American system, with a president "ruling by himself" yet elected by the people. And in fact, while Jabotinsky's attitude toward fascist Italy, whose diplomatic support for Zionism he was not against courting, was ambivalent, his condemnation of fascism as a political system was not. Electoral democracy, he had written in 1926, on one of the many occasions when he declared himself its sworn partisan, was the way of "every civilized community" except one:

> There is today a country where "programs" [approved by an electorate] have been replaced by the word of one man. Whatever he says is the program. Popular vote is scorned. That country is Italy; the system is called Fascism; to give their prophet a title, they had to coin a new term — "*Duce*" — which is a translation of that most absurd of all English words, "leader."
> Buffaloes follow a leader. Civilized men have no "leaders." Civilized men and women elect stewards, executives, simple trustees, who are entitled to act as long as their views coincide with those of the majority and who depart when this is no longer the case.

This was genuine. Yet after he was unanimously elected to preside over Betar in perpetuity at the organization's first international conference in 1929, the Hebrew title given Jabotinsky of *rosh Betar*, "chief of Betar," by which he was always referred to in the movement, had a *Duce*-like flavor. Little by little, against his not always strongly voiced protests, he was to be turned into the supreme commander that "The Idea of Betar" described, even if he did not want to be it.

The tensions in Jabotinsky's thought between freedom and duty, personal autonomy and authority, and self-fulfillment

and social responsibility, already present when his philosophy of "individualism" clashed with his attraction to Zionism
in Odessa, were most thoroughly explored by him in his remarkable novel *Samson the Nazarite*, which he finished writing in Russian in 1926. (Serialized in *Razsviet*, it was published
the following year in Berlin.) Although its historical setting is
far too richly embroidered, and its characters too realistically
embedded there, for it to be read as mere disguised autobiography, the novel was clearly intended, not only as an imaginative excursion into the world of ancient Palestine from which
the Israelite nation emerged, but as a commentary on the inner
conflicts that its author had been living with for years.

Jabotinsky's Samson is of mixed race. His mother is an Israelite from the tribe of Dan; his father, an unknown, physically
imposing Philistine, her chance sexual encounter with whom is
turned by the biblical narrative—or perhaps by the lie she tells
her husband—into the annunciation of an angel that the son
she bears must be raised as a consecrated Nazarite forbidden
to drink wine or cut his hair. Like the reader, Samson does not
learn the truth about his paternity until the novel's end, when
it comes as both a shock and a revelatory insight. Psychologically, however, he is half-Israelite and half-Philistine from the
start and torn between these two parts of himself.

As opposed to his fellow Danites, simple farmers from the
foothills of Judea who fear and shun the more powerful Philistines of the coastal lowlands and are their vassals, Samson is already drawn to Philistine society as a boy. Its worldly sophistication and refined grace appeal to him, and as an adolescent he
often leaves his Israelite village to seek the company of young
Philistines his age. Accepted and admired by them for his fear-
lessness, exuberance, and great physical strength, he can speak
their language, mimic their ways, share their pranks and jokes,
and play their games as well as any of them. Although his hair

remains long beneath the Philistine hat that he wears when among them, he drinks their wine with abandon.

Jokes and laughter are important to the Philistines. Theirs is a playful culture. They take nothing too seriously, not even their gods and religion—nothing, that is, except the military power that enables them to rule their neighbors and the social organization that makes such power possible. Among the peoples of Canaan, they alone possess the art of making iron weapons, which they guard zealously. It is their capacity for order and discipline, so seemingly at odds with their frivolity, that attracts and puzzles Samson the most, since there is nothing in the somber, quarrelsome, individualistic Israelite society he was born into, with its jealous God and contentious prophets, that enables him to account for it. "Its precise, highly articulated hierarchy that extended into the tiniest details," the narrative tells us,

> its distribution of tasks and responsibilities, with strict rules for every rank of leadership—all this was beyond his grasp and seemed like a great confusion. And yet he could see clearly that there was nothing confused about it, but on the contrary, an all-encompassing harmony.

Play and order combine in games and art, activities the Israelites have no conception of. Their pedagogical importance is realized by Samson while witnessing a grand religious pageant in the Philistines' capital city of Gaza:

> When the music struck up, all froze—both the dancers in the stone-paved plaza and the crowd surrounding them. . . . Not a crease stirred in the dancers' costumes; the women's bared breasts as though ceased to breathe. The clean-shaven priest paled, his gaze boring into those facing him, whose eyes probed his in return; his pallor increased; it was as if the mighty force of the thousands of performers was so compressed in his chest that he would choke to death on it. Sam-

son, too, felt flooded by it; another moment and he would
suffocate. Just then the priest lifted his baton with a slight,
almost imperceptible gesture and all the white-clad figures
in the plaza dropped to their left knees and raised their right
arms skyward in a single quick movement, an abrupt, per-
fectly synchronized rustle of accord . . .

The entire dance was composed of such poses, all struck
at the wave of the baton, some suddenly, some slowly. Although it didn't last long, Samson left the celebration deep in
thought. . . . He was stunned by the spectacle of thousands of
limbs moving in unison to a single will. The magic of it ob-
sessed him. Although he could not have put it into words, he
vaguely sensed that he had just had revealed to him the secret
of all state-building peoples.

How the separate members of a society can function in
perfect unison is a secret Samson yearns to understand, because
he leads a double existence: the same young man who is the life
of the party at the Philistines' revels and a bedder of their sexually free women, so unlike those of the puritanical Israelites, is
also an Israelite patriot with a band of young followers, known
as "Samson's foxes," that daringly raids the Philistines' outposts
and ambushes their patrols. As much as he chafes under the
provincial backwardness of his own people, he is flesh of its
flesh and cannot shake off its claim on him. No one else has the
ability to organize and lead it in its struggle for independence,
which is a mission he is unable to refuse. Nor is it unworthy
of being led, for it has one thing the Philistines lack: a sense
of spiritual destiny and purpose. When he is betrayed by his
Philistine lover who clips his strength-giving hair, and is given
the choice by his captors of either defecting to them or being
dealt with harshly, Samson answers, choosing the grimmer fate:

> I love you and I don't love Dan. . . . Dan has no overseer; he
> plows his fields every which way—hastily, with no order and
> no plan. . . . The farmer hates the shepherd, Benjamin hates

Judah, the prophets hate everyone. But beyond all this, all share one thing in common: a hungry heart, a craving for all that can and cannot be seen. In each single one of them smolders the revolt against ordinary existence. From every heart comes the cry: There must be more! There must be more!

In the long run, Samson is convinced, their perpetual dissatisfaction with the status quo will enable the Israelites to outlast the Philistines and overcome them. By itself, however, this is not enough. At the novel's end, blinded and kept by the Philistines as their plaything, he is asked by one of his "foxes," a follower named Hermesh, if he has a last message for the group. "Tell it two things from me," he replies.

> The first is: iron. Get hold of iron. Give whatever you have for it: money, wheat, olive oil, wine, your flocks, your wives and daughters. . . . The second thing is: a king. Tell Dan, tell Benjamin, tell Judah and Ephraim: a king! One person at a signal from whom thousands will raise their arms all at once. That's how the Philistines do it and that's why they're the lords of Canaan.

"But don't you have anything to say to those who loved you?" Hermesh asks, craving to part on a more personal note. Turning his head to hide the tears in his blind eyes, Samson answers: "Nothing."

> Hermesh walked away slowly. Suddenly, Samson called to him. He turned around. Carefully wiping the wet back of his hand, Samson said: "I've changed my mind. Tell them from me that there are three things, not two. Get hold of iron, make yourselves a king—and learn to laugh."

Soon after this, his shorn hair grown back, he brings down the great temple of Gaza on his and the Philistines' heads.

Not *mere* autobiography—but autobiography nonetheless, for the character of Samson is clearly a projection of Jabotinsky himself, just as the biblical Israelites are his fellow Jews; the Philistines, the Odessans, Italians, and Englishmen he had lived among; and the novel's events, the course his life had taken. To be the baton or scepter that will fashion a people into a disciplined force is not Samson's deepest ambition; it is unsuited to his anarchic nature; but it is a role that has to be played by someone and he alone has what is needed to play it. His real downfall is not his capture and blinding. It is the sense of responsibility that makes him choose to become a leader when he is too free a spirit to succeed as one. Success will have to wait for the king who comes after him.

Iron, a king—and laughter. Without laughter, there is no play. In 1936, a decade after the publication of the novel, Jabotinsky wrote an essay called "The Revolt of the Elderly." A paean to the liberalism of the nineteenth century and an attack on the totalitarian politics of the twentieth, it was the closest he ever came to a reasoned analysis of the contradictions that lay at the heart of *Samson*—and of his own political thought. All human activity, he proposed in the essay (written two years before the Dutch historian Johann Huizinga published his influential *Homo Ludens*, a more sustained intellectual treatment of the same subject), can be resolved into the two categories of necessity and play, of which the latter is the driving force in human progress. "The esteem for political freedom that characterized the nineteenth century," Jabotinsky stated,

> has its roots in a fathomlessly deep, a priori belief in "play." All honor to play, make room for it! . . . Let every human desire find its niche: from such chaos will arise a new world order. "Discipline" was something the nineteenth century reserved for special occasions, for emergencies, when publics and peoples were faced with singular trials that demanded to be overcome in short order. It was, in other words, a bitter medicine, good for its time and no other.

· The Jewish people was in a state of emergency. The politics of "Yes, a machine!" were the medicine. And there was play—the play of the great pageant of Gaza—even in that.

Early in 1924, the Jabotinskys moved again. The hyperinflation raging in Weimar Germany had made life there insupportable, and together with *Razsviet* and Hasefer they left Berlin for Paris, where they rented a dark flat on rue de la Tombe-Issoire, a street in the 14th arrondissement near Boulevard Montparnasse. Jabotinsky's office was in the living room, which Eri remembered as being "full of papers, maps [for Hasefer's atlas], dictionaries, and other books strewn over the chairs, the cabinet, and the floor." Before long, the family moved to a larger, sunnier place around the corner in a new, seven-floor apartment building on rue Marié-Davy.

Paris was to be Jabotinsky's home for most of the next twelve years. It was there, in April 1925, in the Latin Quarter's Café de Panthéon, that he and a group of supporters centered around the editorial board of *Razsviet* founded a Union of Zionist Revisionists, with offices on rue Blanche, next door to the Théâtre de Paris. (These were later transferred to rue Pontoise, between Boulevard Saint-Germain and the Seine.) Its platform included the goal of a "Jewish commonwealth" in Palestine with a Jewish majority enjoying "self-rule"; Jewish control over all immigration to Mandate territory; the restoration to the latter of Transjordan; the expropriation, with full compensation, of all untilled Palestinian land for the purposes of Zionist colonization; a revived Jewish legion as part of the Mandate government's military presence; and a Jewish Agency directorship entirely chosen by the Zionist Organization. The term "Revisionist," in retrospect an awkward one, was chosen for its double meaning of "revising" and "re-visioning," that is, correcting the course that post–World War I Zionism had taken and returning to Herzl's original conception of a Jewish state rapidly achieved by the international charter that had now been provided by the Balfour Declaration and the League of Nations mandate.

Thus was born the Revisionist movement, which Jabotinsky headed until his death. At first, the question of whether it would function as a political party within the framework of the world Zionist Organization was left undecided. He himself was initially opposed to this; he had resigned his membership in the organization two years earlier and did not wish to recant or tie his hands by resubmitting to its authority. In the end, however, he was overruled by the new movement's executive committee, which voted to participate in elections for the fourteenth Zionist Congress that was to be held in Vienna in the summer of 1925. With little time to prepare for them, the Revisionists ran their own slate and garnered barely one percent of the vote, electing only four of the 311 delegates—a majority of which belonged to an informal grouping of pro-Weizmann factions known as the "General Zionists." Jabotinsky spoke twice at the congress, at which he presented the Revisionist program. An ominous portent of the future were the crowds of Nazi sympathizers who taunted and threatened the delegates on their way from their hotel to the conference hall.

Soon after the congress, Jabotinsky set out on a tour of Germany, Lithuania, Latvia, Rumania, and Czechoslovakia to spread the Revisionist message. Well attended, his lectures helped shore up his finances, which were shaky as usual; Hasefer had failed to turn a profit and a part of his income was going to help support *Razsviet*. Yet a similar circuit of the United States, undertaken shortly afterwards and sponsored by the noted Jewish impresario Sol Hurok, was a flop. Boycotted by the pro-Weizmann American Zionist Organization, Jabotinsky spoke to half-empty houses, and Hurok, faced with heavy losses, cut back on the number of his appearances and their fees.

Unable to send Ania the money he had hoped to, Jabotinsky cast about for other alternatives. One involved the American Jewish fraternal lodge Bnai Zion, which broached the possibility of his taking an executive position with a new insurance company it planned to start in Palestine. Another was the New York Yiddish press, for which he now began to write. In one of his first articles there, published in the daily *Morgen Zhurnal*, he mused on America's childlike qualities—its love of fantasy, its dreams of adventure, its sense of unlimited possibilities—and observed that these were what had given it and its literature their great influence on European youth.

He returned to France in the summer of 1926 and departed again for Palestine in late September, both to visit his mother and sister, now living in Tel Aviv, and to touch base with a country he had not been in for four years. Despite the large crowds he drew, he came away discouraged. Though the population of the Yishuv had grown to over 125,000 and Tel Aviv was now a bustling town of 35,000 inhabitants, the rate of growth fell short of Zionist hopes. Unemployment was severe and Jewish immigration, which had hit an all-time high of 34,000 new arrivals in 1925, most urban-oriented, lower-middle-class Jews from Poland, had decreased sharply. (Dropping to 14,000 in 1926, it would plunge again to 3,000 in 1927.) Jabotinsky's family was affected by the downturn, too. His sister Tania, a teacher by profession, was out of work, and she and his ailing mother were supported by her son, a trained engineer forced to take a menial job.

For Weizmann and the Labor Zionists, the crisis was a vindication of their belief that a middle-class population was economically unsuited for Palestinian life. For Jabotinsky, it proved the opposite. In an article called *Basta!* (Italian for "Enough!"), he argued that the Yishuv was paying the economic price of a collusion between the Labor Zionist–controlled Histadrut and the Weizmann-controlled Zionist Executive. In return for politically backing Weizmann's soft line toward the British and his Jewish Agency expansion plan, the Histadrut had channeled to it large sums of money, mostly raised from American Jews, that gave it a choke hold on the Yishuv's economy to the detriment of all not organized in its ranks—businessmen, small factory owners, shopkeepers, petty tradesmen, and independent craftsmen and professionals. The private urban sector was discriminated against in favor of collective agriculture; employers, threatened by constant strikes, were unable to enforce discipline or make demands on their workers; the self-employed could not compete with Zionist-subsidized Histadrut enterprises or obtain the social benefits granted Histadrut members; and in the absence of competition, productivity was low and workmanship was shoddy. In the early years of the Mandate, Jabotinsky conceded, when private capital had been unwilling to invest in Palestine, a socialized economy might have been necessary. Now, however, capital was available because Jews wished to transfer it out of Europe but was not flowing into Palestine because the Histadrut frightened it off. The Histadrut was the reason for the Yishuv's economic doldrums.

Though he had increasingly distanced himself from the socialist beliefs of his youth, Jabotinsky was never an advocate of laissez-faire capitalism. He accepted, as did most economic liberals of the age, the need for laws to protect workers and regulate business, and he went beyond liberalism in calling for compulsory arbitration in all labor disputes. Influenced by the views of the Viennese social and economic reformer Josef Popper-Linkaeus, he advocated an extensive welfare state, arguing that governments should take responsibility for providing, free of cost, not only education and medical care, but the basic housing, food, and clothing requirements of every citizen. Yet the traditional proletariat, he was convinced, far from being destined to seize power in advanced capitalist countries, stood to dwindle in size and importance as industrial automation grew. The problem of poverty would be solved by technology, not by the expropriation of wealth—one more way in which, of all Zionist thinkers, he was closest to Herzl, whose faith in the social benefits of technological progress was great.

Meanwhile, however, the Revisionist Party's political prospects depended on convincing shekel payers that it had immediate solutions for Jews wishing to settle in Palestine. With elections for the fifteenth Zionist Congress scheduled for the summer of 1927, Jabotinsky threw himself into the fray. Twice he went on the campaign trail, concentrating on Poland with its Jewish community of three million, Europe's largest. The enthusiastic turnouts made him hopeful that, with the help of potential allies like the Mizrachi Party, he might wrest control of the congress from the pro-Weizmannites. His one complaint was the hero worship he was met with. "I'm beginning to be made a myth of," he wrote Ania from Łodz.

> The main roles I'm cast in, of course, are of the Legionnaire and Acre prisoner, but I'm also credited with all kinds of things that I've never remotely done. . . . Not even my paunch and my bald spot can save me. In Warsaw, where the stairs leading up to the platform were very steep, I had to be helped from tripping by a young Scout who dragged me up them like a sack—yet the newspapers reported that I strode onto the stage with a brisk military gait, etc. The worst of it is that the legend is taking on *Duce*-like proportions . . . I fear more and more that this—not our ideas or our program—is of all things what will bring us (God help us!) "to power."

When the electoral results were in, however, the Revisionists had done badly, winning only 8,400 of approximately a quarter million votes and increasing their representation to a mere 10 delegates. Jabotinsky's fears had turned out to be justified, if not quite as he had conceived of them: his personal appeal notwithstanding, he did not yet command a fully functional political organization or strong campaigners apart from himself. A General Zionist–Labor Zionist coalition controlled the congress and chose an Executive composed entirely of Weizmann's backers.

Jabotinsky's response was to decide to move back to Palestine. Despite his and Ania's reservations about life there, it was the place, he now judged, where he could be most effective. "You know it's of no great concern to me where a man lives," he wrote to a friend, "but the atmosphere of discontent in Palestine is such that even one person can be the drop that makes the cup overflow." His initial plan of opening a law office fell through when he was unable to obtain documentation from Soviet Russia of his University of Yaroslavl degree. Then, however, he was contacted by Bnai Zion: its Palestinian insurance company, called Judea, was finally about to be launched and he was being asked to serve as vice-president at a salary of five hundred dollars a month. A handsome sum, it was accepted by him, and he sailed from Marseilles to Jaffa in the autumn of 1928. Ania, who had declared her grudging willingness to follow him if he could promise her comfortable circumstances, stayed in Paris for the time being with Eri.

Judea had its offices in Jerusalem, and Jabotinsky rented a room there near Prophets Street, not far from where he had lived in 1919–21. Although Judea got off to a good start, the local market for insurance, it quickly became apparent, was limited; soon he was thinking of expanding to other countries, with Egypt as a first possibility. Meanwhile, his workload was light, and when he was offered a second job, the editorship of the Jerusalem *Do'ar ha-Yom* or "Daily Mail," a right-wing, tabloid-like newspaper with a small circulation that its publisher hoped he would be able to enlarge, he decided to take it. Ania, now assured that her conditions could be met, prepared to join him.

Jabotinsky set to work at *Do'ar ha-Yom* diligently, hiring

new editors and writers and turning the paper into an openly pro-Revisionist organ. Its "Levantine period," he confidently stated, was over; he was going to make it a European-class publication. But although the outside talents he recruited, among them contributors like Arthur Koestler, the Hebrew poet Uri Tsvi Greenberg, and the Hebrew prose fiction writer Avigdor Hameiri, lived up to his expectations, the in-house staff did not. Its lack of professionalism—technical blunders, sloppy language, typographical errors—exasperated him despite the paper's expanding circulation. Levantinism, it seemed, was not so easily eradicated from the Levant. To Koestler, he confided that he felt more in exile in Jerusalem than in Paris.

Still, *Do'ar ha-Yom* was a fighting newspaper and Jabotinsky was at his best in a fight. One of the paper's causes inherited by him was that of the Wailing (or "Western," as it was called in Hebrew) Wall, the last standing remnant of the Second Temple compound. Rising above a narrow lane at the base of Jerusalem's Temple Mount, the Muslim *haram esh-sharif* on which stood the Dome of the Rock and the el-Aksa Mosque, the wall had been an uncontested site of Jewish prayer for centuries. Now, however, driven by nationalist emotions, the Muslim religious authorities claimed it for Islam. A battle for jurisdiction broke out, and on the fast of Yom Kippur, two weeks before Jabotinsky's arrival in Palestine, Muslim protests against the introduction of benches for the Jewish worshipers and a partition to separate the sexes had set off a scuffle in which the offending innovations were removed by the British police. "Scandal at the Western Wall," *Do'ar ha-Yom*'s banner headline read. "Police Desecrate Yom Kippur in Jerusalem."

With Jabotinsky as its new editor, the paper continued to insist loudly on the exclusive Jewish right to the wall. Led by the Grand Mufti, Muslim spokesmen warned darkly of a Jewish plot to usurp the Temple Mount. Jews were harassed at prayer by the playing of loud music and Muslims were encouraged to treat the cramped space in front of the wall as a pedestrian thoroughfare, even driving their donkeys through it. The British did nothing. Jabotinsky ran editorials condemning their inaction and urging a strong Jewish response. The liberal *Haaretz*, closely identified with Weizmann and the General Zionists, accused him of deliberately inflaming religious emotions. *Do'ar ha-Yom* hit back. "Even when our official leadership has ceased to exist, there are honest people who feel the pain of the nation," an editorial proclaimed on August 6, 1929. "One thing is necessary: that we rise and take action!"

On August 15, the fast day of Tisha b'Av, the annual commemoration of the Temple's destruction, several hundred Jewish youngsters, many of them Betar members, staged a demonstration at the wall. Shouting "Down with the anti-Semitic government," they raised the blue-and-white Zionist flag and sang Hatikvah, the Zionist anthem. The next day angry Muslims assaulted Jews at the wall and burned their prayer books. On August 23, Muslim crowds burst from the Temple Mount after Friday prayers and attacked Jewish neighborhoods. The riots spread from Jerusalem to the rest of the country. In Hebron, 67 Jews were killed and the city's ancient Jewish community was destroyed. Eighteen Jews were killed in the old quarter of Safed. The violence continued for a week. Jewish casualties when it was quelled were 133 dead and 339 wounded.

The Arabs held *Do'ar ha-Yom* and the Revisionists responsible for having triggered the events with their Tisha b'Av "provocation." Voices on the Zionist Left concurred: Jabotinsky, they charged, had been deliberately fomenting violence since his return to Palestine. "The vitriol of propaganda," wrote *Haaretz*, "dripped from [*Do'ar ha-Yom's*] columns day after day until it poisoned the atmosphere." The British appointed a commission of inquiry, as they had done in 1921.

Jabotinsky was in Europe when the riots broke out, having gone for the sixteenth Zionist Congress that convened in

Zurich in late July. The Revisionists had doubled their strength to 21 out of 315 delegates, but the Zionist Left had also gained and now had 81 seats, compared with the General Zionists' 137 and Mizrachi's 50. Their sights now set on dominating the Zionist Organization and the Zionist Executive, the Labor Zionists viewed Revisionism, despite its still small numbers, as their most dangerous rival; not only was its ideological opposition to them the fiercest, but it alone inspired the passion in its followers that they did in theirs. At a pre-congress session of Palestinian delegates in Tel Aviv, the two factions battled each other physically, and Jabotinsky had to be escorted out of harm's way by a Betar bodyguard. He blamed the Left for it. "They hate us organically and necessarily," he wrote to his fellow Revisionist Yeshayahu Klinov. "As far as they're concerned, it's either them or us." In the *Morgen Zhurnal*, he recalled thinking how relieved he felt, aboard the ship taking him to Europe, to be leaving Palestine and the hostility directed against him there. "Is this the feeling a man departing his homeland should have?" he asked rhetorically.

The major resolution passed at the sixteenth congress, with only the Revisionists and a scattering of others opposed, adopted Weizmann's Jewish Agency expansion plan. Jabotinsky gave a short speech explaining his vote. As the undemocratically chosen representatives of Jewish wealth, he asserted, the non-Zionists in the Agency directorship would be involved in making crucial decisions about the Jewish future that no Zionist organization had the right to entrust them with. When he was finished speaking, he led a Revisionist walkout.

He spent two weeks vacationing with Ania and Eri in the Alps, after which they moved to temporary rooms in Paris. The rue Marié-Davy apartment, which Ania had just finished packing up, had been let to others; now, however, the bloody events in Palestine had made her change her mind about living there. Jabotinsky informed Judea and *Do'ar ha-Yom* that he was taking a leave of absence, and he and Ania moved back to rue Marié-Davy soon afterwards. His second attempt to settle in Palestine, shorter-lived than the first, was for all purposes over. Although he was thinking of a visit there in the coming months, he planned it to be a brief one.

He had no way of knowing it would be his last. He arrived in the first week of December 1929 with the intention of testifying in Jerusalem before the commission of inquiry, which was headed by the British jurist Sir Walter Shaw. Given the accusation that he and *Do'ar ha-Yom* had provoked the riots, there was every reason for his being heard. Yet the Zionist Executive, tasked with presenting the Jewish case, intervened to block his testimony and he left Palestine in late December without giving it. Two days before his departure, he spoke at an outdoor rally in Tel Aviv.

His exact remarks there were a matter of debate. According to records in British archives, possibly based on police reports, he declared that a "social rapprochement" between Jews and Arabs was impossible, since the two peoples were too different and had opposed interests. He himself stated afterwards in a letter to the Austrian newspaper *Reichspost:*

> I never said [as *Reichspost* reported] that no agreement with the Arabs is possible. . . . Nor did I say [as the paper also claimed], "All of Palestine must be given to the Jews. The Arabs have enough deserts in which to pasture their camels." [I believe that] Forcing the Arabs out of Palestine is totally out of the question. Palestine will always be the country of more than one people—and as long as it has a Jewish majority, this is perfectly acceptable to me.

Ya'akov Veinshal, on the other hand, who was present on the occasion, remembered Jabotinsky declaring: "Everyone talks about peace in this country. There is no peace and there never will be."

In the end, he was allowed to testify before the Shaw Commission in London, in January 1930. Shortly afterwards he sailed to South Africa with Ania on yet another speaking tour. He was there in March when the commission published its report. Like the Haycraft Commission's findings in 1921, it apportioned blame to both sides. The Arabs, it asserted, had started the violence; however, the Jews—particularly "one Hebrew daily paper"—were also to blame for it; furthermore, its underlying cause was the thwarting of the Arabs' "political and national aspirations" and their fear of losing their land and livelihoods to Jewish colonizers. Several days later, while in Johannesburg, Jabotinsky was notified that the high commissioner of Palestine, Sir John Chancellor, had issued an edict banning his return there.

The formal reason given for the ban was Jabotinsky's "incendiary" Tel Aviv speech. Yet whatever he had actually said in it, this was obviously a pretext. He was, the British clearly had decided, a danger in Palestine, which would be better off without him.

More difficult to understand was his reaction. His first and only recourse to the British government did not come until June, when he was back in Europe. Discovering that, without his knowledge, the directors of Judea had petitioned to have him admitted to Palestine for a limited period in order to conclude unfinished company business, he wrote the colonial secretary Lord Passfield, the anti-Zionist British intellectual Sidney Webb, that he was not interested in such an arrangement and would accept nothing less than the full restoration of his right of residence. It was the closest thing to a formal request for the ban's revocation that he made.

A few days later, answering his Revisionist colleague Meir Grossman, who suggested mounting a public campaign to reverse the edict, he wrote:

Thank you for your letter and for your offer to make a fuss. I don't think, however, that it's our business to make one. This should be done by the Zionist Organization and the Jewish masses who are offended by my banishment. I've asked [Joseph] Schechtman not to say a single word [in the name of the Revisionist movement].

Two weeks later, Jabotinsky wrote Grossman again to object to the intervention of the Zionist Organization, too. He had heard that the Anglo-Jewish mathematician Selig Brodetsky, a Zionist Executive member and staunch Weizmannite, had made overtures on his behalf to the British government. Though he had the highest respect for Brodetsky's motives, he said,

I'm not at all sure that the intervention of the Zionist Executive is in the interest of the Revisionist movement or would redound to its honor or to the honor of its president [himself]. I suggest, therefore, that the movement's executive committee thank Professor Brodetsky personally for his kind concern but abstain from all cooperation with him or with the Zionist Executive if such a prospect is broached.

He made his peace with his banishment quickly. To the American Zionist Abraham Tulin he wrote in September 1930 that "the revocation of my visa hasn't particularly upset me — after fifty years on this earth, a man like me develops a thick skin." In a letter that same month to the Russian-born Revisionist Sioma Jacobi, he declared, "I have been prohibited from returning to Palestine, so I resigned from Judea and intend to stay in Paris for ever." And the president of Judea in New York was told by him: "I can't ask my wife to keep packing, starting all over, and packing again. . . . I hate to admit it, but our enemies have won this round — they've thrown me out of Palestine for a long time."

The subject of the ban was to come up in his correspondence only once more. In 1934, he signed and sent to King George V the first copy of a Revisionist petition, about to be circulated worldwide, in which he demanded his right as a Jew to settle in Palestine. The following month, a rumor spread in the Jewish press that the king had granted him a residence visa. His sister Tania wrote to ask him about this and he replied, "About the visa given me for Palestine, I know only from the newspapers. I've gotten no official announcement. I never asked anyone for a visa. My appeal to the king was not for a visa, but for a change in the immigration laws."

The following year, in 1935, he did apply for a tourist visa. The British embassy in Paris rejected his application and he did not make a public issue of it. He never set foot in Palestine again.

Although Jabotinsky's Revisionist followers regarded the British decree as a bitter blow that their leader bore with stoic fortitude, a view accepted by his biographers, it is quite clear that he not only refused to fight for its repeal but forbade others to do so, too. This is particularly baffling when one considers that the chances of success would have been good. The banishment, while not technically illegal, rested on dubious grounds; Jabotinsky, despite the enemies he had made, was a popular figure in the Jewish world; not even his Zionist opponents could condone the symbolism and potential precedent of a Jew's expulsion from the Land of Israel; any campaign against it would have received widespread support and only enhanced the Revisionists' strength and prestige. What was there to lose by staging one?

Was it Jabotinsky's pride that stood in the way, as perhaps can be inferred from his letters? It had always been great. He was a man who could be made to grit his teeth but not to go down on his knees. He would sooner hold his head high and carry on than beg the British to relent.

Perhaps. But perhaps, too, whether consciously or not, he found the ban convenient. The man who demanded the right of every Jew to live in Palestine—who called on Jews to exercise that right—had not felt at home there. Twice he had been defeated in his own efforts to live there. His wife was against it. They were happier together in Europe. This may or may not have been a source of private grief; it was certainly a reason for public embarrassment. The British, without intending to, had provided him with a way out. No longer the leader who failed to practice what he preached, he was now the one cruelly prevented from doing so.

But it was a way out that came at a high price. As the Yishuv, recovering from the economic stagnation of the second half of the 1920s, began to grow rapidly again in the '30s with the arrival of hundreds of thousands of European immigrants fleeing pauperization and the shadow of Hitler, it was increasingly, not just the raison d'être of Zionism, but Zionism's living center. Zionist Congresses continued to be held in Basel, Prague, and Lucerne; Zionist parties in Poland, Lithuania, Czechoslovakia, Rumania, and elsewhere battled fiercely with each other and with non- or anti-Zionist parties for the allegiance of millions of Jews; these Jews were desperate to get out; many who had never been Zionists by conviction now became so by necessity. Yet they lived in a world that was collapsing.

In Palestine, a world was being built. An immigrant-fed economy was booming at the same time that the Great Depression cast its pall over Europe and America. New cities, towns, and villages were springing up; new forms of life were coming into being; a new culture and society, speaking an old-new language, were being fashioned. Not just one but two semi-underground Jewish military forces had emerged from the original nucleus of the *Haganah*. (The second, many of its members Betarniks, split off from the parent body, which was affiliated with the Histadrut, in 1931. At first known as Haganah B, it eventually took the name of Ha-Irgun ha-Tsva'i ha-Le'umi, the "National Military Organization.") Zionist institutions were moving from the Diaspora to Tel Aviv and Jerusalem. Once, the Yishuv had looked to Europe for help and guidance. Now, Europe looked to the Yishuv.

From all this, Jabotinsky was cut off.

4

Racing the Clock

THE SHAW COMMISSION report led to the Passfield White
Paper of October 1930. Openly pro-Arab, the White Paper
amounted to an all but total abandonment of the Balfour Declaration. It called for Jewish immigration to Palestine to be
severely curtailed; for all Jewish land purchases to be ended; for
the new Jewish Agency to be denied special rights or powers by
the Mandate administration in Jerusalem; and for the Zionist
leadership to renounce "the independent and separatist ideals
which have been developed in some quarters in regard to the
Jewish national home"—in other words, to give up all hope for
a Jewish state.

The Arabs celebrated. The Jews protested. Weizmann
resigned as head of the Zionist Organization. Jabotinsky demanded that the Palestine mandate be returned by Great Britain
to the League of Nations for reassignment to another country,
possibly Italy, England's rival for hegemony in the Mediterra-

nean. The Labour government of Ramsay MacDonald, faced with pro-Zionist sentiment in its ranks and in Parliament, backtracked by shelving the White Paper and appointing a new high commissioner for Palestine, General Arthur Wauchope, who was more sympathetic to Zionism. Now the Jews celebrated and the Arabs protested. It was a typical British zigzag that concluded with the restoration of a status quo with which no one had been happy.

Yet within the Zionist movement, the last vestiges of confidence in England's reliability had been eroded. What had been decided in London in contravention of all prior British-Zionist understandings and reversed under pressure could be reversed again under counter-pressure. Weizmann's policy of trust in British intentions now seemed naive even to his backers, and he only exacerbated his situation by defending England with the claim that a Jewish state in Palestine, as opposed to a "productive, autonomous Jewish society" there, had never been Zionism's aim to begin with. His General Zionist supporters were greatly weakened. In hard-fought elections for the seventeenth Zionist Congress, held in Basel in the summer of 1931, they won only 84 of 254 seats. The Labor Zionists captured 75 seats, with Achdut ha-Avodah and Ha-Po'el ha-Tsa'ir now united as Mapai, a Hebrew acronym for Mifleget Po'alei Eretz-Yisra'el, "The Workers Party of the Land of Israel." The biggest gainers were the Revisionists, who tripled their strength to 52 delegates and 20 percent of the vote.

The congress was a volatile one. The Revisionists introduced an anti-Weizmann motion declaring a Jewish state to be Zionism's goal. Mapai joined the General Zionists in rejecting it as an unnecessary provocation of the British and Arabs. Jabotinsky stood on a chair, tore up his delegate's card, shouted, "This is not a Zionist congress," and was carried out of the hall on Revisionist shoulders. Weizmann then fumbled his victory by stating in a newspaper interview that he had "no understanding or sympathy" even for the objective of a simple Jewish majority in Palestine. This was too much for many of his supporters as well. Passing him by, they voted with Mapai, against Revisionist opposition, to elect his follower Nachum Sokolov as the Zionist Organization's new president. A compact Zionist Executive of two General Zionists, two Mapai members, and one Mizrachi member was chosen to serve under Sokolov.

Jabotinsky had been ambivalent all along about participating in Zionist Organization elections. Although he recognized the symbolic importance of a body founded by Herzl and widely recognized as Zionism's legitimate international representative, he was unwilling to sacrifice Revisionism's freedom to conduct its own relations with whatever political forces or governments it pleased, unimpeded by the Zionist Organization's collective discipline. Now, he found himself in the middle of a fierce intraparty dispute. On one side, encouraged by their electoral success and averse to fracturing the unity of the Zionist movement, were those who argued for remaining in it and winning control of it by democratic means. Arranged against them were the proponents of secession; the route of congress elections, they maintained, was too long and uncertain, and Revisionism would only lose its independence and momentum by taking it. The Zionist Organization loyalists commanded a majority in the party's executive committee and numbered several of Jabotinsky's old friends and associates, such as Yisra'el Rozov, Richard Lichtheim, and most prominently, Meir Grossman, who ran the party's "foreign affairs desk" in London. The secessionists had strong backing in Jabotinsky's Razsviet-Paris circle, in Betar, and in the party's Palestinian branch, which was led by young right-wing militants like Abba Achimeir and Eliyahu Ben-Horin.

Jabotinsky's inclinations aligned him with the latter group. A man with little tolerance for outer constraints, he was always happiest going his own way; it was his nature to plunge ahead and expect others to follow. Coming to power within the Zionist Organization meant working with other parties; the horse-trading of coalition politics was distasteful to him; more appealing was the prospect of conquering the Zionist movement from without. Yet at the same time, he feared driving men like Grossman and Lichtheim, whom he valued and depended on, out of the Revisionist camp. He knew himself well enough to realize that their sobriety was a useful check on his own impetuosity, which the Achimeirs and Ben-Horins would only be a spur to—especially since voices in both Palestine and Betar were now calling on him to play the authoritarian role he feared being forced into. "Sir, why do you consult with us so much?" wrote Achimeir, an admirer of Italian fascism. "Command us more! We have to obey your orders." And a secessionist manifesto published in the Palestinian Revisionist newspaper *Hazit Ha'am*, "The People's Front," ended with the cry: "Long Live the Leader! Long Live the Kingdom of Israel!"

The movement was close to schism. In September 1931, its executive branch met in the French port town of Calais, half-way between London and Paris, in an attempt to find a solution. After two days of debate, a compromise was reached. The Revisionist Party, it was agreed, would give its members freedom of choice. Those who wished to retain their allegiance to the Zionist Organization could go on paying the shekel. Those who did not could stop. Within the party itself, all would have equal rights.

It was not a workable arrangement. A party half in and half out of the Zionist Organization could not function well in either sphere. Nor was the Zionist Executive willing to accept the Calais agreement. Speaking in its name, Chaim Arlosoroff, one of its two Mapai members, warned the Revisionists that unless all of them paid the shekel, they would have to "face the consequences."

Jabotinsky was willing, even eager, to face them. The

Grossman faction was not. The infighting grew harsher. In a letter to Lichtheim, Jabotinsky sketched several options. One was to make a last, supreme effort in the elections for the eighteenth Zionist Congress that were to be held in the summer of 1933, and "if that doesn't work, to agree that it's over with and found an independent Zionist organization." It was, he made clear, the course he intended to follow.

The year 1933 began badly. In January, Adolf Hitler was appointed chancellor of Germany. In March, his National Socialist Party won new elections. Immediately afterwards, the Reichstag granted him emergency powers. In May, he banned all trade unions, and in July, all political parties apart from his own.

Although the immensity of its consequences was not yet evident, the Nazi dictatorship had begun. Barely a week after Hitler's elevation to the chancellorship, Jabotinsky published a newspaper article cautioning against the wishful assumption that the Nazis would probably not remain in power for long and would govern pragmatically if they did. Hitler and his cohorts, he wrote, were not fools or buffoons and could not easily be kept from consolidating power or acting on their beliefs, especially those regarding the Jews. It would be "facile optimism" to draw a line between their anti-Semitism and the rest of their ideology. Anti-Semitism was not just another part of Hitler's program. It was the crux of it.

Yet Jabotinsky was now brooding about assuming dictatorial powers himself. To Yisra'el Rozov he wrote, with the fatalism of a man who feels driven by the winds of events: "Clearly, all this [the dispute with Grossman] must be ended. . . . It looks like the movement needs a single head—a 'Leader,' even though to this day I can't abide that word or its implications. But if that's what has to be, that's what will be."

In March 1933, the Revisionist leadership met in a hotel

in the Polish city of Katowice in a last-ditch effort to avoid a split. Jabotinsky refused to give ground. Grossman threatened to oust him in an executive committee vote and replace him as the party's head. The talks broke up in acrimony. Jabotinsky took a night train to Łodz. There, the next day, he dismissed the executive committee in a bulletin that announced:

> I, the president of the Union of Revisionist Zionists, pro-claim that as of today I am personally assuming full com-mand of the Union and of all the worldwide affairs of our movement. All activities of the movement's central institu-tions are hereby suspended.

Grossman labeled the move a "putsch" and accused Jabotinsky of "Führer-like" behavior. "It's beyond me," he declared, "how democratic principles can co-exist with the dictatorship of a single man, who has now bared himself in front of the world like a belly dancer stripping off her veils."

The accusation that Jabotinsky had been plotting all along to seize one-man control of the Revisionist Party was foolish; the comparison with Hitler was ugly. Revisionism was a volun-tary movement, not a state that could punish and coerce, and Jabotinsky's "putsch" had endangered no one's life or liberty. Moreover, while there was some sympathy among the move-ment's rank-and-file for Grossman's pro-Zionist Organiza-tion position, there was little or none for deposing Jabotinsky. Forced to choose between him and the executive committee, the great majority of Revisionists would not have hesitated to back him.

Nevertheless, the figure of the man of destiny who em-bodies the popular will in circumvention of conniving politi-cians was a centerpiece of fascist ideology. Jabotinsky had vio-lated both democratic norms and his own movement's by-laws; coming on the heels of Hitler's takeover, this could not fail to arouse sinister associations. It was a period in which, in one

Central and Eastern European country after another, dictators were taking over the machinery of government: Piłsudski in Poland, Smetona in Lithuania, Ulmanis in Latvia, Gömbös in Hungary. Grossman was not alone in regarding Jabotinsky's action as cast in the same mold.

Jabotinsky, stung by such criticism, sought to give his move legitimacy by submitting it to a Revisionist referendum. Although the vote was boycotted by the Grossmanites and the turnout was low, over 90 percent of the ballots cast were in Jabotinsky's favor. Confident that he had the movement behind him despite Grossman's decision to found a separate Democratic Revisionist Party, he turned his attention to the eighteenth congress elections, scheduled for late July.

No Zionist elections were ever more bitterly contested. With the General Zionists hobbled by the loss of Weizmann and the discrediting of his views, the battle turned into a showdown between the Revisionists and Labor Zionists. Ben-Gurion took a leave of absence from his activities in Palestine and spent the months before the vote in Eastern Europe, personally supervising the Mapai campaign. Tirelessly going from town to town, he spoke at one rally, conference, and strategy session after another, from morning till far into the night. Jabotinsky did the same. In a letter written in mid-May from the then Rumanian city of Czernowitz—he had just come from Kishinev and was about to depart for Bucharest—he apologized for not answering his correspondent sooner and explained, "I'm on the run all the time and haven't been home [in Paris] since February 20. I give public speeches [at least] four times a week; the nights are spent on railroad trains, the days at meetings." A typical week in Poland, where support for him was strongest, found him in Lublin on Friday, in Nowogrodek on Saturday, in Pinsk on Sunday, in Ostrowice on Tuesday, in Pabianice on Thursday, and in Brisk two days later.

His speeches—mostly given, like Ben-Gurion's, in Yiddish—focused on three main themes: only the Revisionists could lead the fight for a Jewish state; only the Revisionists could end the Labor Zionist–promoted "class struggle" in Palestine that was wrecking the unity and economic development of the Yishuv; only the Revisionists could conduct a successful Jewish campaign against Nazi Germany by organizing a worldwide economic boycott of it. Negotiations, managed on the Zionist side by Chaim Arlosoroff, were then being conducted between the Jewish Agency and the Nazi government for the purpose of enabling the growing number of Jews leaving Germany to salvage their wealth by exchanging it for German-manufactured goods exported to Palestine. Justified by Ben-Gurion as a way of enriching the Yishuv while encouraging immigration to it, this "transfer agreement," as it was known, was fiercely denounced by Jabotinsky for treasonously undermining the economic war against Hitler. Although his role in the Slavinsky affair made him vulnerable to charges of hypocrisy, Nazi Germany was not just another anti-Semitic regime for him. It represented a qualitatively different kind of evil, a country to be placed beyond the pale.

The elections turned into a Jabotinsky–Ben-Gurion duel. The two men stood out among the Zionist leaders of their age. Each had an ability to empathize and communicate with the Jewish masses of Eastern Europe. Each had an unshakable faith in himself and his own judgment; neither doubted its correctness even when colleagues disagreed with it or events appeared to belie it. Jabotinsky was the more captivating speaker and personality; Ben-Gurion, the superior political tactician. Though a highly sociable man, Jabotinsky did not excel at organizational work; generous, sometimes to a fault, in delegating responsibility to those he trusted, he was stingy at sharing it when he thought it should be his own. Ben-Gurion, the more abrasive personality, was also the more disciplined team player; while devoid of the sense of humor that Jabotinsky possessed in abundance, he had a patience for detail and drudgery that Jabotinsky did not have at all. Both men had a wide range of intellectual interests, pursued by Jabotinsky with a casual sophistication and by Ben-Gurion, the less formally educated of the two, with an intense and sometimes quirky curiosity. Jabotinsky had an artist's imagination, Ben-Gurion a savant's love of fact.

Each respected and scorned the other. Both shared the goal of a Jewish state; Jabotinsky thought it could be achieved only by campaigning for it openly, Ben-Gurion that it was better camouflaged while the Yishuv built up its strength on the ground. Each recognized in the other the greatness he felt in himself and saw in it a danger to Zionism and the Jewish people. Each was certain that, within his own camp, he alone was a match for the other.

Both drew large and boisterous crowds, especially in Poland, where worsening anti-Semitism and deteriorating economic conditions had made emigration to Palestine a potential lifeline for many Jews. Groups of demonstrators interrupted and heckled both men. Violent brawls were frequent. In Warsaw, Ben-Gurion was attacked with Revisionist stink bombs and bricks; in Brisk, Jabotinsky was stoned by a Labor Zionist mob. The level of invective was fierce. Jabotinsky called the Zionist Left "lackeys of Moscow." Ben-Gurion referred to him as "Vladimir Hitler," an epithet given resonance by the brown-shirted squadrons of Betarniks who accompanied him everywhere. (It was actually pure coincidence that both Betar and the Nazis wore brown for their marching colors, which had been chosen for the Betar uniform long before Hitler's rise.) Nor did it help that Achimeir and *Hazit Ha'am*, in which Jabotinsky frequently published, praised the Nazis for their anti-Bolshevism and cult of the leader while condemning only their anti-Semitism. Jabotinsky was irate over this. "I'm asking you," he wrote in mid-May to the chairman of the Revisionists' executive committee in Palestine, "either to crack down on *Hazit Ha'am* or to close the paper and dismiss its crackpot staff. . . . I will not put up with any defense of Hitler. All their verbiage [about Nazi Germany] is a knife in my back—and a filthy one at that."

Worse was to come. On the night of June 16, Chaim Arlosoroff was murdered by two men while walking with his wife Sima on a deserted Tel Aviv beach. Immediate suspicion fell on the Revisionists. Robbery did not appear to be a motive, Sima had not been molested, and Arlosoroff had just returned to Palestine from successfully negotiating the transfer agreement that Jabotinsky had inveighed against. Moreover, Achimeir and *Hazit Ha'am* had repeatedly defended the use of violence against the Left; the former had even published, that same year, a tract justifying political assassination. The Revisionists were still smarting from an assault by Mapai toughs on a march of theirs in Tel Aviv several weeks earlier. What could be more logical than the assumption that they had committed the crime?

Within two days this assumption seemed confirmed when the British police arrested a twenty-seven-year-old Betar member named Avraham Stavsky, a recent immigrant from Poland who was identified by Sima Arlosoroff as having shone a flashlight on her husband while a companion shot him with a pistol. Also detained for conspiring to commit the crime was Abba Achimeir. A month later, a third Revisionist, Tsvi Rosenblatt, was picked by Sima from a police lineup as the gunman.

The Zionist Left made the most of it. Immediately after the first arrests, Ben-Gurion issued a statement labeling Jabotinsky the "mastermind" behind the crime. Although no one accused him of actual involvement in it, he was blamed for having primed the gun. The "fascist dictator" was now an assassin, too. In Palestine and Europe, the Left hammered away at his guilt. Calls were made for outlawing the Revisionist Party.

Arlosoroff's murder turned into the central issue of the election campaign and threw Jabotinsky and the Revisionists on the defensive.

Jabotinsky himself had no doubt from the outset of the accused men's innocence and took precious time off from campaigning to help organize their defense and raise money for their legal fees. Although his initial reaction was purely intuitive—the killers, he felt sure, must be Arabs, since no Jew, much less a Betarnik, would do such a thing—it was soon strengthened by the facts that emerged. Achimeir, quite clearly, had nothing directly to do with the case. Stavsky and Rosenblatt had strong alibis. It was all but impossible for them to have been at the scene of the murder when it took place, nor could they have known in advance that Arlosoroff would be there; the only real evidence against them was the testimony of Sima Arlosoroff, a woman recollecting a terrifying few seconds on a dark strip of beach. In addition, half a year later, in January 1934, an Arab from Jaffa, while jailed on a different murder charge, confessed to having been one of Arlosoroff's killers. He and a partner, he told police, had meant to rape Sima but had run off after shooting her husband.

This confession, however, was subsequently retracted, and Stavsky and Rosenblatt, following Achimeir's release, went on trial in May 1934. Rosenblatt was acquitted. Stavsky was convicted and sentenced to death. In July 1934, a court of appeals reversed his conviction and freed him.

By then, though, the damage had been done. Over half a million shekel payers, an unprecedented number, took part in the 1933 elections, and while the Revisionist vote rose to 95,000 from 56,000 in 1931, its share of the total fell to 16 percent. Mapai, with 44 percent, was the clear winner. Dominating the congress, it took control of the Zionist Organization and the Zionist Executive. For the first time in its history, the Zionist movement was in the undisputed hands of the Left.

It was a bitter blow for Jabotinsky. The Arlosoroff affair, though tarring his image, was but one factor in his defeat. He himself was another. He had managed to confuse many Revisionists. Nearly 12,000 of them had voted for Grossman's party—yet if Jabotinsky had intended to contest the elections in any case, what had been the point of precipitating the crisis leading to his "putsch"? Why declare in advance that he would leave the Zionist Organization if he lost, thereby influencing those of his followers who favored secession not to vote? Deep down, he confessed in a letter to the Polish Jewish journalist Alexander Poliakow, he may even have wanted to lose, for "in my heart, I'd like to fail and be free of the entire burden [of politics]." His weariness was not just emotional. The year before, complaining of fatigue, he had seen a doctor and been diagnosed with diabetes.

Still, a triumph as decisive as Mapai's could not have been averted by different behavior on Jabotinsky's part. When all was said and done, voters preferred the optimistic Labor Zionist message of striding with the forces of progress toward the victory of socialism in Palestine, and of a united front against fascism in Europe, to Jabotinsky's starker vision of a Jewish people with only itself and the dimly flickering conscience of a dog-eat-dog world to fall back on. In the global struggle between Left and Right that defined the 1930s, the Left, which was relatively untainted by anti-Semitism and spoke the language of human brotherhood, had a natural hold on Jewish sympathies. Ben-Gurion exploited this hold skillfully. In any contest between worse news and better, the better will usually win.

"The times are hard, old man," Jabotinsky wrote to Sioma Jacobi a month before the eighteenth congress elections.

Sometimes I begin to wonder—have I done wrong? A strange thing has happened: too much hatred has been created around me. . . . I would be happy to go back to our Paris apartment and devote myself to literature, but I can't allow myself to: many thousands want to follow me and their numbers grow daily.

In fact, he had been devoting himself to literature all along. In his letter to Alexander Poliakow, he had announced that "in these hectic weeks, I've been mostly busy finishing *The Five*."

He was not as close to finishing as he thought. *The Five*, his greatest literary achievement and one of the finest twentieth-century Russian novels, was concluded only in 1935 after having been serialized like *Samson* in *Razsviet*. Yet the fact that he managed to find the time and concentration to work on it at all in a period of feverish political activity is astounding. When and where were the hours for it stolen? Early in the morning and late at night at rue Marié-Davy? Between one meeting and the next at the Revisionist office on rue Pontoise? After finishing that week's newspaper article or day's round of correspondence, which might include a dozen or more letters in half as many languages? Before starting another chapter of his memoirs, written in the same years? While riding trains and sitting in train stations, in notebooks pulled from coat or jacket pockets? Waiting in hotel rooms to be picked up for another speech or appearance? His capacity for work aroused wonderment. Joseph Schechtman speaks of more than once conferring with him until the early morning only to be woken a few hours later by his voice on the office telephone saying, "Get a move on, you lazy corpse, you've slept enough!"

On the surface, *The Five* reflects nothing of this. Its opening pages, set in Odessa in the first years of the 1900s, suggest a wistfully nostalgic divertissement far removed from the political battles of the 1930s. Like an étude played by a harried pianist to keep out, if only for a few moments, the sounds of the menacing street, they hark back to a happier and more innocent age.

"The Five" are the children of the Milgroms, a well-to-do, semi-assimilated Jewish family whose father, Ignatz Albertovich Milgrom, is a shrewd grain merchant, and whose mother, Anna Mikhailovna, is a woman of insight and cultivation. Their eldest child, Marusya, is about twenty when the narrative begins; Viktor or Torik, the youngest, is thirteen or fourteen; and in between are Sergei or Serezha, Marko, and Lika. As often happens in large families, all five are very different, each having carved out a space that is in no danger of being occupied by a rival. Marusya is an attractive redhead, lively, funny, unconventional-minded, and sexually provocative; yet while it is never quite clear how much her verbal flamboyance is matched by deeds, she does clearly have a more serious, soulful interior that she is hesitant to reveal. Serezha is a *Wunderkind*, adept at everything: sports, music, poetry, mechanics, card tricks, friendships. "In general," Ignatz Albertovich says of him, "he's a charlatan; I love charlatans." Marko is more slow-witted and idealistic; short-lived in his enthusiasms, he gets, his father says, "a new dream every month or so." Lika is the family rebel and malcontent; sullen and withdrawn, she lives like a nun in her bare room and reads revolutionary literature. Torik is just the opposite, a polite, friendly boy who does well in school.

The narrator of *The Five*, a young journalist, befriends the Milgroms and gets to know them well. His closest relationship is with Marusya. Although it never becomes a romantic one, it sometimes teeters on the edge, and its unspoken restraint at such times is what makes their bond so strong, for it is one of those friendships between a man and a woman that is instinctively understood by both to be too precious to be squandered sexually. Only toward the book's end does the subject of physical love come up between them. Marusya is now married—improbably, so it seems, to a hard-working, conscientious, and rather dull pharmacist named Samoilo Kozodoi—and is the happy mother of a small boy. The narrator has come to visit her in the provincial town she and her husband have moved to from Odessa; Samoilo is away and the two of them stay up till late at night, talking intimately in the guest bedroom. When Marusya finally rises to go, she lingers by the door and then says:

> I'll confess. I was standing here thinking: I ought to say good-bye to you in a special way—perhaps we'll never meet again. But as you can see, I've reconsidered. You and I have missed all our deadlines; in general, it's unnecessary; let things remain as they've been.

Her premonition that it is their last meeting comes true, because shortly afterwards she dies in a fire.

Marusya's death forms the somber denouement of a book that darkens as it progresses, for she is not the only one to end badly. So do all the Milgrom children. Serezha falls in with a crowd of cardsharps, gets involved in an extortion racket, and is blinded in an acid attack. Marko, having taken up and abandoned one cause after another, ridiculously drowns while jumping off a bridge to rescue a woman he mistakenly thinks is screaming for help. Lika joins the Bolsheviks and becomes a secret agent, living a double life as the glamorous mistress of a high Tsarist police spy. Torik grows up to be a successful law-yer and an apostate, converting to Christianity because, as he tells the narrator,

> everyone else has already jumped ship or has inwardly re-solved to; besides, there are plenty of lifeboats all around and there's room for everybody; and the ship isn't really sinking; it's merely uncomfortable, dirty, and crowded, it isn't going anywhere, and everyone's sick and tired of it.

By now, the reader realizes what Jabotinsky is up to. *The Five* is not a divertissement at all. It is a classic *Verfallroman*, the story of the decline of a pre–World War I Russian Jewish society doomed by forces stronger than its own innocence. Despite its very different setting, style, and register, the work of fiction it most resembles is Sholem Aleichem's *Tevye the Dairyman*, in which each of the children of a large Jewish family similarly undergoes a representative fate. Lika, like Tevye's Hodl, chooses the Revolution. Torik, like Tevye's Chava, converts. Marko and Tevye's Shprintze both drown—the latter a conscious suicide, the former a perhaps unconscious one. Shprintze's boyfriend who jilts her, Aronchik, is a cruder version of the Milgroms' Serezha, a hedonistic playboy with no inner core. Their five children have given Ignatz Albertovich and Anna Mikhailovna only one grandchild, Marusya's son.

But who is Marusya? In trying to understand Jabotinsky's intentions in *The Five*, her death is perplexing, for the most inward and self-aware of the Milgrom children, she is the only one whose fate is seemingly determined by a mere accident. While she stands in the kitchen one morning warming milk for her son Mishka, the sleeve of her nightgown brushes the stove and catches fire. Afraid Mishka will be engulfed by it, she pushes him into the hallway with a broom handle and shuts and locks the kitchen door. Only then does she try to tear off her burning nightgown—too late. Her last, apparently pain-crazed act is to crawl to the open window and throw away the key to the door, which is later found in the street.

But as reconstructed by a colleague of the narrator's, a crime reporter, there is nothing crazed about it:

> It's clear. At such a moment anyone, not merely you and I, would first of all want to escape. Madame Kozodoi is, after all, only a human being, and she, too, wanted to escape; the worse it grew, the more she would want to. . . . But Mishka's out there. Let's say the key was still in her hand. Or perhaps it was different: the key was still in the lock, and a fraction of a second arrived when her hand all on its own was stretching out to reach it. Then Madame Kozodoi says to herself: "No.

It's forbidden." And so there wouldn't be any argument, she hurls the key into the street.

Rather than try to save herself by fleeing the burning kitchen, Marusya thinks only of saving Mishka. Hers is the act of a woman with a will of steel that has lain coiled in her all along. As frivolous as she may once have appeared to be, she is the only one of her brothers and sisters to understand what another friend of the narrator's, a lawyer, explains to him in accounting for their generation's moral vacuity:

> From time immemorial the moral equilibrium of humanity has rested on the fact that we hold certain axioms: some closed doors bear the inscription "Forbidden." Simply "forbidden," with no explanation; these axioms stand firm, doors are locked, floorboards don't crack and planets continue to revolve around the sun according to their established order. But if only once you pose the question: "But why is it forbidden?"—these axioms come crashing down. . . . Not only the rules of conventional morality, such as "don't steal" or "don't lie," but even the most instinctive, most innate reactions of human nature—shame, physical squeamishness, the voice of blood—everything dissolves into dust.

It is this "moral equilibrium," which she alone has retained, that causes Marusya to marry Kozodoi, an older man whom she respects but does not love. Even as she plays the teenage flirt in Odessa, she is intuitively aware that she will choose him one day, because she knows that he will be, unlike the young men she has her flings with, a loyal husband and good father, and that when the time for youth and its freedoms has passed, one either renounces them for the obligations of maturity or gets dragged down to destruction.

Who, then, is Marusya? A marvelously realized character, she may have been modeled on someone Jabotinsky knew in Odessa. Yet she was also, like Samson, a fictional projection of himself. A carefree young man of immense talent, he had not been forced to shoulder the burden of Zionist politics. But the Jewish house was on fire. Had it not been, he might have, like Torik, walked away from it with a clear conscience. As it was, though, that was forbidden.

A fanciful interpretation? After Jabotinsky's death, the Hebrew actress Miriam Bernstein-Cohen wrote a short recollection of him that critics of *The Five* have overlooked. In it, without referring to the novel, she relates that Jabotinsky once said to her: "I had two gates in me, one to my people and one to culture, literature, my writing. To keep it from hindering my work for the Jewish people, I locked the second gate with my own hands, took the key, and threw it as far into the depths as I could."

He had, he once said, eleven unwritten novels in his head. Two were biblical ones about the figures of Jacob and David, meant to form a trilogy with *Samson*. Of the others, we only know that he never wrote them.

The virulence of the 1933 election campaign did not abate at the eighteenth Zionist Congress that met later that summer in Prague. Mapai refused to give the Revisionists the seat on the presidium traditionally reserved for a representative of each party. Jabotinsky stayed away from most of the proceedings. He addressed the congress twice, once to press the case for an economic boycott of Germany and once to demand an open discussion of the Arlosoroff case. Both proposals were kept from coming to a vote. Toward the end of the congress, Ania, who had accompanied her husband, was shoved by a Mapai delegate. A Betar contingent came to her defense. A fistfight ensued and the police were forced to intervene.

Mapai-Revisionist violence continued to escalate after the congress, especially in Palestine. Two new controversies inflamed matters more. One was the Revisionists' founding of their own National Labor Organization to compete with the Histadrut. The Histadrut sought to intimidate workers from joining the new union; those who did were turned away by Histadrut-run employment offices and harassed at work when they found it; they, for their part, refused to participate in Histadrut strikes and were accused of scabbing. Although they numbered only seven thousand, barely ten percent of the strength of the Histadrut, the latter, fearing management would exploit them to suppress wages, struck plants and businesses that hired them. In January 1934, in what Jabotinsky called with some exaggeration a "pogrom," the retaliatory refusal of two Revisionist building contractors in Haifa to employ Histadrut construction workers led to a rampage by Mapai gangs in which Revisionist facilities were sacked and more than thirty people wounded. Groups of Betarniks attacked Histadrut picket lines and rallies in return.

An equally contentious issue was that of immigration certificates. The situation in Europe had caused immigration to Palestine to reach new heights, rising from 12,000 in 1932 to 38,000 in 1933, 45,000 in 1934, and 65,000 in 1935. Although the Wauchope administration increased its annual quota of visas, the demand for them greatly exceeded the supply. Issued to applicants by committees appointed by the Jewish Agency, they were apportioned on a political basis, with each Zionist party getting an allotment to distribute to its members based on its strength in the Zionist Organization. The Left, now in control of these committees, used the Revisionists' hostile attitude toward the organization as a pretext for denying them their fair share. Jabotinsky responded by ordering his followers in Europe to boycott the committees while seeking visas in the "assured jobs" category through agreements with Palestinian farmers and factory owners willing to contract for their labor in advance. Mapai threatened such employers with reprisals. The Revisionists struck back by vandalizing the offices of the immigration committees.

By mid-1934, the Yishuv had reached a boiling point. Alarmed by the prospect of civil strife, in which the Revisionists, with their lesser numbers, were likely to get the worst of it, and fearing a loss of support in Eastern Europe if he could not provide his followers with immigration certificates, Jabotinsky decided to sue for peace. In July 1934 he wrote a letter to the Mapai leadership suggesting that representatives of the two parties sit down together. No answer was received. In September, he asked his friend Pinchas Rutenberg, then staying in London, to mediate. Rutenberg turned to Ben-Gurion, with whom he was on good terms, and the Mapai leader agreed to talk. On the evening of October 10, Ben-Gurion and Jabotinsky came to Rutenberg's London hotel room.

It was a dramatic moment. Though the paths they traveled on had often crossed, the two men had not met in years. From afar, they had hurled thunderbolts at each other; now, Ben-Gurion entered a room in which Jabotinsky was waiting. "I said hello without putting out my hand," Ben-Gurion wrote in his diary. "He rose, held out his, and asked, 'Don't you want to shake?' Taken aback, I murmured something and gave him my hand."

The atmosphere warmed up quickly. Jabotinsky expressed the hope that Ben-Gurion would "speak as Ben-Gurion does, fearlessly," and Ben-Gurion assured him that he was ready to discuss everything, from Mapai-Revisionist relations to Zionism's ultimate goals. Jabotinsky had in fact come with a detailed proposal for a détente. It included a joint pledge to cease all violence and inflammatory language; mutual recognition by the two labor unions and the establishment of a national labor arbitration board; the restoration of Revisionist immigration rights; and a shared diplomatic offensive on behalf of a Jewish state. Although pleasantly surprised by Ben-Gurion's open manner, he did not have high hopes. "Our talks will apparently go nowhere, but we have to pursue them," he wrote to Ania the next day. A short note to Schechtman said, "Yesterday I spent four straight hours with B.G. . . . It's hard to believe that it will end in anything spectacular."

In the days that followed, the two men corresponded and met intermittently, with Jabotinsky shuttling back and forth between Paris and London. Contrary to his predictions, progress was made. Ben-Gurion genuinely wanted an agreement and offered unforeseen concessions, such as a readiness to recognize the National Labor Organization and accept the principle of arbitration. On other things, however, positions remained far apart. Ben-Gurion insisted on the Revisionists' full return to the Zionist Organization. Jabotinsky was no less adamant about the party's keeping its independence.

After the first week, the two men exchanged Rutenberg's hotel room for the London apartment of Sioma Jacobi, whose wife Edna was on a visit to her native Australia. In expressive if at times imperfect English, Jabotinsky wrote to her high-spiritedly:

> Dear Edna,
>
> Please: when washing up tea-cups and other machinery, is it really indispensable to wash the outer side of them, too? Kindly cable expert advice.
>
> Otherwise there's no trouble. There is a distinct by-scent of youth in this double bachelorhood. . . . Every sardine tin opened without feminine assistance, and especially every saucer dried without disaster, has the taste of a glorious achievement, reminding me of my undergraduate days in Italy . . .
>
> Edna, your house is the historic stage of most of my conversations with the fire-eatingest of all Left Labour men in Palestine, Ben-Gurion. Our mutual friendliness and cor-

diality is a surprise for both of us, and when his party learns about how he broiled eggs on your gas-grille for us to eat, he'll be lynched. He still makes a feeble pretense to believe that Stavsky and Rosenblatt "did it"; but Sioma and I have laughed it out of his innards, I'm sure. As to whether these negotiations will have any earthly use in the end, [that's] quite another matter. But in any case, in the name of both our exalted parties, I offer you my gratitude for your unconscious hospitality.

In the end, a limited agreement was reached that called for a cessation of all violence, a modus vivendi between the rival labor unions, the Revisionists' agreement to respect the immigration committees, and the renewal of their certificate quota — all subject to the approval of the two parties. Ben-Gurion was more apprehensive on this score than Jabotinsky. "It's too good to be true," he noted in his diary on October 27. "My dear Jabotinsky" he wrote the next day, omitting the customary "Mr.":

> I hope you won't be upset with me if I address you as a comrade and friend without the ceremonial title.
> We parted yesterday after 15 consecutive hours of intensive work. I'm not a sentimental man, nor do I think you are. I haven't bared my heart to you, and I won't do so now. . . . Yet whatever happens can never change the fact that we two met in reciprocal trust and respect, that we managed for many hours to put everything behind us, and that our deep concern for the [Zionist] movement and its success led us to make this joint effort.

Jabotinsky wrote back:

> My dear friend Ben-Gurion,
> I just received your letter of yesterday. It's difficult for me to tell you what an impression it made on me. It so happens that I am sentimental (and not in the least ashamed of it), but it's much more than sentimentality that causes me

the deepest emotion when after all these years—and what years!—I hear the words "comrade and friend" from you. I had long ago forgotten that such a way of speaking exists, and perhaps I've been the cause of its being forgotten between us. . . .

In January 1935, Jabotinsky presented the agreement for approval to the annual Revisionist convention that met in Cracow. The Palestinian delegation accused him of ceding too much, as did some of the Eastern Europeans. When it came to a vote, however, he commanded a large majority.

Ben-Gurion, as he had anticipated, met stiffer resistance. It was widely felt on the Left that he had accepted a ceasefire with the Revisionists just when Mapai had them on the run. His language of the previous summer now boomeranged against him: how could one suddenly befriend the fascists and murderers of yesterday? In March 1935, Mapai members went to the polls in a referendum. Nearly sixty percent of them voted against the agreement.

Jabotinsky received news of this in America, where he was once again on a speaking tour. From Chicago, he wrote to Ben-Gurion:

> I'm not sure if I'll send this letter when I finish it. Even the strongest spirit can be influenced by his environment, [such as] the environment you encountered [in Palestine] after returning from London. Perhaps you'll read these lines with changed eyes. I, for example, confess that when I heard [of Ben-Gurion's difficulties with Mapai], an inner frailty in me whispered: "Thank God we're done with all this—and maybe B.G. is thinking the same thing!" And yet nothing has changed in the appreciation for B.G. the man and his aspirations that I learned to have in London.

A month later, when he was back in Europe, he received a reply. "It may be," Ben-Gurion wrote, that our joint labors in London have gone up in smoke, at least publicly—but beyond matters of public policy stand human beings, and when I look back on our days in London, I don't think we wasted our time. . . . Our London episode will remain in my heart. I can forget many things, but not that. If we're doomed to war with one another, I want you to know that among your "enemies" is someone who esteems you and shares your anguish. The hand that you thought unwilling to take yours when we first met will be held out to you in the heat of battle.

Jabotinsky answered:

Your letter made me very happy. It came as a comfort. Recently, I've begun to hate this way of life; my soul is weary of all the constant, endless bitterness stretching beyond the horizon. You've reminded me that perhaps there is an end to it after all.

One short, "philosophical" note. I can vouch for there being a type of Zionist who doesn't care what kind of society our "state" will have; I'm that person. If I were to know that the only way to a state was via socialism, or even that this would hasten it by a generation, I'd welcome it. More than that: give me a religiously Orthodox state in which I would be forced to eat gefillte fish all day long (but only if there were no other way) and I'll take it. More even than that: make it a Yiddish-speaking state, which for me would mean the loss of all the magic in the thing—if there's no other way, I'll take that, too. In the will I leave my son I'll tell him to start a revolution, but on the envelope I'll write: "To be opened only five years after a Jewish state is established." I've asked myself several times if these are my true feelings; I'm certain that they are.

Jabotinsky returned from America in April 1935. The bridges to the Zionist Organization were now burned. He was free to do as he pleased—which was to pursue his petition plan and set about supplanting the parent body with an offshoot that would, as he saw it, represent the true interests of Zionism. In August, worldwide elections were held for delegates to what was officially called the New Zionist Organization. No shekel-like payment was required, and 713,000 voters turned out, two-thirds of them in Poland, exceeding the numbers that had taken part in Zionist Organization elections that spring.

The NZO's first congress convened in Vienna in September. Jabotinsky gave the keynote address in German. Appealing for a *Hochzionismus*, a "high-minded Zionism," he sounded two new themes in addition to his old ones. One was a call for the elimination of the Diaspora by means of a massive "evacuation" of world Jewry to the future Jewish state, starting with an emergency campaign, reminiscent of Max Nordau's post-World War I plan, to bring a million and a half European Jews to Palestine within ten years. It was the first time he had openly associated himself with the radical Zionist school of *shlilat ha-golah* or "Diaspora negation," which viewed Zionism not merely as an antidote to Jewish exile but as a final end to it. It was a position for which, especially in Poland, he was to be taken to task in Zionist circles. *Haynt*, the country's largest Yiddish newspaper, which for a long time had published him despite its pro-Labor Zionist policy, accused him of delegitimizing Polish Jewish life and abetting the anti-Semites, and even the pro-Revisionist *Moment* echoed the criticism.

Herzl, to be sure, had assumed that the Diaspora would gradually wither once a Jewish state existed as an alternative. Yet Jabotinsky, as far back as the 1906 Helsinki Conference, had been a strong advocate of what was known in Zionist circles as *Gegenswartarbeit* or "working in the present"—that is, intensively investing in Diaspora life so as to strengthen it for the long haul ahead. Now, he no longer thought it had that kind of time. He had always believed there was such a thing as an "objective anti-Semitism," a hostility toward Jews stemming not from irrational prejudice but from unavoidable majority-minority conflict, and in a Europe afflicted by the misery and chaos of the 1930s, the benefits of exploiting such conflict were great; they were both political, as in Germany, where anti-Semitism had helped propel the Nazis to power, and economic, as in Poland, Rumania, and other countries, where government-supported boycotts and discrimination were wresting jobs and businesses from Jewish hands. The "Bartholomew's night" he had half-flippantly foreseen as a young student in Bern now loomed as a reality. Haunted by what he called in his Vienna address "the approaching catastrophe in our worldwide ghetto," he had come to view Zionism as a race against the clock.

For the first time, too, he resorted in his rhetoric to religious imagery, speaking of a "second exodus from Egypt" and "the messianic birth pangs" of national redemption. Never hostile toward Jewish religious tradition like many secular Zionists, he nevertheless had kept an intellectual distance from it; in Vienna, he took a step toward closing the gap. Although the anti-clericalism of nineteenth-century liberalism had been justified, he told his audience,

> it has led to the banishing of God—and one may doubt, and more than doubt, the desirability of this. Yes, religion must remain a private matter . . . but it cannot be a private matter whether there are temples of worship [in a society] or not; whether Mount Sinai and the Prophets remain living spiritual forces or are embalmed behind glass in museums like mummified Pharaohs and Aztec relics. . . . It is imperative for a "state"—and for us as a nation—to keep the eternal flame from going out, so that amid the innumerable cross-currents that buffet contemporary youth and sometimes toxically lead it astray, the purest of them, the spirit of the Lord, be preserved; that a space be maintained in the public arena for those who preach and contend in its name.

In its struggle with the Left, Revisionism had a natural ally in the religious Zionist camp, and Jabotinsky's reevaluation of religion's role in a future Jewish state was seen by many as an opportunistic attempt to reach out to Orthodox Jews and make room for them in the New Zionist Organization. There was a measure of truth in this; in time, indeed, the NZO came to have an organized Orthodox faction. Yet it would be doing Jabotinsky an injustice to deny that his Vienna address also reflected a genuine evolution of his thought. This was expressed in a letter he wrote in Hebrew to Eri, who had been raised in a totally secular home. Concerned about his son's reaction to the stress on religion in Vienna, Jabotinsky explained:

> I don't need to tell you that I still advocate freedom of thought, etc. Nor do I see any sacredness in ritual. The matter is deeper than that. . . . Everyone agrees that there are truly sacred principles in the Bible of the sort that need to be inculcated; but these principles, it so happens, are moral ones that can be espoused by any atheist too, so why inculcate them under the banner of religion? Precisely here, in my opinion, lies the crux of the matter. One can of course seek to formulate the noblest moral system without bringing the divine into it; this is what I've done all my life. Now, though, I'm convinced that it's more correct *to treat ethical fundamentals as connected with superhuman mystery* [the italicized words were written by Jabotinsky in English]. . . . I'll go even further: the pathos of religion, in and of itself, is needed. I'm not sure it can be rekindled in anyone's soul—perhaps, like musical pitch, it's an innate trait that few people are born with. Still, if it were possible to create a generation of believers, I'd be pleased.

At the age of fifty-five, Jabotinsky had not found God. Rather, he had lost the optimistic belief, shared by most European intellectuals of the late nineteenth and early twentieth centuries, that a firm moral conscience could be internalized in the average person without recourse to God. He had never believed in the natural goodness of man; now, he had come to the conclusion that an atheistic acceptance of the binding nature of moral law, while possible, was not mass-producible. Society needed religion, even if not every individual did. It was no accident that the two monstrous totalitarian regimes of the era, Nazi Germany and Soviet Russia, were both ideologically anti-religious. A Hitler or Stalin could not be worshiped alongside a God who had commanded, "Thou shalt have no other gods before me."

Early in 1936, the New Zionist Organization moved its main office from Paris to London. Free to conduct its own diplomatic relations, it could do so better from the capital that held the reins to Palestine. For the Jabotinskys, the move was difficult. They had lived longer as a married couple in Paris than anywhere else and now had to uproot themselves again.

The NZO established its headquarters on Finchley Road, in north London, and Jabotinsky and Ania rented rooms in Belsize Grove, in nearby Hampstead. Their plan was to buy a small house, their first, but they could not raise the money for a down payment. His political differences with *Haynt* and *Moment*, both significant sources of income in the past, had caused Jabotinsky to stop writing for them, and not only did he draw no salary from his political work, he occasionally had to cover Revisionist debts from his own pocket. Receiving a check for $666 from Paramount Pictures for the film rights to *Samson*, he passed it on immediately to the NZO. (The Cecil B. DeMille movie, starring Victor Mature and Hedy Lamarr and listing Jabotinsky in the credits, grossed $11 million at the box office when it was finally produced in 1949.)

In March of 1936, Hitler sent troops into the Rhineland.

In May, Italy completed its conquest of Ethiopia, and in July, the Spanish civil war broke out. In the middle of all this, mass Arab violence erupted in Palestine. Accompanied by a general strike, it was triggered by unmet Arab demands to implement the Passfield White Paper and establish the long-promised national legislature that would be a step toward Palestinian independence. In a country whose four hundred thousand Jews were still less than a third of the total population, this would have been disastrous from a Jewish point of view.

But the Jewish share of the total was growing rapidly. It had almost reached the 30 percent that, in 1922, Jabotinsky had predicted would mark the start of the "real battle"—and this battle now commenced, for the "Arab revolt" of 1936–39, as it was called, was of a different magnitude from the disturbances of 1921 and 1929. Supported by neighboring Arab countries, it lasted far longer and involved larger, better equipped, and more organized forces that at times resembled a guerrilla army. Besides attacking Jewish neighborhoods and villages, ambushing Jewish settlers and vehicles, and burning thousands of acres of Jewish farmland, the rebels fought British troops, cut roads and railroad tracks, and repeatedly blew up the pipeline bringing oil from Iraq to the large British refinery in Haifa.

Faced with a semi-wartime situation, the Yishuv responded in two opposing ways. One of them, advocated by Mapai, the Histadrut, and the Haganah, was to limit Jewish reaction to defensive measures while collaborating with the British as closely as possible. Known in Hebrew as *havlagah* or "self-restraint," this approach held that, since the British were now openly aligned with Palestine's Jews against its Arabs, everything should be done to cement the alliance; independent Jewish military activity would only force the British to combat it, too, and so play into Arab hands. Inasmuch as tit-for-tat retaliation, moreover, was sure to result in the loss of innocent Arab lives, *havlagah* was also a moral imperative.

Havlagah as a policy was not inconsistent with Jabotinsky's analysis of the situation, and at first he supported it. Despite his disillusionment with England, he saw no realistic alternative to its rule. There was no one else to take its place as the mandatory power, especially now that Mussolini was openly in league with Hitler, and Britain would not agree to cede control of so strategically important a country as Palestine anyway with another major European war in the offing. Not only that, but the Mandate government quickly began enlisting Jewish units, procured largely from the ranks of the Haganah, to strengthen its undermanned forces. This was precisely what, in the form of a permanent Jewish legion, Jabotinsky had fought for back in the 1920s. He had always wanted the Yishuv to have an official role in policing Palestine, which he had deemed politically preferable to clandestine militias. The Arab revolt had finally brought this about.

But the Irgun, which numbered some three thousand potential fighters, saw things differently—and in a no less Jabotinskyan vein: when attacked, it argued, always hit back. Nothing indeed had characterized Jabotinsky more over the years than his insistence on responding forcefully as a Jew to aggression, and it was hard for him to disavow such a principle now, even though the Irgun was disturbingly indiscriminate in applying it. Already in the revolt's first days, it struck twice in revenge for the murders of Jews by killing three Arabs who bore no responsibility. In Tel Aviv, egged on by Betarniks, Jews fell on Arab workers and peddlers and drove them from the streets. Jabotinsky reacted with a mixture of denial and disquiet. "The expulsion from Tel Aviv of Arab wagon drivers and shoeshine boys would be worthy of criticism if true," he wrote in a letter to Refa'el Rozov, his old friend Yisra'el Rozov's son, but I doubt that it is. As far as I'm concerned, Palestinian Arabs in Tel Aviv are [as though] in their own home, because otherwise I can't imagine law and order in Palestine. But even if this guideline isn't followed, I could still forgive [the Jews involved] if they had gone [to the Arabs] and politely asked them to leave without laying hands on them. If there were blows or shoves, or seven Jews ganging up on one Arab, I only hope that our people [i.e., Revisionists] weren't part of it. I would consider such a thing beastly, even if it happened during a pogrom [of Arabs against Jews].

The temporizing of "It probably didn't happen and let's pray it wasn't us if it did" reflected the dilemma Jabotinsky was in. On the one hand, he believed in the "ethical fundamental" of punishing only the guilty. On the other, besides identifying with the instinct to lash out against one's assailants, he assumed that his followers in Palestine were the object of Mapai slanders like those that had accompanied the Arlosoroff affair. His absence from the country made it difficult to ascertain the truth and impossible to impose his own standards, which Palestinian Revisionists felt were quixotically detached from reality. As if "politeness" had anything to do with combating Arab terror! He had little or no control over them. "I'm very worried, almost tragically so, about the state of the movement in Palestine," he wrote in May 1936 to Ya'akov Hoffman, a founder of Betar in Latvia then living in Tel Aviv. "If we can't straighten things out there, I really don't know what will happen."

In a move to strengthen his influence, Jabotinsky appointed his son Eri, now working as an engineer at a hydroelectric plant on the Jordan, as Palestinian head of Betar with the special mission of coordinating its activities with Revisionist and NZO leaders. One of Eri's first acts was to tighten relations with the Irgun, and in December 1936 an agreement was reached affiliating it with the NZO under Jabotinsky's formal command.

Many Irgun members were opposed to this, and the organization split in two, half of it rejoining the Haganah. Those that
remained were almost entirely Betarniks.

With the outbreak of the revolt, the British did what they
habitually did when Arab violence surged in Palestine and created another commission of inquiry. This one was headed by
Conservative politician Lord William Peel, whose two stints as
secretary of state for India had familiarized him with the problems of a British colony beset by ethnic hostility. The commission sat in Jerusalem from mid-November 1936 to mid-January
1937. Although Jabotinsky requested to appear before it there,
he was again denied entry to Palestine. In February, he testi-
fied in London.

By then the first stage of the Arab revolt had died down
and there were signs that the commission, having concluded
that it was impossible to harmonize the pro-Jewish and pro-
Arab clauses of the Balfour Declaration or the demands of the
two sides, was considering a radical new solution: Palestine's
partition into separate Jewish and Arab states. Jabotinsky, still
unreconciled to the loss of the land reserves of Transjordan,
objected strenuously in his testimony to the even more drastic
territorial surgery now contemplated. Comparing the Arabs,
who had many lands, and the Jews, who had none, to a full and
a starving man, he told the commission that the claims of hun-
ger outweighed those of satiety; to accuse the Jews of greed was
like blaming Dickens's orphaned Oliver Twist for crying out
"More!" at mealtimes when all he meant was, "Will you just
give me that normal portion necessary for a boy my age to be
able to live?" "I assure you," Jabotinsky went on, "that you have
here today, in the Jewish people with its demands, an Oliver
Twist who has unfortunately no concessions to make. What
can be the concessions? We have got to save millions, many

millions." A truncated corner of Palestine could not possibly be enough for that.

Both Ben-Gurion and Weizmann, who had renewed his alliance with Mapai and again stood at the head of the Zionist Organization and the Jewish Agency, favored partition. Weizmann openly supported it in his testimony; Ben-Gurion, for tactical reasons, did not. By feigning opposition to it, he reasoned, he could extract better terms—and indeed, when the Peel Commission published its report in July 1937, he professed satisfaction with its recommendations. These were that Palestine be divided into three zones: a Jewish state composed of the Galilee and most of the coastal plain, an Arab state in the remainder of the country, and a British enclave running from Jaffa to Jerusalem and including both. Although the Jewish state was allotted only a quarter of the land west of the Jordan, nearly all of Palestine's Jews outside Jerusalem stood to be in it. The commission, moreover, sought to make its small area more palatable by proposing that its Arabs be resettled elsewhere.

Not only the Revisionists reacted to the Peel plan with outrage. The religious parties objected to surrendering large parts of the Land of Israel sacred to Jewish tradition, especially Jerusalem, while within Mapai, too, prominent voices were raised against the plan. Weizmann and Ben-Gurion defended it, although for different reasons. Weizmann thought it territorially sufficient. Like Ahad Ha'am, he had never believed that most or even much of Diaspora Jewry could be concentrated in a Jewish state, which only needed to be large enough for a culturally distinctive Jewish life to flourish in it; although it would serve as a beacon for the world's Jews, it could not serve as a refuge for them. Ben-Gurion dissimulated once more. Publicly, he took a line close to Weizmann's: even a small state that could absorb only a part of European Jewry was better than none. In private, he made no secret of his conviction that this state, once consolidated, would expand into the rest of Palestine—peacefully if possible, by military force if necessary.

Jabotinsky was aware of Ben-Gurion's thinking. Apart from his aversion to Machiavellian politics, he considered it unrealistic. The military option, he believed, would indeed be resorted to—but by the Arabs first. Strategically speaking, he asked a group of British parliamentarians he met with after the release of the Peel Commission's report, how would it be possible to defend this Jewish "pale" from a concerted attack? The most heavily populated part of it would lie in lowlands overseen by its enemies in the hills above. Arab artillery stationed within range of Tel Aviv and Haifa could devastate both cities, which would be overrun no matter how brave their defenders.

Nor was Jabotinsky enticed by the idea of Arab resettlement. People might call him an extremist, he said, but at least he had never dreamed of asking Arabs in a Jewish state to emigrate. If there would not be enough room for Arabs in a partition state, this was only because neither would there be enough room for Jews. It would be a "death sentence" for Zionism.

Jabotinsky's stand against partition was pragmatic. In his appearance before the Peel Commission, he had little to say about the Jewish emotional connection to the Land of Israel or Jewish historical rights there. In part, this may have been because he doubted whether such concerns would speak to the British public; in the years since World War I, the old Bible-based Christian philo-Semitism had declined in England while an awareness of the Jewish plight in Europe had increased. But in part, too, this was not what mattered to him most. Palestine was not sacred ground for him. It was simply the only possible ground on which the Jewish people could be rallied. This was why he had voted against Herzl's Uganda plan—and a partition state was simply another Uganda. A small piece of Palestine was no better than a larger piece of somewhere else. Neither satisfied the needs of what he had now come to call "humanitarian

Zionism"—a Zionism that sought to save a maximum of Jewish lives rather than to establish, as he scathingly remarked in alluding to Weizmann's Ahad Ha'amism, an "amusement park for Hebrew culture."

A month later, the twentieth Zionist Organization congress met in Zurich. After a stormy, week-long debate, it adopted a resolution that, while falling short of approving partition, authorized the Zionist Executive to enter negotiations over it with the British government. These never took place. A pan-Arab congress, held in Syria with Palestinian participation in September 1937, rejected partition categorically. All of Palestine, it declared, was Arab land. Not an inch would be surrendered to the Jews.

Following a lull, the Arab revolt flared up again. The British appointed yet another commission, chaired by former Indian administrator Sir John Woodhead, to review the Peel Commission's findings. Although its members could not agree among themselves, all concurred, in a report issued in November 1938, that any Jewish state would have to be smaller than the one proposed. This was not acceptable even to Ben-Gurion and Weizmann—nor would it have mattered if it had been, since the Arabs remained adamant about yielding nothing. Jabotinsky had been confident all along that this would be the case. "I can't say too often that the partition plan is an impossibility," he had written the Revisionist journalist Wolfgang von Weisel immediately after the publication of the Peel Commission report. "The harder it's pushed, the deeper it will be buried."

The second stage of the Arab revolt, starting in the autumn of 1937, was bloodier and harder-fought than the first. At its height, the rebels had close to ten thousand fighters in the field; large areas of the countryside fell under their control, which even extended for a few days to the old city of Jerusalem. The British responded with a heavy hand, throwing up to fifty thousand soldiers into the fray. They inflicted collective punishments on towns and villages suspected of harboring and aiding insurgents, bombed them from the air, razed entire neighborhoods, rounded up thousands of prisoners, and executed over a hundred. More than fifteen thousand Haganah fighters took part in suppressing the uprising, ranging from constabulary units to Captain Orde Wingate's "special night squads," known for their daring counterinsurgency tactics. (Wingate was later to acquire a lasting military reputation as the commander of anti-Japanese guerrillas in Burma during World War II.) An irregular force when the revolt broke out, the Haganah emerged from it larger, better trained, and with tested combat capabilities.

Nevertheless, while it participated in actions that went far beyond the previous limits of *havlagah*, the Haganah was subject to British command and lacked the freedom to respond directly to Arab assaults on Jewish life and property. Unhindered by such restrictions, the Irgun launched a campaign of fighting terror with terror, responding to the murder of innocent Jews with the murder of innocent Arabs. In the summer of 1938, when its offensive peaked, its bombs and bullets in Arab streets and marketplaces took nearly one hundred lives.

Jabotinsky knew little or nothing in advance about the specifics of such attacks. In his contacts with Irgun emissaries in Europe, he established a system of cabling his coded approval of the scope and timing of Irgun reprisals while leaving their details to the Palestinian command. When attempts were made to consult him further, his standard response, delivered in Yiddish, was *Men fregt nisht dem tata*, "One doesn't ask Papa"— which could only convey that he didn't wish to know more. It was a way to avoid compromising the Revisionist Party and its institutions while easing his own discomfort. He would have preferred more selective retaliation but felt unable to press for it from afar. On a brief stopover in Alexandria in July 1937 to meet Revisionist leaders from Palestine on his way back from a second South African tour, he reportedly told them, "I see nothing heroic about shooting an Arab peasant in the back for bringing vegetables on his donkey to Tel Aviv."

Yet as the cycle of violence increased, his reservations weakened. They vanished entirely with the execution in June 1938 of Shlomo Ben-Yosef, a young Irgun and Betar member arrested with two comrades for firing on an Arab bus while it negotiated the hairpin turns of a road in the Galilee. Though none of the passengers were injured, the British, who had hanged Arabs for no worse, decided to demonstrate their fairness by hanging Ben-Yosef, too. Jabotinsky fought tooth and nail to have the sentence commuted. In an imploring letter to British colonial secretary Malcolm MacDonald, Ramsay MacDonald's son, he wrote:

> I know all that can be said in support of the sentence: [that] the law should apply equally [to Jews and Arabs], etc. . . . [But this is] a theory repellent to the very essence of public decency. I urge you to remember that the Arab terror has by now lasted two years; I beg you to visualize it, to try and realize palpably what these two years mean in sorrow and humiliation. . . . The whole atmosphere is madness. The Jewish people would never get reconciled to a situation which first drives youngsters to the verge of madness and then hangs them.

The plea that Ben-Yosef was the victim of a form of collective insanity to which the Yishuv had been reduced was not in itself an endorsement of Jewish terror. Among Jews, however, Jabotinsky now spoke differently. Shortly after Ben-Yosef's execution, he referred to him as a shining example of the "new spiritual race" he had first envisioned in his 1928 missive to Betar in Latvia. And on the first anniversary of Ben-Yosef's death, he published a memorial tribute to him in a Warsaw

Hebrew weekly. This began with a recollection of Jewish self-defense in Odessa before declaring that the time for mere defense had passed:

> There's no point in returning to the childish argument about the moral value of *havlagah*. . . ."Don't you dare punish the innocent" [we are told]—what a superficial, hypocritical thing to say! In war, in *all* war, both sides are always innocent. What crime against me has the "enemy" soldier committed? He's a poor beggar just like me, conscripted against his will. . . . If [another European] war breaks out, we'll all demand an embargo on the enemy's country in order to starve its inhabitants with their women and children; the first air raid on London and Paris will lead to retaliation against Stuttgart and Milan, which are full of women and children, too. . . . Damned be every war, in every form! There's no difference between defense and attack. If you don't want to harm the innocent, you can die. If you don't want to die, shoot and don't blabber. This lesson was taught me by my teacher Ben-Yosef.

These were impassioned words. They were also a traditional justification of terror, which is no more immoral in its consequences, its defenders have always maintained, than any other form of warfare. "Is a situation moral in which one side can commit any crime or murder and the other is forbidden to react?" Jabotinsky asked in a speech to a Polish Jewish audience. Two years previously, he had wanted Arabs to feel at home in Tel Aviv. The year before, in Alexandria, murdering an Arab vegetable peddler had seemed wrong to him. Now, he declared:

> Jews can't let themselves be seen on the roads of Palestine—but the Arab in Tel Aviv feels at home. He gets up in the morning and sets out and knocks on the Jew's door and says, "Good morning, I've brought some vegetables"—and nothing happens. He's not afraid of being harmed. . . . How long

can this go on? Forever? Why, under such circumstances, should the Arabs stop what they're doing? . . . Who doesn't understand that the greatest enemy of equality for Jews is he who says that the means used by the Arabs in their war against us must not be used by us against them?

The Arab vegetable peddler had become a legitimate target. But Jabotinsky's questions were legitimate, too. If anti-terror terror had a deterrent value that could save even a single Jewish life, was it not defensible from a Jewish point of view? The moral calculus has yet to be invented that can deal with such equations. All that can be said is that, in the madness of the times, the commander-in-chief of the Irgun had chosen to ignore what the author of *The Five* had insisted on—that the "moral equilibrium" of humanity rests on age-old inhibitions that, though they may retain their power when breached in practice, crumble to dust when challenged in theory. Kill an innocent peddler and you have but killed an innocent peddler. Ask "But *why* should killing an innocent peddler be forbidden?" and nothing is forbidden any more.

In March 1938, Germany forcibly annexed Austria. In September, British foreign minister Neville Chamberlain signed the Munich agreement with Hitler. In October, the German army marched into the Sudetenland.

England, despite Chamberlain's promise of "peace in our time," prepared for war. Determined to keep the Arabs on its side, it zigged in Palestine again. Following the final crushing of the Arab revolt and the foreordained failure, in February 1939, of a Jewish-Arab "round table conference" in London at which an Arab delegation refused to share a table of any shape with a Jewish one led by Ben-Gurion and Weizmann, a new White Paper was issued by Ramsay MacDonald. It proclaimed that since 450,000 Jews now lived in Palestine, the Balfour Declaration's promise of a Jewish national home had been fulfilled, and it proposed that 75,000 more Jewish immigrants be admitted over a five-year period, after which the gates of the country would be shut and a Palestinian state with a permanent Jewish minority would be established. This time, there was no zagging back. The MacDonald White Paper was approved by the House of Commons over Zionist remonstrance and took effect as government policy.

With the Germans threatening to overrun the rest of Europe, its Jews were trapped. At an international refugee conference in Évian, in the French Alps, in the summer of 1938, only the tiny Dominican Republic, which lacked the means to make good on its offer, expressed readiness to take in more than a token number of asylum seekers. In Germany, a nationwide pogrom in November 1938 resulted in the murder of ninety-one Jews and the deportation of twenty thousand to concentration camps, heralding the lethal turn that Nazi anti-Semitism was about to take. In Soviet Russia, the favorable attitude that had prevailed toward Yiddish culture in the early years of the revolution had given way to a brutal repression of all expressions of Jewish national feeling. In Poland, Lithuania, Latvia, Rumania, and Hungary, Jews faced official discrimination, daily attacks, joblessness, and even starvation. In the maelstrom of another war, many were certain to be whirled to their destruction.

Ben-Gurion returned from London to Palestine in a grim mood. He had reached the conclusion that Jabotinsky had reached long before. Socialism could wait. A Jewish state able to save as many Jews as possible was the immediate priority — and it would have to be won by force of arms, no matter how great the odds against this were. The commanders of the Haganah were told to prepare for such an eventuality while stepping up the smuggling of Jewish immigrants into the country.

Illegal immigration was an activity the Irgun was engaged in, too. Now, there were calls in the organization for an armed

Jewish insurrection against the British. Jabotinsky opposed this as impractical. Over the years, pressure from the ranks had forced him at times to take more extreme positions than his better judgment might have inclined him to; this time, better judgment prevailed. For two decades the standard-bearer of militant Zionism, he found himself accused by young Revisionists of hesitancy and weakness. At a tumultuous Betar conference in Warsaw in late 1938, he clashed angrily with his critics, headed by Menachem Begin. It was "nonsense," he told them, to think that conditions existed in Palestine for a Garibaldi-like Jewish war of liberation. As long as they didn't, it was incumbent on Zionism to pursue policies that would enable it to appeal to the world's conscience. "To say," he declared, "that conscience no longer exists—this is despair. . . . Conscience rules the world. I respect it. It is forbidden to mock it and ridicule it."

Never had he and Ben-Gurion been so close in their views. With his encouragement, the Irgun negotiated an agreement with the Haganah for a united front. Jabotinsky was ready to sign. Ben-Gurion was not. Although far less divided him from Jabotinsky than in 1935, the Mapai leader stuck to his demand for the dissolution of the NZO and a Revisionist return to the Zionist Organization as a precondition for joint action.

The NZO, however, could not be dissolved, not least because it gave Jabotinsky a platform from which to deal with heads of state. After a period of indecisive groping, he had discerned, he believed, a path of action. Conscience could be linked to interest. England, weary of the mandate, had chosen to end it by granting the Arabs victory. But the governments of Eastern and Central Europe had a Jewish problem that an Arab victory did nothing to solve. Increasingly attracted to the revolutionary Left, their Jewish minorities that could be absorbed neither socially nor economically constituted a threat. The only way to dismantle it was via Jewish emigration; the only possible destination for such emigration was Palestine. Zionism, therefore, needed to prevail on these governments to get England to change its mind.

Nazi Germany was not an eligible partner: Jabotinsky never wavered from his policy of avoiding all contact with it. Nor was there any possibility of approaching the Soviets, whose ideological opposition to Zionism was unyielding. But he had no qualms about talking with other regimes, even if—indeed, precisely because—they had anti-Semitic leanings. He had done it with Petliura and he was ready, no matter what was said about him, to do it again. He visited Rumania several times, meeting with King Karol II and Foreign Minister Nicolae Petrescu-Comnem. He had talks with Lithuanian president Antanas Smetona, with Latvian foreign minister Wilhelms Munters, and with others. Everywhere he was received cordially. For the most part, nothing came of it. His interlocutors were sympathetic, but their influence over England was slight and they did not wish to waste the little they had on a cause whose chances of success they deemed slim.

Poland was a different story. It was a larger, more powerful country formally allied with France and England against Germany, and Jabotinsky's discussions with its foreign minister Josef Beck, its prime minister Felicjan Sławoj-Skłodkawski, and its army chief-of-staff Marshal Edward Rydz-Śmigly, as well as with lesser officials, yielded tangible results. The Poles agreed to host Betar and Irgun training camps on their soil, to help the two organizations obtain lights arms, and to assist Polish Jews to depart illegally for Palestine. To Jabotinsky's frustration, however, they, too, were reluctant to press Zionist demands in London. Their alliance with the British was too important for them to risk putting strains on it.

Jabotinsky alternated between gloom and prophetic exaltation. In Vienna, in 1934, he had spoken of "the birth pangs of the Messiah," using the traditional rabbinic imagery for the final deliverance of the Jewish people in a paroxysm of suffering and blood. Now, he believed that the moment had arrived. It exasperated him that a passive European Jewry failed to grasp this. In a speech in Warsaw two months before the German invasion of Poland, he told his audience:

> I must say to my shame that [the Jews] are behaving as if their doom had been already sealed. I know of nothing like it in all the history books; not even in novels have I ever read about such submission to fate. Do you know what it's like? It's as if all were put in a wagon—twelve million educated, well-mannered people—that was driven toward the edge of a cliff. What do they do? One cries, one smokes a cigarette, one sings, but not a single person can be found to jump to his feet, grab the reins, and change the wagon's direction. That's the mood all are in. They might as well have been chloroformed by their worst enemy.

Yet the very hopelessness of the situation inspired hope: the worse things got, the greater the pressure on the gates of Palestine would become. To the Tel Aviv Revisionist Felix Danziger, Jabotinsky predicted after the Évian conference: "I very seriously think that a 'Nordau plan' will soon be accepted as England and the world's policy for Palestine." "The Jewish State of Palestine," he wrote in another letter that same month, "will probably be a fait accompli before the world is five years older." And in April 1939, he told his old friend Shlomo Saltzman: "Within five to seven years there will be a Jewish state in all of Palestine—*if* there will still be any Jews left. I think there will be."

But the clock was ticking ever faster. In March 1939, the Germans dismembered the remainder of Czechoslovakia. In April, their general staff was ordered to stand by for an invasion of Poland. In July, Hitler threatened immediate war if the Poles did not cede Danzig.

The time for diplomacy and appeals to conscience had run out. In August, Jabotinsky decided on a desperation measure. A year earlier, he had dismissed such thinking as "nonsense"; now, he transmitted a plan to the Irgun command in Palestine for an armed insurrection that would begin with the seizure of British administrative buildings in Jerusalem while ships of Irgun and Betar fighters arrived from Europe with him aboard, like Garibaldi landing in Messina, to raise the flag of independence. What he envisioned happening next was unclear. An uprising of the entire Yishuv, joined by the Haganah, in which a Jewish state would be declared on as much territory as could be held while tens or hundreds of thousands of immigrants were hurriedly brought to its shores? A capitulation to superior British forces, followed by a worldwide campaign to return the Palestine mandate to a League of Nations that would honor its original terms? The Irgun command, which had doubts about the plan's sanity, was not sure itself. It was obvious that the British navy would intercept whatever invasion force could be mustered and that any part of it managing to reach shore would be hopelessly outnumbered and outgunned.

As it was, there was no time to debate the matter. By late August, a German attack on Poland was imminent. On August 31, Jabotinsky met in his Belsize Grove quarters with Berl Katznelson, the influential editor of Mapai's daily newspaper *Davar* and a confidant of Ben-Gurion's. The two men felt comfortable with each other; they had been acquainted since the days of the Jewish legion, in whose 39th Battalion Katznelson had served, and the talk between them lasted from ten in the morning until seven at night. Katznelson found Jabotinsky "bitter and despairing." When they finally parted, he later reported to Mapai's central committee in Tel Aviv, Jabotinsky said to him:

"You've won. You still have America with its rich Jews. All I had was the poor Jews of Poland. Now they're gone. The game is up for me."

One pictures a gray London day imperceptibly darkening into night beyond rain-streaked windows. The next day, the Germans invaded Poland.

Jabotinsky had not expected a major war to take place. The destructive technology of modern weaponry, especially air power, had become so much greater in the two decades that had elapsed since 1914 that the major European powers, he had predicted, would no longer dare engage in all-out hostilities. Yet while he doubted that the conflict would escalate into a total one even after the attack on Poland and the Anglo-French declaration of war on Germany, which led to no immediate military confrontation, he was certain that millions of European Jews would be left destitute and homeless by it. For the moment, they had disappeared behind the flames and smoke of the German onslaught. "The main feature of the new situation," he wrote the South African Revisionist Michael Haskel shortly after the fall of Warsaw, "seems to be this: East-European Jewry, which was the mainstay of all Zionism, and particularly of our school of Zionism, has been smashed. . . . Politically, we Jews are simply not on the map."

The quarrel with Great Britain had to be laid aside for the war's duration. Meanwhile, Zionism's sole objective could only be helping the British and French vanquish Hitler while putting itself back "on the map" for the renewed struggle for a Jewish state that would follow. The best way to achieve this, Jabotinsky thought, was by the creation of a Jewish army, a greatly enlarged version of his World War I legion that would take part in the fighting and arouse worldwide sympathy for the Zionist cause. Marshaled by the NZO, more than a hundred thousand volunteers, he estimated, could be found in Palestine, the United States, and other countries.

Characteristically grand in conception and ambition, the idea was a chimera. It had taken years of negotiating with a pro-Zionist English government during World War I to raise a force of three Jewish light infantry battalions that the British general staff had had no interest in. A Jewish army of a hundred thousand men, complete with mechanized divisions, an armored and artillery corps, and transportation and logistics units would divert precious military resources from elsewhere and serve no political purpose from a British point of view. England had agreed to arm and train a "Free Polish Army" after Poland's collapse because it viewed it as a tool for establishing a democratic, pro-Western Polish government after Hitler's defeat. It did not wish to establish a Jewish state in Palestine and had no reason to create a military force that might one day be enlisted in the fight for one.

Jabotinsky was grasping at a straw—but straws were all he had to grasp at. Eastern and Central Europe were lost. With the wartime disruption of normal channels of communication, he was more removed than ever from Palestine—where, under the auspices of the Haganah and the Jewish Agency, many thousands of the youngsters he was counting on for his Jewish army were signing up for wartime service in British ranks. His failure to build a political base in the United States had left him without a structure of support there. Overnight, the New Zionist Organization had become an empty shell. Dream though he might, he was a commander whose troops had melted away.

For several months he remained in London, trying in vain to find a key to the doors of influence. He was met with stony politeness. Great Britain had no time to waste on fantastical projects. By midwinter, he gave up and decided to travel to America. There, at least, he would have a large Jewish community to turn to and politicians who, especially in a presidential election year, wanted its votes.

He sailed by himself in early March 1940. Ania was not given a visa: strict U. S. immigration procedures granted entry for extended stays to only one half of a married couple so as to ensure its return to the other half. Nor was she was keen on making the trip. The previous month, Eri had been arrested by the British aboard an illegal Irgun immigrant ship he was in command of, the Turkish freighter *Sakarya;* now he was imprisoned with the rest of the crew in Acre, in the same fortress in which his father had been held in 1920, and Ania did not want to be even further away from him. Jabotinsky had misgivings about leaving her. He felt, he told a friend, that he was deserting her in her hour of need.

In New York, he moved into the Mayflower Hotel on Central Park West, near Columbus Circle, and set about promoting his Jewish army plan with the help of a small group of young Revisionist aides (including Ben-Zion Netanyahu, the future father of an Israeli prime minister). Reactions were cool. The American Zionist establishment was firmly in the Weizmann–Ben-Gurion camp and did nothing to assist, and American Jews were loath to send their sons to fight in foreign embroilments and afraid, as Jabotinsky put it in a letter, to be accused of "war-mongering." ("I have never seen American Jewry," he wrote, "so scared of local anti-Semitism as now.") The U.S. public was in an isolationist mood. Germany, England, and France seemed to have settled down to a war of words. "The Jewish army issue," Jabotinsky wrote on April 14, "is not even on the horizon right now, with this phony war slipping off to the back pages of the newspapers and America feeling proud to be out of it." He was thinking of taking time out to visit South America, particularly Argentina, whose sizable Jewish community Revisionism had not yet tapped.

The South American trip did not take place. On May 10, the so-called "phony war" ended with a German invasion of Holland, Belgium, and France. That same day, Chamberlain resigned as British prime minister and was replaced by Winston Churchill. In early June, British forces in France were evacuated at Dunkirk along with much of the French army. France surrendered on June 22. On July 10, the Battle of Britain began with the first large-scale German air raids on England.

Churchill had been relatively pro-Zionist over the years and Jabotinsky was encouraged by his appointment. With a Revisionist-sponsored public rally scheduled in New York, he cabled him in early June:

AMERICAN PUBLIC OPINION LITERALLY SEETHING JEWISH ARMY PLAN STOP URGE YOU TO CLINCH MATTERS BY SANCTIONING STOP IMPORTANT ACCEPTANCE REACHES US BEFORE JUNE NINETEENTH GREAT RALLY MANHATTAN CENTER NEW YORK.

Disappointingly, however, a negative reply was received via the British ambassador in Washington. The rally was held in Manhattan Center—the original Metropolitan Opera House—on Eighth Avenue and Thirty-fourth Street. Jabotinsky spoke, as did the ever faithful John Henry Patterson. Although the hall was filled and several thousand dollars were raised from the audience, not a single American Zionist leader or prominent U.S. politician was in attendance. He had tried putting a brave face on it, but Jabotinsky knew well that when it came to the war and the Jewish situation in Europe, American public opinion was hardly "seething." It was rather characterized, as he wrote in a private memorandum on July 3, by "an atmosphere of hesitation and half-heartedness." Without British backing, his Jewish army campaign stood no chance.

Money was a constant problem. The campaign was operating on a shoestring. In May, Jabotinsky moved from the Mayflower to the Hotel Kimberly, on Seventy-fourth Street and Broadway, to economize; finding that too costly as well, he rented a one-room apartment in a nearby brownstone. He was not in good health. He was suffering from chest pains and had been told by a doctor that he had a heart condition caused by his diabetes. He had kept this a secret and told no one, not even

Ania; those who met him, however, remarked on how tired and drawn he looked.

He wanted Ania by his side, but her visa had still not come through. Increasingly worried about Eri, she had begun to drink to calm her nerves. In mid-May, he wrote her:

> Eri is not the most important: you are. You've again men-
> tioned the bottle in your letters. Of all the reasons I can't get
> myself to do the simplest thing, this is the greatest. If people
> [in the U.S. government] weren't so pig-headed, I could get
> them to make the [American] embassy in London issue you
> a visa in spite of everything and I would send you a telegram
> imploring and ordering you [to come]. But people *are* pig-
> headed; they won't do it or else they'll keep dragging it out.
> And you won't give in. For a while now, I've been thinking
> of returning to London. My head is spinning. And the world
> looks like it's turning upside down.

He now found himself in a nightmarish bind. His Nansen passport had expired without his knowledge and there was no way of renewing it in America—yet without it, returning to London was impossible. Germany was threatening to invade England and the thought of Ania by herself there, with German bombs already falling on London, was maddening. On June 18, he wrote a letter to U.S. secretary of state Cordell Hull, beg-ging him to intervene. Ania sought to reassure him. "My dear-est," she wrote on June 20, "Don't worry about me. I'm healthy and feel sure everything is going to be fine and that Erinke will be with us soon."

The next day, however, news arrived from Palestine that all the *Sakarya* prisoners had been freed except Eri. "It's very hard for me to write," Jabotinsky wrote Ania.

> It feels as if all this mess is my personal fault; [as if] there's
> something I haven't done. And I'm terribly ashamed of
> having followed a will-o'-the-wisp to this place of comfort

when at any time you could be hit by a shell. A fine ending for a life!

Throughout July, his chest pains worsened. On August 2, he was told by a doctor that he needed to rest. On August 3, he received a telegram from London that Ania's U.S. visa application had been turned down. He dashed off a cable to the pro-Zionist Labour parliamentarian Josaiah Wedgewood, who had been seeking to obtain permission for him to reenter England:

ENTREAT YOU SPEED UP ENABLING MY RETURN.

That same day, he was driven from New York City to the Catskills for several days of relaxation at a Betar summer camp. On the way, he asked to be taught the Kol Nidrei prayer, with which he was unfamiliar because it had never been his habit to attend synagogue even on Yom Kippur. Reaching the camp, he reviewed a Betar honor guard and collapsed. He died, like Herzl, of a heart attack, on August 4, two months before his sixtieth birthday.

His will, written in English in Paris in 1935, was a simple one, leaving everything to Ania. The last of its five paragraphs stated:

It is my desire that I be interred or cremated (it makes no difference to me) in the place where my death occurs, and that my remains (if I am buried outside the land of Israel) only be returned to the land of Israel at the order of a Jewish government in that country, a government that will surely come to be.

He was buried in a cemetery on Long Island. Eri was released immediately after his death. Ania, finally granted her visa, came to New York in 1941 and died there in 1949. She did not, she said, wish to leave her husband all alone.

After the establishment of the state of Israel, the imple-

mentation of the last paragraph of Jabotinsky's will came up
several times for discussion. Each time, it was vetoed by Ben-
Gurion. Only when he stepped down from the prime minister's office in 1963 did it become possible. In 1964, Jabotinsky
and Ania were reburied together on Mount Herzl in Jerusalem
in a ceremony attended by Eri, by then a professor of electrical
engineering at the Haifa Technion, and Prime Minister Levi
Eshkol.

Epilogue

IF I COULD RAISE any of the great figures of Zionist history from the dead for an hour's conversation, I would choose Jabotinsky. Herzl would awe me into silence. Weizmann would not think me worth his time. Ben-Gurion would harangue me. Jabotinsky would chat affably over a beer in La Coupole, his favorite brasserie on Boulevard Montparnasse, delighted to see it was still there.

In the 1930s, La Coupole was a gathering place for Picasso, Sartre, Malraux, Jacques Prèvert, Chagall, Édith Piaf, Josephine Baker, and others, but there is no indication that Jabotinsky knew any of them or that they had the slightest notion who he was. At most he would have been the short, boyish-looking middle-aged man with the glasses, double-breasted suit, firm chin, and gray cowlick of hair at the next table, laughing and joking with his friends and colleagues in Russian or foreign-accented French. Serious conversations took place at that table, too, of course; the one rule laid down by him was never to talk politics after work. Books and literature—by all means; theater, films, science, philosophy, friends, women, travels, food, goings-on about Paris, reminiscences, memories of Russia and Odessa—all welcome topics. Zionism, though, was *hors-jeu*. There had been enough of it during the day.

He had given his life to it but needed to keep a space free of it. Ultimately, Vera Weizmann may have been right that politics were not his true vocation. Herzl died young and thwarted, but he had created political Zionism. Weizmann ended as an irrelevance, the figurehead first president of a Jewish state he had never wanted to fight for; yet he was instrumental in keeping Zionism alive in the years after Herzl's death and in obtaining the Balfour Declaration, without which it could have gone no further. Ben-Gurion, more than anyone, could claim credit for the establishment of Israel, at whose helm he imposingly stood in its first years; his rupture in old age with a Mapai leadership he had fallen out with was a melancholy postscript to a triumphant career. Jabotinsky, apart from his partial success with the Jewish legion, which did not substantially change Zionism's course, was a political failure, the perennial leader of the Zionist opposition.

More prescient about most things than the men he opposed, he never had their power to influence events. He was one of the first to anticipate that England would win World War I and drive the Turks from Palestine, and that Zionism's future lay with it. He foresaw ahead of others that British governments would betray the Balfour Declaration unless sufficient pressure was exerted on them not to. He understood from the start that socialism could not develop the economy of Palestine fast enough to attract massive Jewish immigration and was not in the long run a viable economic system. He grasped early on that European Jewry was on the verge of a catastrophe from which it could be saved only by a Jewish state. He realized before anyone that the struggle for Palestine would be decided by a Jewish-Arab war. Weizmann and Ben-Gurion eventually came to see these things, too, Ben-Gurion sometimes sooner than Weizmann, but Jabotinsky saw them sooner than either of them.

Was he responsible for his own failure? Could he have gained control of the Zionist movement had he made less stubborn, less prideful, tactically wiser decisions—fought, say, to return to Palestine in 1930, or chosen to stay in the Zionist Organization in 1934? History has no answers to what-if questions; neither can it tell us whether, had Jabotinsky been in Weizmann and Ben-Gurion's place in the years before World War II, he could he have done anything they didn't. Were the grandiose plans that he hatched—petitions with millions of signatures, diplomatic pacts with European governments, a Jewish army landing on the shores of Palestine or fighting the Wehrmacht—ever more than the wild fantasies they were derided as by the Zionist Left? Was he, who so trenchantly criticized the Left's delusions, the victim of ones at least as great?

He was a man of contradictions. He had enormous literary talent and wrote a vast amount, most of it journalism and political polemic in which this talent was but dimly reflected. He dedicated himself to a people and a land that he never found particularly attractive. A firm believer in "individualism," he developed a philosophy of revolutionary Zionism that called for the utter subordination of the individual to the group. He abhorred fascism, yet founded a political party and a youth movement that were repeatedly accused of it. In his personal relations with others, he scrupulously treated them as equals; as a political leader, he allowed a personality cult to form around him. The author of a novel that condemned the loss of the concept of "the forbidden," he sanctioned the spilling of innocent blood.

If there was a common denominator in all this, it was of someone who became what he did by acting against his deeper instincts—or rather, whose deepest instinct was to overrule all his other instincts in the name of a single, willed goal. This self-denial had a brio that made it seem like self-assertion. It *was* self-assertion. Perhaps here lies the resolution of the paradox of freedom and duty that had already occupied him as a young man in Odessa.

But the contradiction I want to talk to him about is another one. "I need to ask you something," I say.

"Please."

"You were always a territorial maximalist and a political democrat. One can't say that of Ben-Gurion, Weizmann, or Herzl. Weizmann and Ben-Gurion supported partition—once in your lifetime and again in 1947. Weizmann was a social and cultural elitist. Ben-Gurion was a Leninist in his younger years. Herzl would have settled for Uganda. He thought a Jewish state should be an 'aristocratic republic,' because the masses couldn't be entrusted with political decisions. You alone cared passionately about the right to all of Palestine *and* the rights of all who lived there. You wouldn't concede any of it and you said that the moment Jews formed fifty-one percent of its population, you would grant full equality to every Arab."

"I meant it."

"But how could a Jewish fifty-one percent have ruled an Arab forty-nine percent without being an ethnic dictatorship?"

"It couldn't have. But it wouldn't have remained fifty-one percent for a day. Millions of Jews wanted only to leave Europe. As soon as there was a Jewish state to take them in, they would have arrived by the boatful. Fifty-one percent would have become sixty percent, seventy percent, eighty percent, in no time. That's the same ratio of Jews to Arabs that you have in Israel today, excepting the Palestinians in Judea and Samaria."

"I see you've managed to keep abreast of things."

"Only in Israel. I don't follow much else. You'd be surprised how much that matters when you're living no longer does when you're dead."

"I don't have to tell you, then, that since 1967 we're a country torn in two: the party of territory and the party of democracy, the land of Israel versus the rights of man, the Right against the Left. I need to know where you stand."

"I'm a man of the Right."

"Of course. And that's how you're remembered today: the fiery nationalist, the unyielding Jewish patriot, the man of 'Both sides of the Jordan are ours'—unless you're simply the name of a street in every city and middle-sized town in Israel. But you were more complicated than that. So is the situation. We control all of Palestine now—and those millions of European Jews don't exist any more."

"No, they don't." His hands clench and unclench on his knees. "I was lucky not to live to see them die. If only I could have seen Israel born, though!"

"But what should Israel do now?" I ask. "Return to its 1967 borders for a dubious peace? Going on ruling millions of Arabs against their will and the wishes of the world? Not all of us have taken sides. Some of us are split down the middle just like the country. There's no one whose opinion would matter to us more than yours."

"Get the best deal you can," he says.

I look at him.

"I've disappointed you? You would have liked me to be more specific? A Palestinian state, the settlements, Jerusalem? I agree, the details are everything. I just don't have the head for them any more. I had the reputation of a zealot, but I was the least ideological of all Zionists. The best possible deal for the Jewish people was all I wanted. For that, though, we had to be tougher and smarter than we were. There's no other way to survive in this world: I learned that as a boy in Odessa. Well, you have the state I dreamed of. It came too late for too many Jews, but it's there. Don't lose it."

"But what *is* the best possible deal?" I persist.

He glances at his watch. "That, my friend," he says, "you'll have to figure out for yourselves. If you want my advice, never take advice from a dead man. I really do have to go now. Ania will be worried."

I reach for the check on the table.

"Permit me," he says. "We get an allowance for things like this." He takes a bill from his wallet and regards it with curiosity.

"It's called a euro," I say. "Francs haven't been used for years."

He smiles. "You see what I mean about keeping abreast. Will this be enough?"

"It's plenty."

He hands it to the waiter. "S'il vous plaît, monsieur," he says.

SOURCES AND ACKNOWLEDGMENTS

Jabotinsky published prolifically, mostly in Russian, Hebrew, and Yiddish, and wrote many thousands of letters, some in English, French, German, and Italian as well. I have been able to read him in all of these languages apart from Russian—alas, the most important. Yet all his major Russian work, as well as the Russian correspondence in the twelve volumes of his letters that have appeared in Israel to date, has been translated into Hebrew.

The situation in English is different. Although nearly the entirety of Jabotinsky's prose fiction—*Samson*, *The Five*, and the short stories in his collection *A Pocket Edition of Several Stories, Mostly Reactionary*—exists in English translation, this is true of little else that he wrote. A great deal written about him is not available in English, either. For this reason, I have not annotated my sources in this book, though I have generally tried to indicate what they were. To fill numerous pages with footnotes referring English readers to texts that few could read would have been pointless.

Still, readers seeking to broaden their knowledge of Jabotinsky beyond the confines of this book are not without recourse. Two excellent comprehensive biographies are at their disposal: Joseph Schechtman's three-volume *The Life and Times of Vladimir Jabotinsky: Rebel and Statesman* (1956) and Shmuel Katz's two-volume *Lone Wolf: A Biography of Vladimir (Ze'ev) Jabotinsky* (1993). I have made extensive use of both works, especially Schechtman's, while often discussing matters unmentioned in them and arriving at different interpretations and conclusions.

In addition, a one-volume selection from Jabotinsky's writings can be found in *The Political and Social Philosophy of Ze'ev Jabotinsky* (1999), and his younger years are the subject of several thoughtful chapters in Michael Stanislawski's *Zionism and the Fin de Siècle: Cosmopolitanism and Nationalism from Nordau to Jabotinsky* (2001). Writing after the dissolution of the Soviet Union, Stanislawski had access to archival materials, such as Jabotinsky's first two plays and much of his early journalism, that Schechtman and Katz lacked.

I, too, was able to read a good deal of this material, in addition to Jabotinsky's World War I reporting, the Russian letters in his still unpublished correspondence from the years 1939–40, and some of Ania's letters to him, with the help of two Israeli assistants, David Kriksinov and Andrei Pshenitsky, whom I wish to take this opportunity to thank. They reviewed, summarized, and translated into Hebrew or English many pages, which I then retranslated or revised when quoting from them.

Secondary translation is never an ideal method, but when the translators are competent—and Jabotinsky has been fortunate in his Hebrew ones—it need not yield unsatisfactory results. I have also resorted to it in quoting from many of Jabotinsky's articles, essays, and speeches; from parts of his memoirs; from *Samson* (citations from *The Five*, on the other hand, are from Michael R. Katz's English version of the novel); from his play "A Strange Land"; from his poetry; and from much of his correspondence. His poem "There Is a Sea That Men Call Black" was translated directly by me from its original Italian, and "The Song of the Prisoners of Acre," from its original Hebrew.

My thanks go also to the Jabotinsky Institute in Tel Aviv and its two archivists, Ira Berean and Olga Gekhman-Prosmushkin, for their always gracious assistance; to the Avi Chai Foundation and David Rozenson, its former director in Russia, for their kindness in sponsoring a trip to Odessa; to Anya Misyuk for being an attentive and knowledgeable guide there; to the two editors of this series, Anita Shapira and Steven Zipperstein, for their patience and support, and for reading my manuscript and making useful observations and suggestions; and to Yale's manuscript editor Phillip King for painstakingly doing the same. All contributed to this book and I am grateful to each of them.

INDEX

JEWISH LIVES is a major series of interpretive biography designed to illuminate the imprint of Jewish figures upon literature, religion, philosophy, politics, cultural and economic life, and the arts and sciences. Subjects are paired with authors to elicit lively, deeply informed books that explore the range and depth of Jewish experience from antiquity through the present.

Jewish Lives is a partnership of Yale University Press and the Leon D. Black Foundation.

Ileene Smith is editorial director. Anita Shapira and Steven J. Zipperstein are series editors.